The Life & Times of the Boy from Tacarigua

This book was compiled by Capt. Ernest Garth Fidler Lyder, D.F.C., F.R.MET.S., M.I.N., A.M.TECH.I., GRAD.A.I.A., ably assisted by his wife June Rose Bruford Lyder (left) and daughter Jenny Lynne Lyder LLB. (Hons.), F.C.C.A. (right).

Garth Lyder

The Life & Times of the Boy from Tacarigua

An Autobiography

First Edition 2010

Design and Layout by Paria Publishing Company Limited
Typeset in Berling and Dorchester Script
ISBN 978-976-8226-22-8
Printed in the United States of America

Table of Contents

Lilla May Fidler Lyder

Dedication

This book is dedicated to my mother, Lilla May Fidler Lyder, 18/12/1878 to 02/06/1958, a most remarkable woman by any standard who brought up six children to the glory of god single handedly after her husband died at the young age of 43. The oldest child was Glory Gwendolyn Lyder who at that time was 10 years old and who gave her life to the church and to keeping the family together. The second in line was Deryck Maund Lyder CBE, who was then 8 years old, who joined the Methodist Ministry and became the Chairman of the District exactly 100 years after his great grandfather, the missionary, the Reverend William Fidler was so honoured. The third in line was Ernest Garth Fidler Lyder, who was then 6 years old, who grew up to serve in the RAF in World War II as a flight commander DFC and later as a Captain on commercial flying. The fourth in line was Patricia Joy Lyder, who was then 4 years old and who became a secretary in the United Nations League in Geneva. The fifth in line was Edwin Hope Lyder, then 2 years of age and who became a bank manager. The last child was Marguerite Elise Lyder, then a babe in arms and who became a senior secretary in the commercial world.

Mother & Father

The chauffeur, my father, mother holding Glory (the first child) and Aunt Charlotte.

My Family.
Front row: Deryck, Mother & Edwin.
Back row: Marguerite, Glory, Garth & Pat.

Me in front of the house where I was born
(4 Broome Street, Port-of-Spain)

Deryck Maund Lyder CBE

Per Ardua ad Astra

(Through adversity to the stars)
Motto of the R.A.F.

Sauviter in Modo
Furtiter in Re

(Gentle in manner, resolute in execution)
Motto of the 180th Squadron

Preface

BY ANTHONY ROSTANT

Nowadays, hero status is heaped upon young athletes and performing artists. Kids look up to and idolise and try to model themselves upon them. Talented individuals, no doubt, but all too often they fall out of grace, caught up in some scandal of crime, drugs, gambling or the sort. All this, while our elders in society, those with a lifetime of experiences and wisdom to share, are scoffed at as having nothing to contribute to this new, high-speed, digital age that we live in. So sad for our children, who are all the poorer for our not telling their stories, often and loud, for our not ensuring that they are indelibly written into the pages of our little country's rich history.

Here is the tale of one such son of our soil. I have known Ernest Garth Fidler Lyder, "uncle Garth" to me, almost all my life, always as mild mannered and a devoted, loving family man. I have sat for many a wonderful hour listening to the author tell and retell the stories you are about to read, stories of virtue, of perseverance, courage, loyalty, responsibility and love and duty to family and country. Stories about always doing what is right and good even at one's own peril. Stories of navigating life's most treacherous storms and piloting a true course to the journey's end.

My Childhood

I was born at No. 4 Broome Street, St. Clair, Trinidad at 4.30 am on 5th January 1914 to Lilla May and Edwin Hugh Donneville Lyder.

I was the third child following Glory Gwendolyn and Deryck Maund. Following me came Patricia Joy, Edwin Hope and, last of the six, Marguerite Elise Lyder. My father was brought to Trinidad as a child two years of age in 1878 by his parents Edwin Ernest Augustus Lyder and Arabella Ketura Lyder of Bath Village, Barbados, along with a brother named Julian, who was slightly older. Both grandparents were born in Barbados of two different Lyder families, who were settled on small-holdings at a date I cannot trace. I understand that grandfather's father was a retired ship's captain who took up residence there in the mid-19th century.

My mother Lilla May Lyder was born in Trinidad on 18th December 1878 at 6.00 am to parents Carlton Sydney and Eliza Cook Fidler. She was the fifth child of six, preceded by Carlton Sydney, Eliza Wale, Edith Shenton and Jessie Louise, my mother Lilla May, and last Charlotte Alison. My parents lived at No. 4 Broome Street next door to R.A.M. Cambridge and family, who was the Principal of Queen's Royal

College. "Ram Ram", as he was affectionately called by the pupils, had four children: Tom, Elizabeth, Miriam and John. Mr Cambridge used to have the weekly *Mirror* paper sent out to him so that he could keep abreast of happenings in England, and he passed them on to us when he had read them. Tom Cambridge, the eldest son, joined the Civil Service and became the Governor's Representative in Tobago, known as the Warden, whilst my brother Deryck was posted there as the Methodist Minister many years later and they ran the island together. Tom's sister Miriam, known to us as "Mimim", became the Ladies Tennis Champion of Trinidad and reigned as such for many years.

In those days, Napoleon Arthur Robinson was studying Law and Deryck made his office available to him to pursue those studies. During Deryck's mission in Tobago, Mr Hassanali was posted there as Magistrate and the three of them became fast friends. When later on Mr Robinson became Prime Minister, he appointed Mr Hassanali as President and Deryck, who was then in Barbados as Chairman of the Methodist Church, was invited to Government House in Trinidad to a special reunion luncheon along with their wives.

My father was the Manager of the grocery department of Stephens, the number one store on Frederick Street in those days. My mother worked in the main office where they met, and eventually they married in Tranquility Church at the corner of Victoria Avenue and Tragarete Road. They were married by the Reverend Maund in the presence of the then Chairman of the

Methodists, the Reverend Sam Hawthorne, known to us later as Uncle Sam. My mother was a staunch Methodist, having descended from a long line of Wesleyan Ministers, one of whom was her grandfather, the Reverend William Fidler who became Chairman of the Methodists in this region. He built the Bethel Church in Bridgetown, Barbados, where my brother Deryck was laid to rest aged eighty-three. As a matter of historic interest, my brother Deryck was inducted in that same church as Chairman precisely one hundred years to the minute after his great-grandfather the Reverend William Fidler had been so honoured.

Broome Street was the last row of houses heading west, in those days, after which came the River Bridge at the start of St. James where there is the police barracks followed by Long Circular Road, the latest residential area at that time. The Western Main Road ran through what was an Indian village down to Cocorite and into Diego Martin, which was mainly waste or agricultural land. I remember as a young boy, my father coming home from work and taking Deryck and myself for a ride on the tram-car through St. James and into the coconuts to its terminal in Cocorite. The tram would spend several minutes there before the backs of the seats were turned over and the tram driven from the other end back to Port-of-Spain. The memory of those days is quite nostalgic.

When we lived in Broome Street at the back of us was number 4 Havelock Street, where a very nice family lived named Aleong. There were Mr and Mrs and two children Barbara and Kevin. My mother was very friendly with Mrs Aleong, who was a seamstress and made several dresses for her.

Mrs Aleong adopted a young boy named Julian and when he grew to maturity, he left to make his way in America. He eventually learnt to fly aeroplanes and started a flying school in the south and when Mussolini invaded Ethiopia, he went there as Colonel Julian, to offer to train Selassie's two sons to fly and defend their country. I never heard any more but thought I would mention it as another example of a Trini making a contribution to the world.

We enjoyed our lives there and father was moving on. He left Stephens and bought a bakery, then another and another and thought he would start the first biscuit factory in Trinidad. He bought some machinery through the German family Boos and secured a site on the north side of Queen Street, between Frederick and Henry Streets. Boos got a so-called engineer named Gormandy to assemble the machinery, but somehow they did not get it to work properly. Though I remember going down to the factory one day and trying the biscuits, which were very like the "Crix" of today. Unfortunately it was costing more money and my father had to give it up. He had extended himself and his finances too quickly and was running out of money. In those days, the only bank was the Colonial Bank, which later became Barclays Bank, and loans were very difficult to obtain, so he had to rein in his ambitions, working too hard taking over from other managers and eventually fell ill. Life had become difficult and when I was only six years old and Marguerite a babe in arms, he died. I vividly remember meeting the hearse at the top of Victoria Avenue to follow it down to Tranquility Church in my white suit next to Deryck, each with a wreath over our arms.

Our lives changed drastically from that day. We had to leave our happy home and had to move into a City Council-owned house, named "Shamrock Villa" up Bournes Road. Our grandfather, who had retired as the Senior Overseer of the Orange Grove Estate in Tacarigua, took a job as Warehouse Manager in Claxton Bay for Phoenix Park Sugar Estate so that he could pay the rent on Shamrock Villa, which saved our lives as it had plenty of room for us and was sited on approximately three acres of land with numerous fruit trees. Mrs St. Hilaire lived in the large estate house further up Bournes Road, which was called "Rosslands", and had a son named Jack and a daughter whose name I cannot remember now, but Jack used to come down to play with Deryck and myself. We would also go to his house and enjoy a large plunge bath which they had. More of him later.

To backtrack a bit, we had a very enjoyable life at No.4 Broome Street, when father and mother had a number of friends who would visit as well as their families. Particularly Auntie Blanche Legge, a most exuberant character who worked at the Government Main Post Office, then in St. Vincent Street, who would pound away on the piano "Chin-chin-chinaman, chop, chop,

chop" and other such ditties and we all sang along, gathered around her.

Glory, Deryck and myself attended Mrs Springer's Elementary School on New Street. Mrs Springer was a widowed English lady who used her house to hold classes for a select group of friends' children and was a strong disciplinarian, teaching good manners and behaviour alongside the three R's, and we missed her when we had to move further away. Deryck and myself attended the RC School at the corner of Bournes and Western Main Road until we joined the Tranquility Intermediate Boys School on Victoria Avenue. Mother cleared up father's business and decided to buy a few cows, pigs, a couple of goats and a donkey named Etheline, and ran that as a small homestead. She got a small group of friends to buy milk, which was delivered by donkey with the herdsman Henry, and Deryck or myself accompanying him early in the morning. Mother had to go out to work as a secretary in Port-of-Spain and Glory took charge of the family in her absence. She was only ten years of age when father died.

As I mentioned earlier, mother was one of six. The only boy, Carlton Fidler, married a lady of French heritage and settled on an eleven-acre estate called "Pirraza" in Arima. Auntie Eliza (Cissy) had married Doctor Moister Laurence, who was on the Legislative Council governing the colony at the time and was the Port Health Officer. His job was to visit all the ships and visitors arriving in Trinidad to check on health and sanitation to control the epidemiology of the colony. Aunt Edith remained a spinster throughout her life. Aunt Jessie married Mead Kelshall, who was a solicitor in San Fernando. Aunt Charlotte married one Richard Mole, an English journalist who started the newspaper, *The Mirror,* in Trinidad. This consortium of relatives called a meeting of the clan to decide how to go about helping their fallen member, my mother. This meeting was held one evening at Carlton House on Abercrombie Street, just above Park Street. The house was a magnificent home designed and maintained in pristine condition for entertaining the Governor and other visiting potentates. From the dining room you walked out onto a large pebbled garden with a number of flower-beds resplendent with roses, which Dr. Laurence tended a lot of the time, and he never left the house without a rose in his buttonhole. He ran an expensive car, the "Willis Knight", with sleeve-valve engine built in America. From this house, his eldest son Eric left for Cambridge University in England and was killed serving in the army during World War I. His second son, Noel, won the Island Scholarship from Queen's Royal College and he too sailed to England to study Medicine after the war, but more of that family later.

I must relate what transpired at the meeting of the clan. My mother was handed a plan of action which entailed her keeping the baby Marguerite, who had been born at Carlton House, and would take a secretarial job in town. The rest of us would be split up between the different families. I just cannot remember the details now, but my mother was horrified at the thought and pleaded to be allowed to keep her family intact. They would have none of it. Eventually she was given an ultimatum to accept the deal or get nothing. She picked up her hat, fixed it firmly on her head and stormed out, taking the tram-car back to Bournes Road. She walked up and into Shamrock Villa, throwing herself on her large bed where we had all collected like chickens in a nest, and she burst into tears. We all dissolved into weeping, as our champion had been smitten down and it seemed the end of the world that night at 11 o'clock.

With the dawn of another day, mother spoke to us about our new situation and told us that we should rally around her and stick together as a unit. One for all and all for one, and we faced the world with renewed courage. Glory continued at Mrs Springer's School. Deryck and I went to Tranquility Intermediate Boys School and Patricia to the Tranquility Girls School. Edwin went to Tacarigua to keep grandma company, as grandpa had gone to Claxton Bay where a house was provided by the Phoenix Park Estate, and Marguerite was looked after mainly by Glory, but also by all of us.

St. James was a large village, even in those days, with land extending from the Western Main Road north to the foothills owned by Guthrie and Henderson. Mr Guthrie was a Scottish expatriate, imported as colonial treasurer, who married locally and had a number of children who moved away when adult. He lived in a low sprawling house on the Western Main Road with a crescent driveway, which is now the site of a petrol station, two plots west of Bournes Road. There was a Chinese shop on the corner, which is now a Royal Bank branch, and alongside it a furniture shop. There was a large ravine, running down the north-east side of Bournes Road out to sea at Mucurapo, which has been built over to widen the road, and the east/west roads such as Patna, Delhi etc. had narrow wooden bridges into Bournes Road. I remember being fascinated by a fight between a macajuel snake and a mongoose on the riverbed near our house. The mongoose actually measured its distance from the snake and teased it repeatedly as though it would get closer and when the snake struck, it withdrew just sufficiently to make it miss. This went on until the snake became tired and the mongoose grabbed it by the neck and killed it. Mongeese were brought to Trinidad to combat the snake menace, but found domestic groups of chickens to be much easier prey.

To the west of our land border was a large open area known as the pauper's burial ground, which is now the Western Cemetery. There was a footpath up the hill to join the Fort George Road, which led to a signal station at the top of the hill, looking out to sea. This was manned by a member of the harbour master's office to monitor the approach of ships that were approaching the harbour mouth, and he would identify the ship through a telescope and put out flags on the hilltop flagpost to inform the office in Port-of-Spain of their size, nationality etc. We used to host parties of friends to climb the hill to this lookout spot on holidays, and at one time parties would come from Port-of-Spain for moonlight rambles.

School Days

The time came for Deryck and myself to move on to college and the normal (progress) choice would have been Queen's Royal College, but my mother just could not afford the fees etc. so we joined some of our friends in going to the Trinidad New College, headed by C.L.R. James, who had been a tutor at Queen's Royal College (QRC) and considered as being a promising intellectual.

It was first sited on Jerningham Avenue, but later moved into Belmont, on Norfolk Street, until Mr James packed it in and went to England. Our friends, the Howards, Gibbons and Dates, who were with us there then went to QRC, and Deryck and myself went to Pamphillian High School to finish our formal education. The Principal of which was a Mr Alexis who was nicknamed "Yanko", and the senior teacher was Mr McClean, who was nicknamed "Torpedo" because of the shape of his head, whose son later in life became the Speaker in our House of Parliament in Trinidad. Torpedo used to be called upon by Yanko to officiate at periodic addresses to the whole school, as he was fond of using flowery language and long and uncommon words of the elite English language that would attract loud ooohs and whistles from his audience. Yanko, on the other hand, was given to spouting encouraging bits of poetry to raise enthusiasm for study among the pupils. Here are a couple of his admonishments. "Lives of great men all remind us, we can make our lives sublime, and departing leave behind us footprints in the sands of time", also "heights by great men reached and kept were not attained by sudden flight, but by those, who whilst their companions slept, kept toiling upwards in the night". These had quite an impression on me.

When I first got to the school, Deryck was put in a different class as he was always one class ahead of me. I had certain chores to carry out at home before leaving for school, which made me late in arriving for 8 o'clock start, and Torpedo was scheduled as tutor for my first lesson. Quite rightly, he reprimanded me for being late, and when I arrived at ten past eight the next morning, he sent me to Yanko to be punished. Yanko, who presided at the head of the hall on a slightly raised platform, administered six lashes, three on each hand, with a tamarind rod, in front of the whole school. When I returned to take my seat in class, Torpedo ordered me to stand on the bench behind until his lesson was finished, and this incensed me to such a degree as to make me fight him. So in spite of my newly made friends begging me to come at 8 o'clock next morning, I advised them to look for me at 8.10 am and I arrived precisely at that time, and the same punishment was applied. This went on for three days until Torpedo gave up, and then I would arrive at 8.00 am punctually.

I should have mentioned before all of this that I had been struck down with malaria fever some years earlier, and had become very ill indeed, and when an attack was taking place, which occurred spasmodically at intervals of days, I would shake with ague so badly it was almost like a dog having a fit. At times, I was bed-ridden and Dr. Laurence, our Uncle Moister, would come to see me and give me lots of quinine tablets, which was the only medicine for treating malaria at that time. I became weak and emaciated and must have looked dreadful. I was visiting my grandmother at Tacarigua on one weekend when I overhead her crying while talking to a friend visiting, telling her that she feared that Lilla, my mother, was not going to raise that boy, meaning that I would soon be dead. That pulled me up with a jolt and I made my mind up to do something to make myself fit and well, so I got a length of rope and started to skip, and although I felt dreadful and my head ached awfully, I persevered for the next several months and I saw great results. So I adopted physical culture in a big way.

I joined a group of friends who met frequently at Sidney McIntosh's home at the top of Sydenham Avenue in St. Ann's and I read the *Health & Strength* magazines, trained with their equipment and did a lot of wrestling. This routine made me tough and strong, but it took up extra time in the morning in addition to the domestic chores occasioned by the family situation. That was our private business and I was ever a proud character like my mother, and would never explain to outsiders what we had to do to exist. We just had to survive.

In Trinidad in those days there was no such thing as welfare, and any help that the government provided was for what we call the poor people. We had to depend on friends and precious few remained. When father was alive, there were always business friends in and out of the house at Broome Street, but now only the very staunch of them came to Shamrock Villa. I remember on occasions, going down Frederick Street with my mother and seeing earlier acquaintances approaching us on the pavement, and looking forward to having a chat when we met, suddenly to see them tip their hats while some distance away and cross the road to continue down the other side, to avoid us. My grandmother would often recite, "when poverty comes in the door, love goes out the window".

Deryck left Pamphillian High School on completing his Cambridge examinations and went to Alstons to apply for a job. In those days, there were about five large business firms that we sought to join, Alstons & Co., Huggins & Co., Geddes Grant & Co., Gordon Grant & Co., and Furness Withy & Co., which controlled most of the business that there was. They all sought to employ boys of a certain background to recruit as officeboy trainees who had the potential to move up to directorships.

Deryck applied to Alstons and was accepted in competition with a few others, and joined as officeboy at a salary of TT$15.00 per month. I continued for a year at Pamphillian to sit the Cambridge examinations, and Glory had secured a place at the Cable Office, that later became Cable & Wireless, after taking secretarial training.

Deryck did so well at Alstons that in the July of the following year, one of the directors, Mr Sidney Fitt, who lived on Patna Street, St. James, and knew the family when father was alive, turned to him and asked Deryck, "haven't you got a brother?", Deryck replied "yes sir", "what is he doing now?" and Deryck replied "he is sitting his exams at present". Then came the next question, "doesn't he want a job?", Deryck replied "oh yes sir" and Mr Fitt said "tell him to come to work on 1st August".

When Deryck got home that evening with the news, there was celebration at Shamrock Villa, followed by hasty preparations for me to get ready to be employed. Two long pant suits had to be ordered and a number of things had to be arranged for me to present myself at Alstons, and I arrived at Alstons Head Office with Deryck on 1st August 1929 at 7.30 am. I was shown the routine and introduced to the other members of staff as they came in. I had to fetch the mail from our postbox at the main post office and put out the daily newspapers, the *Port-of-Spain Gazette* and the *Trinidad Guardian,* on file in the Managing Director's office before 8 o'clock. Naturally I was overjoyed to be working as I longed to start earning my keep, and was thrilled at the end of the month to receive my salary of TT$20.00. I realised I had walked straight in on

Deryck's reputation and did my best to prove I was worth my pick.

We moved up the seniority ladder steadily, and Deryck became a salesman in the dry goods department under Gerald Wight, the son of the Managing Director, who later became Sir Gerald. In turn, I was given the job of managing the coffee department and we stayed in those posts until we left Alstons; Deryck in 1937 to study for the Methodist Ministry, and I in 1938 to come to England to train as an air pilot. Deryck journeyed to Jamaica to enter the Methodist College at Caenwood and, on completion of his training, came back to serve in the various islands of the Caribbean.

I should like to say a bit about our grandfather Ernest, who was born in Barbados in the parish of St. George in 1853. He grew up there to the age of 15 when his father, who was a severe disciplinarian, gave him a sound belting for attending the slaughter of a pig next door. So incensed was he that he gathered a few things and went down to the wharf in Bridgetown, where he boarded a Norwegian whaling vessel and applied for a job and was signed on. Years later in his house in Claxton Bay, where we joined him at holiday time, the three boys, Deryck, Edwin and myself, he would hold us spellbound with tales of his youth. First, how he would go out in a small boat from the mother ship to harpoon a whale and the business of swimming to the dying animal to stick a flag into it to identify it for collection by the mother ship as they went in search of others. We enquired how the sharks, which were attracted by the wounded animal, did not attack the men, and he said that very occasionally they would lose someone, but generally the sharks were focused on the blood of the wounded animal. He served some time until he left the ship on one visit to New York, and with an uncle's assistance started training at a medical college. In those days, there were few or no formalities to going into America. The medical course was for three years' duration, but he got tired of it after two years and transferred to another to study engineering instead. Again, he only completed two years of a three year course and got homesick, so returned to Barbados, married his cousin Arabella Ketura, had a son Julian and then another named Hugh, and transferred the family to Trinidad in 1878. He joined the team that was engaged in building the railway until it reached St. Joseph, and then the team building the Caura Royal Road, and eventually settled for a job as an overseer on Orange Grove Estate, which was then owned by a company in England. Grandpa built himself a house on the corner of Eastern Main Road and what was called Dinsley Gap, a roadway where a lot of the people who worked on the estate lived. He was very public-minded, and the large room on the side of the Eastern Main Road was prepared as an office to which the villagers were invited to come for medical attention and he arranged for the doctor from the Tunapuna Hospital to attend twice a week on his way to Arouca and Arima. Being half a doctor himself, he attended to the sick within his capabilities, even to extracting bad teeth etc. My grandmother took on the job of being the Registrar of Births and Deaths and the pair became known as "Papa and Mama Lyder".

He loved horse-riding around the estate and had a buggy and also a smaller two-wheel trap, as it was called. A number of the wealthy residents of Paradise Area owned a sport buggy, so to speak, in those days for quick travel, including one Dr. McLean. There was great rivalry between these owners and grandpa held the record for the fastest time from the river bridge to the tollgate on the east side of Port-of-Spain, about ten miles, and used to regale us with tales of his champion horse which was called "Revolver". We took these tales with a pinch of salt, allowing for the reminiscing of an aging relative, but listened intently.

Many years later, when I returned to fly for BWIA after the second great war, I came in from my swim in the sea at the Beach Hotel when over-nighting in Antigua and the Manager, Bob Smith, called me to meet the Chief of Police who was visiting him. He had mentioned that I was a Lyder from Trinidad and the officer wanted to know which Lyder, so I explained who my parents and grandparents were and he said "oh yes, I knew your grandfather well. He was a member of a volunteer military force known as the Trinidad Lighthorse" and went on to tell us of a horse that my grandfather had owned, named Revolver, that held the speed record from Tacarigua to Port-of-Spain. I gave voice to the feeling that we thought at the time it was the ramblings of an aging person and this Colonel said, "shame on you, that was a fact". My grandfather went up even higher in my estimation and I chastised myself and Deryck for ever disbelieving him. He was truly a great character. He taught us to swim at Claxton Bay, built us a pirogue boat to learn seamanship and to row, and was a staunch Anglican churchgoer. He taught us that Sunday was the Lord's Day and we should keep it holy. Sundays were to be spent quietly reading and enjoying each other's company, and he would sit in his rocking chair, smoking his pipe, and recall his experiences for us to gain insight from them.

He would travel back to Tacarigua by train every fortnight to see grandma, who was riddled with rheumatism, to make sure she was cared for. She had a live-in girl name Tilly, who was a gem and a wonderful help. Grandma would remember, indeed she lived for those visits, and when he would be due, asked Tilly to remind Mr Battoo, a lovely, elegant, grey-haired Indian man who used his buggy as a taxi ferrying locals to and fro, to meet him at the station. Mr Battoo had two sons named Meg and Dally who grew up to build the Battoo taxi and bus services in Port-of Spain.

Alas, in life there is continual change and grandpa's hands were becoming numb. He fashioned a device to fit over his forefinger so that it had a nib on the end with which he would write. In those days there were ink wells and common pens normally used and unfortunately grandpa got stuck in the left hand with a dirty nib and it turned sceptic and he had to go to the

San Fernando General Hospital where he was admitted for treatment. One morning my mother got a phone message to come as it was urgent. Mother hurried to San Fernando by train and the doctor explained that grandpa's left arm needed to be amputated if his life was to be saved, but grandpa refused and would she speak to him. Mother did what she could, but grandpa told her that she was well on the way to security now, that Glory and the two boys were established in their jobs and that he was happy he had helped, but now he was tired and would prefer to go back to his maker with all his parts together. In a couple of days he was gone. His body was delivered to his home in Tacarigua and bathed and dressed by a faithful old Barbadian friend from the Dinsley village. He was laid in the coffin in the living room and later taken to St. Mary's Anglican Church near the river bridge, where he and the family had attended regularly through the years. Grandma followed him just six months later and was laid to rest alongside him in the churchyard.

Mother gave up residence at Shamrock Villa and the family moved into the Tacarigua house. We travelled to work and the younger two to school in Port-of-Spain by train. There was a halt directly outside of the house for the train and the drivers got accustomed to our crowd joining there, so would blow the whistle if they did not see us on the platform and we would come running out still eating the last of our breakfast. We had a very happy stay in Tacarigua with the three Howard boys, sons of the then Manager of Orange Grove Estate, the

Murray boys, sons of the Estate Chemist, the Dates and Gibbons at 5 Rivers Estate and others.

Mr and Mrs Howard had been friends of mother's for many years and they enjoyed her presence. Mr Howard was very fond of cricket, but as we were all busy in jobs, he offered a cup for the game of football and a league was formed from the Eastern Corridor villages from San Juan to Arima to contest for it. Deryck and myself played in the Orange Grove Team, with Deryck as captain, and tried hard but never won that cup. We did win the knockout cup one year, however. Deryck was very keen on cricket and joined the Queen's Park Cricket Club and was progressing well as a batsman and spin bowler, and would certainly have gone on to play for Trinidad and the West Indies had he not gone into the Church. His life seemed to mirror that of Dick Shepherd, the Bishop of Liverpool. I too was wooed to enter the Ministry but realised that it was not for me and with Deryck joining, I had to take on the responsibility of earning enough to restore the family to solvency.

The Flying Bug Bites

I was happy enough at Alstons but realised that I wanted a career so that I could be my own man and not wait for someone else to offer me promotion.

I tried all sorts of avenues including music. I bought a saxophone and a course in music but realised that I would not be very good at that. Then I saw an advert about a course in aviation from America and I sent for it. I had always been interested since my cousin Marjorie Mole, daughter of Richard Mole, the editor of the *Mirror*, sent me a birthday card with a Bleriot type airplane on it and saying "flying to you at a mile a minute with all good things in it for your birthday".

I also remembered my mother telling of a pilot, Boland, who visited Trinidad in his small aeroplane but crashed it in the Grand Savannah and was killed, and the crowds that gathered around the Rosary Church at his funeral. The course was from the American Institute of Aviation and written by Lieutenant Walter Hinton of the U.S. Navy, who was one of the pilots on the very first aircraft to fly from America across the Atlantic to Europe. He was in one of a small formation of four flying boats which flew to Bermuda, the Azores, Lisbon and England in 1920 and returned to the U.S. by ship.

In 1928, whilst Deryck and I were at C.L.R James' New College in Norfolk Street, Belmont, a formation of five Loening amphibian aeroplanes arrived in Trinidad from the U.S.A. and landed on the waterfront at Port-of-Spain and taxied up on to the land at Mucurapo for servicing. A number of us pupils rode our bicycles to the site and I in particular was so fascinated that I spent all my lunch hours and more there, watching as they warmed up their engines, waddled like ducks into the sea and took off to continue their journey to British Guiana. One had a problem and had to stay back, while the other four set course from there in formation.

By this time I was late for the resumption of schooling and rode my bicycle to Shamrock Villa to pad my shorts with extra underclothing, as I was convinced that I would be caned by C.L.R. for being late. When I got back to school, lessons were in progress and I was relieved to be allowed to join the class without chastisement, when I explained that I had to go home because I had had an accident of nature and had to change my pants. My mother was horrified that I had told a lie and rebuked me saying that I should have told the truth and taken the consequences like a man.

I studied this aviation avidly into the nights and was enthralled. In those days we did not have electricity and I had to read at night by candlelight. I completed this correspondence course and received my diploma and a nice recommendation from the Principal that I was a man who finishes what he starts and he had no hesitation of recommending me to a future employer.

Early in 1932, Mikey Cipriani, a prominent lawyer, imported a De Havilland Moth aeroplane into Trinidad. He had obtained a private pilot's licence while on holiday in England and was keen to form a flying club here. He wanted a pilot to fly it commercially, taking passengers for rides, and found one named Lickfold who had flown in the Royal Flying Corps in the First World War, and sent him to Canada to obtain a commercial pilot's licence, buy a plane and bring it to Trinidad.

The plane duly arrived and was positioned at the new Piarco Aerodrome that had recently been built by a local French engineer named Lange. A forested area had been cleared of trees, levelled and drained to make a landing field for Air France to be able to extend its services to Trinidad. Mikey, as he was affectionately called, had a small hangar built for it, quite small as it had folding bi-plane wings, and Lickfold operated it from there.

We were living in Tacarigua at this time and I had a motorcycle and took Billy Howard, my friend from Orange Grove, on the pillion one Sunday morning to see this plane. When we got to Piarco, the plane was airborne, so we waited to see it land. In due course, it arrived and was parked, and the pilot and passenger disembarked. It was an open two-seater in tandem with bi-plane wings and I was very keen to look closer at it, but we kept our distance as we were not known to either Mikey or Lickfold.

However, to my great surprise, Mikey, now garbed in white overalls, came towards us and introduced himself and said that he was going to take it up himself for a brief flight and would one of us like to go. I hurriedly said yes please and so did Billy. He said that he only had a seat for one and he would toss a coin to choose who could go. Well, I just could not believe my luck when I won that toss. He handed me a white helmet with goggles, the same as his, and I went off with him. He strapped me in and explained a few things, he started up and taxied away. We had a primitive tube for communication through which he explained what he was doing and we took off. It was most exhilarating and when he told me to take the dual control stick that was in front of me and fly it myself, I was overjoyed. The droning of the engine, the wind in my face, the feeling of freedom of the space to move in three dimensions confirmed in my mind that this was for me. I thanked him profusely and could not get home fast enough to tell the family. I had found what I wanted to do in life but had to solve the problem of financing it.

I subscribed to the *Flight* and *Aeroplane* magazines posted in from England and avidly read them from cover to cover, and became fully appraised of what was going on in aviation. I became familiar with the names of the famous officers in the Royal Air Force and their achievements and those in Imperial Airways and the aircraft industry in general, and longed to be able to be part of that. I had visited the Pan American Airways base at Cocorite and gawked at the Sikorsky amphibians landing and crawling ashore to be serviced, but now I felt as though I had joined the fraternity.

I heard that Jack St. Hilaire was working there as an apprentice engineer as well as Harry Cadiz. Elmo Bearden had been imported as Manager and when Charles Lindberg arrived on the inaugural flight, I joined the crowds to see him. A new and advanced type of aircraft was introduced, and I went aboard to have a good look around when Mr Bearden invited us to see. Carl Agostini was the latest addition to the staff in the office. When the family left St. James to live in Tacarigua, I missed the frequent visits to the Pan American base but now took an interest in Piarco. I later heard that Cipriani had flown his aeroplane to the Grand Savannah, landed it there and towed it to his garage at his home in Murray Street, Woodbrook. I also heard that Jack St. Hilaire had left Pan Am and was rebuilding the aircraft for Mikey. I rang Jack and asked if I could come to help in the afternoon after work and Mikey agreed. So almost every afternoon I was there.

We stripped the aeroplane completely down to its wooden skin and recovered it and the wings with new cotton and dope, while the engine was sent to the factory in England for overhaul and modernisation. "Red Woodburn", the energetic small powerhouse of a man who was the Chief Engineer at Pan Am, undertook to oversee the job for the issue of the certificate of airworthiness. We worked for months on it. Jack St. Hilaire worked full time on the aeroplane, and I joined him after work, Mikey came when he could spare the time, and Norman Tang, who was the Minister of Health in the Albert Gomes Government and lived nearby, as a frequent handyman, raconteur and comedian.

Mikey secured permission from the City Council to use a site on the waterfront at Mucurapo as a landing field. That site was rough and covered with shrubbery and he hired a team of men to clear and level it and we all helped. Mikey then got a carpenter to build a wooden shed at the Eastern End of the field with a concreted apron extending out to house the aircraft. This site opposite to Fatima College, which came later, is now taken over for the Mucurapo Secondary School and playground.

The aircraft was like brand new and resplendent in a coat of silver paint with lettering in blue on its sides. The registration was VP-TAA, and there was a large circle on the tail fin with the initials MC in the middle. It was towed to the field and assembled there and was eventually signed out as airworthy by Red Woodburn. The test flight was very successful. Lickfold was no longer with us and Mikey the only pilot. It attracted a lot of interest when out of its hangar, and cars would park all along the road to watch.

Mikey often complained about the lack of other aircraft to fly in company with, and he suggested that we should get off one afternoon early enough to fly alongside the Pan Am Duck on the last leg from Guiria to Cocorite, and we actually did that one afternoon. He and I got away from work and rushed to the flight strip, pulled the aircraft out of the shed, opened the wings and were getting it ready, when he shouted to me "there she is – she is coming!" He jumped into the seat and I ran to the front to swing the propeller and got him started, and had to run around the wing to get into my front seat, climbing in while he was taking off down wind. We just managed to fly with it a very few minutes, but it gave him a lift.

The other occasion was when the Graf Zeppelin decided to overfly Trinidad, early in 1934. I cannot remember the date, but Mikey prepared to accompany it for a while. This time he had an ex-1st World War pilot named Essex, I think his name was, employed with the motor car garage owned by Millar on Chacon Street as company. They got off in time to join company with the Graf, which was flying overhead most of the time. Quite an interesting calypso was written about the incident and was very popular, I think I can remember some of it:

One Sunday morning I did chance to hear
a rumbling and a tumbling in the atmosphere,
one Sunday morning I did chance to hear
a rumbling and a tumbling in the atmosphere.
I ran to stare people were flocking everywhere,
gesticulating, gazing and pointing in the air.
It was the Graf Zeppelin which had
come to pay a visit to Trinidad.
As I gazed at the Zeppelin contemplatively,

I marvelled at man's ingenuity,
to see this huge object in the air,
maintaining equilibrium in the atmosphere,
wonderfully, beautifully, gloriously,
decidedly, defying all the laws of gravity.
It was the Graf Zeppelin which had
come to pay a visit to Trinidad."

With mission completed, Jack St. Hilaire had decided to go to England to study Aviation Engineering at the Chelsea College of Aeronautics and booked his passage on one of the liners to leave on the Holiday Weekend of the Kings birthday, 3rd June 1934. But in the meantime Mikey had planned an inaugural trip to Tobago where he had had a team of men clear a strip on the south western tip of Tobago, which in later years became Crown Point Airport. He had arranged with the then Governor of Trinidad & Tobago to take "first flight" letters stamped as such by the post office and that Daisy, his wife, would go with him as she had done to Grenada previously–the first aeroplane to land there.

They obtained media coverage as the flying Ciprianis of Trinidad & Tobago, alongside the flying couple of Lindberg and his wife of America, and the Mollisons of England, and Trinidad & Tobago was moving up in the world.

I happened to be present at the Cipriani house one afternoon, a few days before the flight, when a discussion took place between Mikey and Daisy, who asked Mikey to postpone the flight to another weekend as it had transpired that Jack had booked to leave that very weekend and his passage could not be changed. Daisy had agreed that Jack had done so much for them, the least thing they could do was to see him off. Mikey argued that he could not change the plans at that stage as lots of plans had been made by the Governor for media coverage etcetera and that "the mail must go through", which became a popular phrase used when airmail flying was introduced in the U.S.A. in the mid-20's.

The discussion reached the point where Daisy had dug her heels in and decided that she could not go as she would have to see Jack off, and Mikey turned to me and said "OK, Garth, you come with me". This was a most wonderful opportunity for me but the Good Lord spoke through me and I replied "I would love to Mikey, but think that you should change the date so that Daisy could go on such a flight".

Mike then turned to a young Englishman, Bradshaw, who had come out to Trinidad as an auditor to the firm Fitzpatrick Graham & Co. and had recently attached himself to us and happened to be present and said "very well then Brad, you come with me" and of course he jumped at the offer and that was arranged. I chided myself for holding back but I was ever a shy youngster and fairly introverted.

The weekend of the 3rd June arrived and I awoke at my home, "Sunnyside" in Tacarigua, to a very rainy and overcast sky, so I decided not to go to Mucurapo as I thought the flight would have to be postponed. The day improved, so I got on my motorcycle to ride down as I thought there was a possibility of it leaving at a later time.

I was travelling through St. Augustine when I heard the sound of the engine and saw VP-TAA flying towards Piarco below the clouds and I turned to go home. Again, I thought of having missed a wonderful opportunity but wished the aircraft a safe journey.

At home, a while later, I heard the news that the aeroplane was missing and had not arrived in Tobago. I jumped on my motorcycle and rode to the Pan Am office, which was a hive of activity, and spoke with Elmo Bearden, who told me that he had advised Mike not to go because of the weather, but he had insisted on going. Elmo was in the process of arranging for the Sikorsky, which was on the ramp, to go on a search mission and asked if I would go with it. I agreed, and as soon as the pilot, Shultz and co-pilot, Kowlesky, arrived from the Queen's Park Hotel, we got airborne with the two up front and Harry Cadiz and myself in the back, one on each side of the cabin.

We flew up the Eastern Corridor towards Piarco then turned to cross the hills towards Tobago as low as we dared, and very low over the sea to and fro, but saw nothing and returned to the base after four and a half hours. I rode home and listened for news all the next day, which was a Sunday, and decided to go on foot through the hills on Monday, which was the Bank Holiday, and my younger brother Eddie decided to go with me on the search.

We collected the things we might need, such as a cutlass, torchlight, rope, gun etc. and dressed suitably and took some money and sandwiches and water and rode the motorcycle to Mathura Police Station where I asked for help, but none of the police could go with us, so I sought to hire some local bushmen to take us through the forest.

There were a number of people about and we got three willing to go, but they insisted that I should hire a chap named London, who was the expert bushman. We duly found him and set off into the forest, hoping to emerge at Sans Souci and return along the coast road.

While waiting to collect the search party at Mathura, the police inspector Major Lenegan arrived and asked us if we had any experience of the forest. I said "no" and he was concerned but remarked "at least you look well equipped". We also carried an old white bed-sheet that we had hoped to hang up on trees in the event of finding the wreckage.

We left our motorcycle at Mrs Gordon's house on the coast and set off. London made marks on the trees with his cutlass while cutting a way through the forest, but we saw nothing of the plane and when it got to 2.30 pm, I decided to turn back as we had to get home that night. The men advised against that, as they feared we would get lost. I naively thought that we would follow the marks, which had been made on the trees, and insisted that we would have to turn back. I paid them off and told them to report any findings to the police when they got through to Sans Souci on the north coast.

Within a short while we became lost, unable to recognise the way we had come with the bush closing up behind us after we had passed, and struggled to follow the hand compass we had brought. The terrain was hilly, up and down, uneven ground, and the compass gave conflicting readings in the valleys to those on the crests, so we were left with our instincts. I even climbed a tree, but I could not get near the top and got no better view, so we pressed on until it started to get dark and I told Eddie that we had better pick a cleared spot and settle down for the night.

We came upon a river and an area of ground alongside with enough room for us to lay out a ground sheet and lie down. We were exhausted and fell asleep side-by-side, covered with the sheet to retain some warmth. I was disturbed by a movement across my legs and thought it was Eddie trying to rearrange the sheet, only to find a huge snake slithering across us. We jumped up and when we checked our watch it was 12.25 am, but there was light enough from the moon. We decided to stay awake from then and got the gun ready to use.

The hours dragged and we sat there listening to all the strange sounds emitted by the trees and nocturnal wildlife. At around 4.00 am it started to rain, and as we were in an open area, we got quite wet waiting for daylight. As soon as it was light enough, we packed our things and started to wade down the river in a direction we hoped was east, as we reckoned the river would eventually empty into the sea.

With light increasing in that direction, we decided that we were going the right way and the river was getting deeper. We realised we could not swim with our equipment and would have to get onto the riverbank to proceed. Eventually we saw an improvised raft tied up at the side of the river. We loaded our stuff and climbed onto the raft, cutting it loose and poling our way down the river. We would soon see the sea and the bridge over the river indicating the coast road, where we tied the raft up and continued to walk south along the road.

Within a few minutes a car approached going towards Toco, being driven by Mrs Gordon and chauffeur. She told us that her house was a little further along the road and that we should ask the servant to give us a warm drink and something to eat. On arrival, we relished our mini breakfast and then set out for home on our motorcycle. Mother was relieved to see us and was anxious to hear all about our exploits.

We cleaned up and set out for work, Eddie to Barclays Bank and I to Alstons, with apologies for being late. Our apologies were readily accepted, as the missing of Cipriani was the hottest news in town.

It took a week before a party of scouts found the wreckage and reported it to the Arima police station. We were notified. Frank de Boehmler, who was then a Bush Warden, based in Sangre Grande, and I went in with the police party to the site in the hills of Aripo. The scouts who discovered the crashed plane explained that they did not actually reach the plane, but returned hurriedly to report it, so we assumed that we had been the first to reach the wreck.

I had instructions to retrieve the letters, documents and wallets of the two men when I found them. When I got to them, their bodies were still in the separate cockpits but it became evident that someone had already got to them before us. There were no wallets, and their expensive watches had been removed from their wrists. However, the police were prepared for what they found and removed the bodies from the plane and placed them in body bags as they were very decomposed.

They were carried out, each bag being attached at each end to a slim tree trunk cut from the forest, which was borne on the shoulders of two men fore and aft. When we got out of the forest to the clearing on the Paria Road where the cars were parked. The bodies were placed into lead lined coffins which were eventually sealed. I reported back to Daisy Cipriani, who now insisted that we should take her to the site. The following weekend, Frank and myself took Daisy and Jack's girlfriend to the site. Daisy had previously pressed to see the bodies, but this was refused quite rightly. Mikey and Bradshaw were interred in what was the newly opened Mucurapo Cemetery.

The following weekend, I collected a few men from my work at Alstons and borrowed a jitney and we went back to the site, took off the metal propeller and the tail fin which was intact, and brought them out and gave them to Daisy. I dismantled the engine on site and put the parts into crocus bags and brought them out on poles as we had done with the bodies. I cleaned up the engine parts, put them in a cupboard in the hope that someday I would be able to reassemble it and fit it into another airframe. I paid Daisy $100 for it.

A couple of months later, Jack St. Hilaire returned to Trinidad having abandoned his engineering course in England as he had become homesick, and took up with his earlier girlfriend, Lelia Lynch, whom he later married. Jack came to see me and asked for the engine as he would like to do with it what I had hoped to do. I let him have it as he was in a better financial position to do what I would like to have done. He refused to pay me $100 I had paid for it and that caused us to fall out. He never did use it, as in 1937, he imported a Piper Cub aeroplane from the U.S.A. complete with engine and taught himself to fly, and was the first person to fly an aeroplane to Tobago. But I had left Trinidad for England before that and therefore have no details of that. I heard later that he had crashed his plane and joined the oil industry and did very well in that field from all accounts.

Some time after Mikey's accident, we were paid a visit by "the Goodwill Flyers", who were Professor Forsyth and pilot Anderson, nicknamed "the Chief" in a very nice little two-seater high-winged mono-plane, and they used our landing strip at Mucurapo. The wings did not fold, so it was parked on the concrete apron of the shed.

They were here for a few days being feted and were leaving to continue their journey to British Guiana. A crowd collected on the roadside to wave them off, and they took off to the east waving madly, and the right wing hit the solitary bamboo that had shot up from the small clump and became damaged, and the plane just flopped down in the back yard of a house on the street adjoining the strip. Amazingly the only injury to the two of them was a cut across Anderson's nose. The plane fell between the house and a chicken shed, doing no real damage to the premises. Anderson and the Professor were taken to the hospital for a check up, but were soon free and had to go on to British Guiana by Pan Am.

The wreckage of the plane was collected and housed in our shed on the strip and I went there to help them. While searching the plane, I heard a rattle in the elevator and called Anderson, who cut open the fabric with his penknife and found a small hammer that had been left there in the manufacture. He grabbed it with glee as he could use it as an excuse for the incident. The wreck was duly shipped back to the U.S.A.

Another visitor to our island by air was an Englishman called Lancaster, if my memory serves me well, who landed on the Great Savannah in an Avro Avian aircraft. He put up at the Queen's Park Hotel and was here a few days. He had a party at the hotel the night before leaving, which I was told went on into the early hours of the morning, and when he ventured out at about 5.30 am, he crashed on take off from the Savannah. He was badly injured and was put onto a ship to take him to New York, I think. I never heard how he fared. His wrecked plane was stored in Millar's car garage and was still there when I got back from the war.

I continued in my job as Manager of Alstons Coffee Department, saving up to be able to go to the U.K. and learn to fly. In the meantime, I interested myself in helping any pilots who visited Trinidad and met some very interesting people. One of them was a young, 21 year-old Spaniard named Juan Ignacio Pombo, whose father was one of the first aeroplane pilots in Spain, who went to England and bought a very nice light three-seater aeroplane known as the British Aircraft Company's Eagle, and had it fitted with long range tanks to fly across the South Atlantic.

The story was that he had become infatuated with a young girl of sixteen who was attending school in a convent in Spain, whilst her family lived in Mexico. Her father was a very prominent man there. The father was not too happy for her to have boyfriends so far from home and recalled her to Mexico. Juan

Pombo was a very young, personable man and a private pilot, and thought he would buy an aeroplane, fly to Mexico and present himself, and this he did. He flew from England to his home in Santander, Northern Spain and set out from there to Dhaka, Natal in South America, Trinidad and on to Mexico from here. I met him at Piarco and helped to cover his aeroplane with a large tarpaulin borrowed from a builder, the wings folded so it became compact.

It was our rainy season and very wet. The aeroplane was a pretty little thing built of plywood and cotton-covered, with a Gipsy Major Engine. He took a photograph of Eddie and myself standing in front of the covered plane with Eddie holding a copy of *Flight* magazine. The photograph I sent to *Flight* in England and it was printed in one of their issues with a short progress report on Pombo.

The trip was a total success as he was very well received by the girl's parents. The couple were married and they passed through Trinidad on a cruise-ship on their honeymoon.

The next visitor I helped was a Cuban, José Menendez. He flew into Piarco in a Lockheed Sirius, single-engined low wing. He had over flown Trinidad on his way to Natal, Brazil, to fly up the South Atlantic to Spain, as a return gesture from Cuba, after General Franco's brother, who was the Head of the Spanish Airforce, had paid a courtesy visit to Cuba. In those romantic days of flight, there were many attempts to fly aeroplanes long distances, especially across the two Oceans of the Atlantic, and that one succeeded where many others had failed.

Franco flew as the American Navy did, but in the opposite direction via the Azores, and José Menendez, being the most experienced Cuban in their Navy, was chosen for this flight. He had previously flown for Pan American Airways between Miami and Havana before joining the Navy. He landed in British Guiana and sought help to extend his fuel capacity as he discovered the engine was using more fuel than had been calculated, and he was told to go to Trinidad where Pan American then had a base.

He arrived at Piarco and Pan American Chief Engineer, Red Woodburn, fitted two small extra 15-gallon tanks in the wings, one each side of the fuselage. He cut a section of the plywood wing from underneath on each side of the fuselage. One of those I still have, signed by José Menendez to me as his best aviator friend in Trinidad. This operation took some time and the full moon, the light of which José had planned to use on his Atlantic crossing, was waning, so he postponed departure until the next full moon and spent the time in Trinidad, living at the Queen's Park Hotel.

The Cuban Navy sent another officer to keep him company. My family saw a lot of them as they came to our house, "Sunnyside", on the Eastern Main Road, frequently while going to and from Piarco. There was a family, the Gambals, who lived in St. Augustine, who could speak Spanish. So, two of the girls would come to our home when they could, to help with conversation. I only knew what little Spanish I had learnt at school.

On the first occasion when José brought his friend, lieutenant Gustavo Novo, who was an extremely handsome young man, to visit us, we had invited the Gambal girls up and they were at home to greet them. As Gustavo appeared in the doorway of the drawing room, he heard Mercedes, the elder of the two, remark "oh my god he, looks just like Ramón Novarro". He pulled himself up to his six feet in height and with a flourish of his hand replied "No, no, maybe Ramón Novarro looks like me, but I do not look like Ramón Novarro", which made him immediately acceptable. I would explain here that Ramón was a very handsome, swashbuckling movie actor, who played the lead in the original film of "Ben Hur", which was very popular in Trinidad.

We enjoyed their visit and in time the aircraft was made ready, the full moon came round and José set off to continue his flight. We went to Piarco to see him off and prayed for his safe arrival in Spain. I got a little anxious when the plane took most of the field to get off and watched him make a wide circle to return overhead and give a wave of the wings and set course for Natal. He arrived safely in Spain and wrote me a very nice letter enclosing pictures and newspaper cuttings of his wonderful greeting there.

I think the next visitation of aircraft was a sudden arrival one morning while I was at work in the saw mill building of Alstons. There was an almighty roar of engines and I looked out to see a swarm of British Naval Aircraft in a mock attack on Port-of-Spain. The aircraft carrier "Furious" had launched its aircraft off the north coast before it entered the harbour on a practise exercise and they were enjoying themselves.

I was on the roof of the building when the phone rang and I had to go down to answer it. Captain Roy Alston M.C., my immediate boss, was on the line, "Garth, are you watching this display?" "Yes sir, I was on the roof," I replied. The next question "well what is that aircraft that is beating up the railway yard so close to the ground?" and I was able to tell him the type as I used to read the *Flight* and *Aeroplane* from cover to cover and he said "Gerald Wight says it is so and so," but I assured him that was wrong. It was a Fairy IIIF with a Rolls Royce Kestrel engine, he said "thank you, I'll tell him". There was a standing competition between the two directors, Roy Alston M.C. of the Army and Gerald Wight of the Air Force.

In 1937 an Oilfield Workers strike turned into a riot, which spread to other companies such as the sugar manufacturing ones. The uprising became particularly nasty when a police corporal, who was sent to arrest the leader Uriah Butler, was murdered. When he approached Uriah on the rostrum as he was about to address the large assembly, he was chased by the crowd, ran through a small shop and jumped through a window at the back. He broke a leg and the crowd caught up with him, threw petrol on him and set him alight.

The large businesses in Port-of-Spain, such as Alstons and Huggins etc., called on their staff to go to the aid of the police and Deryck and myself, among many others, went to the Police Headquarters where we were signed up as a voluntary army, given a marching drill in the compound, a rifle and ten rounds of ammunition, and sent out to guard various areas and positions.

The first night we covered the petrol tanks on the waterfront south of Wrightson Road. All was quiet for some time and John Howard, one of the Orange Grove Manager's sons, came to me and mentioned the lack of action and said "I have to fire this rifle, one way or the other, and if nothing happens by 2.00 am, that goat nearby will have to take the shot".

As the early hours progressed, we heard single shots at intervals coming from one area of the waterfront and we became anxious, but had to stay at our separate posts.

The next morning, we were collected by jitney and taken back to Police Headquarters, lined up in the yard and a corporal came around collecting the ten rounds from each man. When he got to a chap named Lambert, who was known for the crazy things he did, Lambert handed in four bullets. The corporal was shocked as every bullet had to be accounted for. When the Corporal asked "where are the others?" Lambert cheerfully told him "Corporal, I got five pelicans with six shots, how's that for shooting?" Of course there was an investigation and hell to pay. Lambert later joined the police force as the first white boy in the ranks, but I never heard how things developed.

After the uprising was quelled, a second battalion of Trinidad volunteers was formed. Colonel Alston asked me to join and a short while after I was promoted to Lance Corporal.

There were other visitors to Piarco, such as Laura Ingalls in a high-winged Lockheed, but they were brief and I did not meet them. The next one I helped was Squadron Leader Bert Hinkler, a small Australian solo in a Puss Moth by De Havilland Aircraft Company. I can't remember where he had come from, but he spent a couple of days at Piarco, preparing his aircraft for the crossing of the South Atlantic back to England. I spent a Saturday helping him clean the spark plugs, gapping them and handing them to him to check and refit to the Gipsy Major engine. He stood by the aircraft and did everything himself. I told him that I would like to do long distance flying myself one day and he said "son, you go to England, join a workshop, learn as much as you can about your aeroplane, then learn to fly and never allow anyone else close to it" and that stuck in my mind.

By this time my brother Deryck was well advanced in his study and preparation for entering the Methodist fraternity as a Minister, and I had completed another homestudy course from the Technical Institute of Great Britain in Aeroengine Design and obtained their Diploma A.M.Tech.I of Great Britain. Unfortunately, I had no one to advise me and I chose the wrong course, engines instead of airframes, which I was to discover later, as an individual can design and build his own small aircraft, but it takes a team to build an engine with years of toil and trial and error. Originally, I longed to go to Cambridge University to study Engineering, but could not afford it, and any course mentioning the term Engineer attracted me. However, the course covered maths, strength of materials etc., which came in very handy when I eventually got to England.

Mother and Glory at the front steps to Shamrock Villa.

Myself patting Etheline, Deryck behind, Marguerite, Pat and Glory behind her at Shamrock Villa.

Mikey Cipriani and his plane as it came from Canada.

The plane rebuilt with Jock St. Hilaire.

Norman Tang and myself at Plymouth.

Strike snap at Woodford Lodge Estate, 1937

Myself having just put up the Alstons flag on their new building.

Mother, Marguerite and Glory on the way to Sangre Grande.

Mother, Glory and Eddie on the way to Sangre Grande.

Lance Corporal G. Lyder, 2nd Battalion, Trinidad Volunteers

Lance Corporal G. Lyder, 2nd Battalion, Trinidad Volunteers and my cousin Kenneth Kelshall.

Off to England

Deryck was duly accepted by the Church and sailed to Jamaica to train at Caenwood College.

I continued to save my pennies and having accrued three months leave over the years, I applied for that leave to go to England.

I was kitted out and booked a passage on the *M.S. Cordelera,* one of two German ships, which at that time provided a service. I was seen off at the St. Vincent jetty by my family on 3rd of August 1938 and taken by launch to the ship that was anchored in the stream. I was shown to my cabin to find that I was to share it with Norman Tang, so was assured of good company en route. We enjoyed the trip to Barbados, but after that, we struck really rough weather and both of us got seasick; in fact we felt so ill after a while that Norman, in the top bunk, called down to say "boy, I wish I could die".

Only a few minutes later, the ship, having gone nose down after surfing the crest of a huge wave, was slapped on the side by the sea, which then gushed through our porthole on our outside cabin, with the exposed propellers whining and having to be throttled back. Norman jumped up shouting "get up Garth, get up, we've struck something", the ship wallowed briefly while the engines were reset and we continued our journey. We never really recovered to enjoy the trip, but survived by staying on deck near the bow with the wind in our faces.

There were a number of young German males onboard, collected from Brazil and Venezuela, going home to do their military service and were convinced that war was imminent. They went into a huddle when I said that I was going to England to learn to fly and one returned to enquire, "military flying?", I said "no, private flying", but they were not convinced. They later opined that war was inevitable between the British and themselves and that I would be involved as they were going to be, and made a pact with me that they would carry a replica of this ship's flag on the ground with them so that I would not bomb them and I should paint the flag on my aeroplane and they would not shoot at me.

After ten long days, we arrived at Plymouth and left the ship on a launch to shouts from the boys "remember the pact". I forgot to mention that halfway through our journey, we crossed the sister ship *Caribia* in mid-Atlantic and hove to for the exchange of greetings between the crews. That gave me confidence that they knew their positions to be able to arrange that.

Norman and I cleared customs and went on our ways. He was met and I boarded the boat train to Paddington, London. It was a lovely clear day and I stood almost the whole journey in the corridor enjoying the scenery, the clean fat cows and horses in the green fields, and thought how my mother would have relished such a journey. I noticed many names of places and buildings familiar to us in Trinidad, such as Sutton Nurseries, Huntley & Palmers, etc.

I was met at Paddington Station by Billy Watson, son of the Reverend Watson, our senior Methodist Minister in Port-of-Spain. Billy Watson had been to Trinidad on several occasions on leave from school and it was great to see him and be taken to his "digs" in Upper Norwood, near the Crystal Palace, where he had arranged a room for me in his house run by a Miss Goodly. He was employed by the Rank Organisation at the time, in the office near Blackfriars, and he escorted me around London whenever he could get away.

I had letters to deliver and friends to visit and saw quite a bit of London before busying myself to seek employment. I went to an RAF office in Kingsway to enquire about the short service commissions, which were being offered at the time to extend the size of the force due to the gathering war clouds, and I was given a letter of introduction to Lady Frances Ryder and her team of Ladies of the Commonwealth who cared for the arriving males from the colonies, offering their services in the threatening situation.

It was a most interesting time, meeting people from Canada, Australia, New Zealand, Rhodesia and South Africa, in fact from every corner of the world, to find we had so much in common with one another and sang the same songs around the piano, which Miss Soley played. We were given tickets for shows, cruises on the Thames and taken to many venues and made very welcome. Lady Ryder had her club at Cadogan Gardens and we met there most days.

My turn for interview to enter the RAF came and I appeared before the senior officers, who asked a number of questions and told me I should hear from them shortly, which I did and the result was negative. In spite of a note saying that 'no reapplication would be considered', I wrote to the office saying how disappointed I was and a Mr Campbell of the Air Ministry asked me to come to see him. He took me to see a single senior officer in a nearby room, a Vice Air Marshal I think he was, and immediately I sensed the atmosphere as anti.

He obviously did not like my questioning the earlier decision and aggressively asked "what did my father do?" and I replied what my mother had called him, "a master baker", which of course he was not, he was a businessman who owned a chain of four bakeries. He then asked "what do you do?" and I told him that I was the manager of a department of a large business company. He then asked "what do you get paid?" and I foolishly divided my annual salary in Trinidad dollars by five to quote him an equivalent figure in sterling, as at that time, the rate of exchange of the Trinidad dollar to the pound sterling was TT$4.80. With that he waved me away as working class instead of officer class.

I had always been shy for speaking up for myself and I realised I had blown the interview. Mr Campbell took me back to his office and suggested that I could still join the RAF as an aircrew member and train as a navigator. On completion of the course, which lasted three months, I would be promoted to Sergeant and could later apply for a commission. At least he thought I was worth one. I rejected that offer and went back to my digs woefully disappointed. On my next visit to Lady Ryder's she asked how I had got on at the interview and I told her that I had been rejected. She looked surprised and said "I do not understand how the RAF works, I would have thought you were a certainty". It was a pity that the RAF did not seek an input from these Ladies of the Commonwealth, who had a wonderful opportunity of assessing the boys as they saw them socially.

I was now faced with looking for a job, a foothold in the aviation industry, and went to Croydon Airport to see Imperial Airways, but had no success, although I explained that I would do anything just to get on the first rung of the ladder. I did enjoy the visit though, watching the aircraft arrive and leave. Imperial Airways operated huge Handley Page Biplanes, in those days named Hannibal, Seylla etc., which took approximately two hours to get to Paris, but were famous as first class moving restaurants. Air France had a fast, sleek, small twin, named Bloche, which slithered over the boundary fence and took most of the field to stop. KLM had just taken delivery of the new, all metal American DC3. I saw the famous Captain O.P. Jones, Captain Emeritus of Imperial Airways, arrive with his goatee beard and was thrilled with the movements at the airport.

I had to get something to do soon or my leave would run out and I would have to return to Trinidad defeated, so I went to the Technological Institute of Great Britain, whose Diploma I held, with offices on Fleet Street, and saw the secretary. He suggested that we go to the restaurant downstairs and discuss matters over lunch, which I paid for, and he promised that he would give me two letters of introduction to colleagues in Bristol, which he did on payment of one guinea each.

I had had a good look around London and looked forward to seeing another city and so took the Great Western Train to Temple Meads station in Bristol. I asked directions to the Bristol Engine Works and I got on a tramcar to Filton and walked down the hill to the Engine Factory. I was interviewed by the Manager, Mr Ramsbottom, who showed me around and said that he could give me a job immediately, but he was more discerning than the RAF and thought I was looking for something more than he could offer. He opened the door of a long hall, with benches holding at least fifty men and women assembling carburettors for their engines and said they were making good money, but he did not think that that was what I was looking for. I agreed and explained that I would like to get into a factory where I could work on building an aeroplane and see it rolled out complete. He said I should go up the hill to the aircraft factory and try to get into the experimental department where the prototypes were built. So off I went but not to the aircraft shop, but to the Chief Pilot's office, where I was received by the Chief Pilot, Captain Uwins. He was quite courteous, but snooty, looking me up and down trying to place me on the social ladder, while I asked him about the possibility of any job so that I could learn to fly eventually. He said that he was very sorry but there was nothing that he could offer.

With that further rebuff, I returned to the room in town that I had booked to lick my wounds, phoned the person named on the second letter and arranged to see him at his home that evening. I can't remember his name now, but he had studied through the T.I. of Great Britain and was now on the staff of the Bristol Aircraft Factory in "the stress office". He was very helpful and he told me that I should aim for the experimental department as they were hiring people at present. The shop manager was a Mr Brown, ex Sergeant Major, really tough but straight-speaking. He would be doing the hiring and I would have to get through him. You will have to sell yourself to him, but that was the place to do what I had explained I wanted. I thanked him and went to my digs.

The next morning, I was up bright and early and made my way by tramcar to Filton and sat at the back of a number of would-be employees in their brown overalls, obviously men with experience in the trade. The whole country was on a huge recruitment drive to secure people to manufacture materials in preparation for war. Mr Brown duly arrived and dealt with each in turn, handing out chits to those he accepted with instructions where to go. At last he had finished and approached me to ask if I had come to see him. I said "yes" and handed him the letter I had received from the Bristol engineer. He read it, then looked me over and said "I don't have anything for you, I am hiring workers", and looking at my manicured fingernails and three-piece blue suit remarked that he did not think I had ever worked in my life. I was up against it but I had to get a start at all costs, so I surprised myself by speaking up to sell myself, explaining that I had rebuilt an aeroplane and he asked "what type?" I said "a De Havilland Moth" and he said "that is wood and fabric, we build metal aircraft here and bolt the parts together" and I retorted that I could do that. I fought back as I have never had to do before and he asked how old I was and I replied "twenty-four", he said "I cannot hire you as a student but a working adult and I will therefore have to pay you the minimum wage which is 4 pence per hour". I told him that I would accept that. He expected me to walk out and was taken aback.

There was a brief silence which I broke by asking, "when should I start", he turned away momentarily saying "I am making a big mistake", but I assured him that he would not regret hiring me. He then said "look, I will give you a try for a fortnight and if you are no good I shall kick you out". I told him he had a deal and again asked him "when can I start?" He said "come on Monday at 7 o'clock". I thanked him and left him shaking his head in disbelief at what he had just done.

I went in search of the Minister of the Filton Methodist Church and found him at home on Charlborough Road. He received me very graciously and we enjoyed a chat, and he promised he would find me digs when I got back on Saturday. This was a Wednesday and I returned to the city by tramcar and took the train back to my digs in London. Billy and Miss Goodly listened intently to my experiences in Bristol.

I settled with Miss Goodly, thanked Billy for all his help and set off to my new venture on Saturday morning. I took the train from Paddington Station and arrived back in Bristol, and went to Filton to the Reverend Fellows and he took me to my new digs, a short distance away. I put my luggage in my room and went into the "Horse Fair Area" and bought some tools for my job. A few to start with and returned to my digs.

There was the owner, his wife and small daughter in a fairly new house, and I had quite a nice room. That afternoon and evening was spent explaining where I had come from and where it was on the map etc. The man worked with a greengrocer downtown and his wife looked after the house. Sunday was spent getting myself settled in and prepared for work at 7.00 am in the experimental shop at the Bristol Aeroplane Company. Again there was a long session of my explaining about the West Indies and why I had come to England. When I mentioned that I hoped to learn to fly, the man was astonished that a mere mortal in the guise of a youth from Trinidad could have such an exalted ambition, as the pilots at Bristol were worshipped as gods. I duly got to Bristol Aircraft Factory early on Monday morning, dressed in one of the two white overalls I had brought with me from Trinidad, shown how to check in using a timecard, which had been prepared in my name and put in a rack alongside the clock.

A supervisor "charge-hand" in the industry took me up on to the gallery and to my work bench and left. I should explain that the shop was a huge shop with prototype aeroplanes and mock-ups on the ground floor and a wide gallery all around it on the next floor up, overlooking a railing to the ground floor. This area contained numerous work benches, each divided into three with three vices to accommodate three persons making parts from drawings supplied from the office. I stood there looking rather spare and not knowing what to do next. Alongside of me was a local named Park, and at the other station alongside him another fitter named Jim Carter. I cannot remember Park's first name as I seldom used it, as he was known as Parks or Parkee. However, he looked at me and said "hello, you are new to this aren't you?" I admitted I had not done this before and he took me to an Irish man who dished out the jobs through a window in his office.

Parkee approached the window with me and told Paddy he had a new one here and could he find me a small job to start with. Paddy handed a drawing to him, which seemed too advanced for me and Parkee got a simpler one that I felt that I could make. Parkee then told me to go to the stores and draw material and when he saw my vacant stare he said "alright come with me" and took me down to the stores and advised me how much duralumin to ask for on the blue work card that was attached to the drawing. He wisely advised me to order twice what I needed just to begin with in the event that I should make a mistake.

We returned to our benches and I started on my job, which was to make a trimmer for the elevator of an aeroplane that would adjust its position. I had to bend the length of duralumin sheet into a triangular shape to be riveted to an extruded solid strip of metal where the two ends met. This I did satisfactorily and I drilled holes at intervals along its 18 inches of length and started riveting. I soon discovered that the extruded filler was moving into a bent curve away from the edges of the trimmer as it stretched while being hammered. I showed Parkee and he chucked it into the bin and said "start again quickly". I did that, but this time I put pins in alternate holes to hold the solid strip between the two ends of the trimmer while I riveted the other holes, and this was a success. I took it to the area where finished jobs were checked and if found satisfactory were passed, and went back to Paddy for another job.

Three weeks had passed and several small jobs completed. I was beginning to feel comfortable and then Mr Brown appeared on the gallery on the far end from us and worked his way round cussing and in some cases firing the chaps who were not satisfactory, and everyone shook in their boots. He got to me eventually and asked what was I doing and I showed him my current job in progress. He asked if I had got any jobs passed and I said "yes sir, several". He then said "come with me to my office". Parkee looked at me with his eyebrows raised as I followed Mr Brown. He sat down at his desk and looking into the shop through the panoramic glass where he observed the workforce and said, "do you remember that I said that I would give you a try for a fortnight and kick you out if not satisfactory?" I replied "that is correct Mr Brown" and turning to look at me said "well boy you have surprised me, so much so that from today your wages will be 5 pence per hour". I thanked him gratefully and he said "I don't want your thanks, just go back and continue as you are going". Well I did and just went from strength to strength in that shop, completing bigger and more difficult jobs and winning approval from the managers and my wages increased time after time without my ever asking.

I had joined Bristol in September 1938 and I discovered a whole new world. I had never known what it meant to be a tradesman and I met a class of person foreign to me and felt somewhat out of place but one spark of light appeared in the form of the only other person in the shop wearing white overalls. He turned out to be Bruce Bleach, a student from Portsmouth who was learning to be an Aeronautical Engineer going through the various departments as he studied at Merchant Ventures College in the evenings towards the Higher National Certificate in Engineering. This was a route taken by most persons who eventually became the masters and designers of the country. As I found that I had little in common with the ordinary fitters, Bruce became a lifeline to me, and perhaps the only person who made it possible for me to continue there. We became fast friends and remain so until this day, for I became very homesick and would cry in my room at my digs and wondered what the hell am I doing here when my family could do with me back home.

The winter arrived and was very severe that year, and I looked forward to going to Cardiff for Christmas where I was invited to spend a few festive days with the Reverend Watson and family who were then ministering to the folk at Tiger Bay. The morning I left Bristol to travel to Cardiff, even the electricity wires were covered with an inch-thick coating of ice. I arrived by train and Billy was at the station once again to greet me, and a very happy reunion it was with all the other members of the family. There were the Reverend and Mrs Watson, affectionately known as Uncle Watter and Auntie Winnie, Billy, Marjorie, Elsie and Donald, the offspring. We had a lovely few days over the Christmas before I had to return to my job at Bristol. I joined the church at Filton and made some nice friends there, many of them also working at the aeroplane factory.

Entering the New Year 1939, I started to look for a convenient school to learn to fly. I went to see the flying club at Whitchurch, but that was difficult to get to without a car and I could not yet afford one. I heard of a club at Weston Super Mare and went down by train from Temple Meads, and discovered that there was a halt a mile or two before Weston Super Mare station, which was right alongside of the airfield. So I got out and walked to the club. This seemed to me to be the answer and in due course, when the weather opened up, I joined that club and travelled down on weekends.

I should mention here that I had changed digs because the owner came to my room and charged me with upsetting his wife, because I had withdrawn into my room and no longer joined them socially in the evenings. I explained that I had a lot of studying to do and letters to write etc., but realised that I would have to move and asked the Reverend Fellows to find me somewhere else. He found me a comfortable room diagonally across the road from him and I was comfortable there until Mrs Riley in turn questioned why it was I took little notice of her daughter of fifteen and did not take her out and about. I had to go back to the Reverend Fellows and he found me another home with two nurses, a Miss Richardson who was retired and a Miss Pemberton who worked at a home for retarded children.

I started flying at the club at Weston – Locking Farm as soon as the weather made it possible, with the Chief Instructor Riley-Sawdon in a "Hornet Moth" two-seater cabin type, which had recently been produced.

Unlike the normal open cockpit type trainers, I could fly without any helmet and goggles and in my normal suit of clothes. This was a new and welcome departure in those days. The De Havilland factory at Hatfield had built this biplane with folding wings to appeal to the private owner who would keep it in a garage like a car.

After giving me a good grounding in the course, I was handed over to a young assistant instructor who took me to the stage of going solo, when Riley-Sawdon gave me a check-out and said "okay, take it round for one circuit as we have just done and bring it back to me" and advised that it would climb faster with one person but that was the only thing different. I did as he said and landed in a lovely three pointer and when I got back to him, he said "well, that was just like blowing the froth off the beer, wasn't it". He congratulated me and said, "you now have one more traditional thing to do and that is to buy us all a round of drinks". So we retired to the bar and I was welcomed into the flying fraternity. I had soloed after 7 hours 20 minutes of training over a rather prolonged period because of weather. I was over the moon and wrote home to say that my ambition was on its way. I duly qualified for and obtained my private pilot's licence that summer, but my flying came to an abrupt halt when war was declared on 3rd September of 1939.

I had joined a few friends at Reverend Fellows' home to listen in sombre silence to the broadcast that Prime

Minister Chamberlain made. I had previously seen on the "Pathe" news in the cinema Chamberlain's return from seeing Hitler in Munich, when he waved a sheet of paper with Adolf Hitler's name on it that war had been averted and that there would be peace in our time.

The War Begins

Immediately the whole country was plunged into a feverish preparation for war. The windows of all buildings had to be blacked out, low wattage bulbs installed in most light sockets, food had to be stock-piled and ration books for food, clothing etc. issued to each and every person.

There was no panic; everyone went about his or her chore with silent prayer and determination. A number of people who were visiting Britain hurried to get out, but I felt it was my business to stay and do my bit for the mother country, and I knew my mother would approve. She was the offspring of a very proud people who had left England as Methodist missionaries to further the cause of Christ to the world and seemed more English than those at home in England. The English could do no wrong. Life in our home was loving and strict and disciplined to a high degree. We were brought up to be clean, honest and not to drink or swear, in fact we had to pay a forfeit if we uttered any swear word, even "damn". Later, when we were earning our own money, we had to put a penny in the huge jar if we did. She taught us to be public-spirited at an early age, and if we saw a standpipe on a road left open or just leaking, one of us would be despatched to try to close it or report it at the nearest police station. She had a book of "poetic gems" she would read to us about the travails of the British people to spread the gospel throughout the world, and eagerly assisted when the Methodist Synod was held every January to review the work of the Church and to re-post the Ministers to the various stations. The senior Church in Port-of-Spain was Hanover on Abercrombie Street, but mother was married at Tranquility Church at the corner of Victoria Avenue and Tragarete Road. We were all christened there and excitedly went there for 5.00 am service on Christmas morning each year to sing the opening hymn "Christians awake" and see the morning gradually open up to daylight.

When we had grown up, Glory, our eldest sister, became a Circuit Steward and later took over the book-keeping of its finances, while the youngest, Marguerite, sang in the choir. I was given the job of going on board the ships to meet the new ministers arriving and help them through Immigration and Customs and on to the house allocated to them. After a busy week, I would enjoy going to Sunday services where I relaxed in our pew and listened to Mrs Worrell playing Handel's Largo and other soothing voluntaries on the organ. I was at peace – the world was, but alas now in England war had broken out and I felt I was born to be part of it, having been born in January 1914 and no doubt influenced by the atmosphere of those early years of growing up and listening to and reading about the dreadful happenings of World War I.

I now applied myself even harder to my job at Bristol helping to build a Beaufort bomber, with the mock-up of the Beau-fighter taking shape full size in the experimental shop close to me. I later had a new one brought off the assembly line for me to modify for Coastal Command duties and regret never getting the opportunity to fly one, but more of that later.

I was on the shop floor when the new Prime Minister, Mr Winston Churchill, addressed the whole population, on the plight of our 350,000 strong expedition force which was beleaguered at Dunkirk, and he appealed to all persons with experience of handling small boats and engines to go forthwith to the nearest police station and offer to help. A number of our workmen downed tools and went and we watched and prayed, whilst a maritime miracle unfolded before our eyes. Some 330,000 of them were rescued and brought back in anything that would float and we gave thanks to the Lord for the quiet sea he prepared for them.

In the meantime, trenches were dug in the grounds of the factory at Bristol and shelters built to house our workforce in the event of bombing raids, and a small shelter supplied for each household called an Anderson shelter. I had grandiose dreams of how I would rescue the Misses Richardson and Pemberton and the lovely red setter named Danny Boy in the event of it being hit in a raid. These dreams were smashed when one night, two loads fell close to the works and I went to look on my way to work. It shook me as one bomb estimated to be a 500 pounder had fallen on a truck, which was the mother to a balloon winched into the air to deter bombers, it had been hit and the whole engine cut out and thrown a distance away and the winching apparatus another distance leaving a huge crater of some 40 feet across and 15 feet deep.

I realised then what bombing could do. The balloon crew were just not there – they may have been cut to pieces. I had a lot to think about then. I followed the exploits of our fighter pilots when the Luftwaffe started in on us in a big way in 1940, and we had to take to the shelters at the factory on several occasions. The tune "Marching through Georgia" would be played on the public address system whenever the bomber raids threatened our area, and we would drop everything and rush to the shelters. On the 'all clear' being sounded, the tune played would be "Colonel Bogey", which meant that we could return to our jobs.

Our fighter pilots were working overtime and I regretted the RAF's decision not to accept me, as I felt as though I was born for this time and would have relished the job of defending our mother country. I thought how short-sighted they were.

After the losses our fighter boys inflicted on them, the Germans called off their dogs from daylight raids and started indiscriminate night bombing of our cities and Bristol was included. My friend Bruce Bleach had joined the Home Guard and his girlfriend the Ambulance and Fire Fighters Brigade as a driver, and

I was truly amazed at the jobs she undertook. She was an extremely brave young woman and I prayed that she would not be hurt. I must back-track a bit as I forgot to mention that on the daylight raids, we at the factory received attention from the German bombers, but the bombs fell on the shelters instead of the factory and caused mayhem.

On one occasion, the shelter next to mine was hit, and lying on the floor, I was shuffled around by the blast, covering my ears to save them from burst drums. There were horrific cries of agony renting the air after the bombers had passed and we emerged to see the shelter alongside ours demolished and the chaps calling for help, those who were not killed outright. We all tried to help and ran to fetch hacksaws etc. to cut through the metal rods holding the broken slabs of concrete together which made them difficult to remove.

We had doctors and first-aid personnel moving around, even crawling into gaps to inject the injured, who were crying with pain, with morphine. Several died before they could be rescued. An all-girls shelter not far away had received a direct hit and just had to be sealed up as a tomb. Some bodies were found in hedges, dead without any appearance of injury, their lungs and heart torn by the blast. This made me think of doing something more active than just building weapons.

I had been making great strides at Bristol and was encouraged by these successes to continue at the factory a bit longer. For instance, a long-nosed Blenheim was wheeled in off the production line and I was called to replace the box-former in the rear end that held the tail-wheel assembly. These boxes made of duralumin were breaking up in service and a quick fix was to replace them with a similar structure in mild steel. I had a look at the job and felt that I could do it without the necessity of removing the tailplane and breaking down the controls of the rudder and elevator as I was told to do.

I went to Paddy in the office and told him what I thought and asked for permission to try it as it would save a lot of time and bother if I was successful. He gave me the OK and I started cutting out the old box-former when one of the senior fitters came up from the aerodrome to tell me that I was wasting time as he was doing one on the airfield and removing the tail section was imperative. I refused to be put off and a row ensued, while he explained that he was doing the job of fitting for fifteen years, while I was swanning around in the West Indies and fishing.

Paddy came out and sent him on his way after betting him 10 shillings that I would succeed. He took it up and departed. Paddy came up periodically to see how I was doing and reminded me that he had a whole pink note riding on me. Having cut out the box structure, I discovered that I could not get the new one in place as the taper of the fuselage presented the box- former notches fitting over the stringers, so I thought out a scheme of cutting the stringers, replacing the former and then fitting patches to the stringers when in place. This is where I drew on the information I gained from courses from the T.I.G.B. I went to the resident air registration officer and explained what I intended and he looked up the air worthiness manual and approved my scheme, so I went ahead and fitted the box-former as planned and had it all pinned in place, ready to rivet when I received a visit from Mr Brown and Mr Johnny Ratcliffe BSc (Cantab) – the manager of the department on the Board of the company, who obviously were following this job with great interest. Mr Ratcliffe, who never had spoken to me before, told me to leave the job now and come into the office and write a report from A to Z of how I had achieved this, as it would be sent to all RAF stations where these Blenheims were grounded and affecting the operations. They got someone else to rivet the thing in place.

The company received a letter of commendation from the Air Ministry in due course, but Paddy was ecstatic and phoned the chap from the aerodrome to come up and see how it should be done and pay him his bet of 10 shillings. The successful completion of that job gave me entirely new status. I was given two young apprentices to work with, named Secombe and the chap we called Tubby because of his shape. I just can't remember his real name but his mother was the leader of a dance band and when 'music while you work' was relayed over the tannoy system at regular intervals morning and afternoon, Tubby would get hold of two screwdrivers or similar and beat taps on the workbench to accompany it. These two went to Merchant Ventures College at night and one whole day on a Thursday for schooling. On one occasion Bruce, who had a bench next to mine with a drawer full of tools and bits of iron of different shapes for riveting in awkward places in the aeroplane, pulled at the tight drawer too strenuously and it came right out of the bench and fell on his foot. He jumped about in pain and Secombe said to him "never mind, Mr Bleach, it could have been worse, think of this, if gravity worked in the opposite sense, it would have hit you under your chin".

These two youngsters became very loyal to me and saved my bacon some time later when a Beau-fighter was brought into the shop to be modified for use with Coastal Command. It had to have its pair of engines upgraded to the Hercules MK VI, a navigator position fitted amid-ships, two Orliken cannons fitted passing under the pilot's seat and firing through the nose etc. etc. The chargehand, Clatworthy, brought me a whole batch of drawings and gave them to me, saying "this is your job, Lyder", and sent a number of experienced fitters to join me. I realised that this was a huge job, but I was always up for a challenge and started handing out the various jobs to those I felt could do each particular one from my knowledge at that time of their capabilities. I soon realised I had a mutiny on my hands when there was a lot of grumbling about them being fitters for years and I was a newcomer from the

Caribbean who had been swanning around and fishing those years. This was a real testing time for me and I tried to reason with them that I was trying to do the best of a job that was handed to me. They were not won over by that and sat on the workbenches swinging their legs and grumbling.

I set out to get on with my job which I had undertaken, to cut into the fuselage and build in a position for the navigator and the two boys moved amongst them asking 'what was their complaint' and saying "Mr Lyder is good you know, and if you make a balls of your job he could fix it". They gradually got off their haunches and got on with their appointed jobs, and eventually the aircraft was wheeled out for service as the prototype. I think the office just looked on to see how I would handle the team, but it was something I had learned to do as a Manager of a department at Alstons in Trinidad. Bruce Bleach came to help every time he had finished a job, but the chargehand, Clatworthy, would come and take him away to another and repeatedly split us up. He felt that Bruce was a student moving around the department to further his experience, but I was hired as an adult and had to produce. Well, I did and went on to join the Air Force while Bruce Bleach journeyed through the various departments, ultimately to become the designer of the cockpit "control cabin" of the "Concorde".

The next big job given to me was to build the nose portion of the Bisley, which was a short-nosed Blenheim brought into the shop to be fitted with armour-plating as they were being shot down in the desert by small arms fire when they strafed German troops. Messrs. Brown and Ratcliffe together approached me and said they had ordered three specially ground and toughened glass fronts for that aeroplane, and two of them had been broken with the fitters trying to fix them in the aircraft. Did I think I could do that? I agreed to take it on and was reminded that it was the very last one.

I duly accepted the challenge and took great care in building up the nose section, and discovered that the bomb-aimers glass panel could just not fit at the angle prescribed on the drawing. So I took the drawing along to the drawing office and asked to see the person whose name was on the bottom of it. I was directed to him and his first remark was, "oh dear, I did that some six months ago, what is the problem?"

I explained the position and he had to do some thinking, but could not give me an answer, so I asked "is it imperative that the glass should be at the particular number of degrees of tilt stipulated on the drawing?" and he said "no". I then said "in that case, I can get it to fit if I can change the angle a few degrees".

He jumped at that suggestion and asked me to go ahead, fit it up and call him to see and modify the drawing. I called him when it was ready in position, all pinned up but not yet riveted, and he did his measuring up and corrected the drawing. The trouble with engineering companies I have found in the UK was that there was little coordination between the workforce on the shop floor and those in the design office. Those who did the jobs with their hands were always ready to criticize the design staff without going to consult with them, and a dreadful mindset of us and them – as though they were two separate companies – pertained. With the nose section pinned up with glass intact and in place ready to rivet, I left to go to Oxford to do my exams for entry into the RAF.

I had hoped to take the whole assembly down to clean off the drilling swaff and paint the joints to make them water-tight, but when I got back from Oxford I found the nose completely riveted. Mr Brown was not taking any further chances and had it riveted as it was. That was the last big job I did at Bristol and I was looking forward to my call-up, which arrived a couple of weeks later. My two boys asked me to leave the tent that we had been working in on the grounds of the factory on my final job for a few minutes, and then called me in to find a table-cloth laid on the ground and laid out with the tea from a flask and cookies as a farewell to me. I was truly touched and thanked them profusely. I often wonder how they got on in life. I was saying my farewells to Carter and Parkes when Parkes produced a small hand compass with a note of good luck and the hope that if I were ever shot down, I would use it to get home.

I presented myself at the College where I was to sit my exam, and on completion of that, I had an interview with three officers of the RAF who interrogated me. The most senior, I think an Air Commodore, asked what did I do at Bristol and I told him that I was a fitter-assembler, and he asked me to explain because that did not mean much to him. I told him that I would go to the office for a drawing that I would use to make a part of the aeroplane and get material from the shop, make the part and hand it in for inspection and that sometimes I might even get to fit it to the prototype myself.

He then said that I was already in a reserved occupation and a very important one, as it took years to train an engineer, but that they could train a pilot in a matter of months. He then held up a letter and said "here is a letter from Bristol saying that you had taken their training for nearly three years and had become a very useful man to them and they did not want to lose you". I explained that they did not train me, in fact they reluctantly employed me, saying "they would try me for a fortnight and if unsuitable would kick me out". I did appreciate the opportunity to use the equipment they had and to practise what I had learned before joining them; besides I held a private pilot's licence and had done all that I wanted to do at Bristol and now needed to move on to flying. If the RAF did not want me I would go to Canada and continue my flying there.

He then asked me a few questions about flying, one being "if you were in a steep turn and the nose tended to drop, what would you do, pull the stick back?" I said "no sir, that would make matters worse, I would apply a bit of top rudder, as moving in those dimensions in the air, the rudder would then become an elevator so to speak". He then said "Lyder, I am satisfied that you are the type we want" and explained that he would have to stamp my application with a multiple choice of pilot, navigator, wireless operator and air-gunner, as that was how they were recruiting. If I failed any one, I would have to be trained as the next one down, but that he hoped I would make it as a pilot and offered his hand, which I shook.

I then went for a thorough medical. I got through that very satisfactorily and returned to Bristol Aircraft Company to await my call-up. In due course, I bade Reverend Fellowes and family and Misses Richardson and Pemberton and of course Danny Boy, the red setter, who had become my fast friends, farewell and journeyed to the Lords Cricket Ground where I was received into the RAF and duly sworn in to serve my king and country, then shown to my billets which were at Abbey Court an unfinished block of flats in the St. Johns Wood area overlooking Regents Park. We were issued a couple of blankets and shown the floor to sleep on amidst the cement dust and smells of fresh paint etc. We, as a platoon, were assembled on the side street and marched to the zoo for breakfast.

On return to the billets, we were ordered to appear in fifteen minutes downstairs to be marched to the tailor for uniforms. We were marched to a warehouse on Abbey Road, which had been a garage, and lined up for measurement before going on to be issued. There was a so-called tailor standing at the gateway to a store opposite a sergeant who was in charge, who would shout "next," the next in line would appear, have a tape thrown around his chest, a number obtained such as "38 regular", which he called out, and you were told to report to the person behind the counter and you would receive the appropriate-sized uniform in battle dress and return with your bundle to await the rest of the platoon before being marched back to the billet.

There was a short chap in front of me named Kent, very talkative and full of life, who couldn't stand still and was observing everything that was going on – yes, one of those busybodies, but a pleasant chap who turned to me and said "look, Lyder, look that tailor is shouting 38 regular regardless of the height or size of the person he measures". I took notice and so it seemed. Anyway the call "next" meant Kent and off he bounded, straight past the tailor and sergeant, shouting "38 regular" himself. A loud shout from the sergeant "come here you smart arse" brought him back and he had the tailor's tape thrown around his chest and was measured as 38 regular. Kent made a gesture to the sergeant to indicate that he was right and that was a waste of time only to be shoved on by the sergeant. I was next and was measured as 38 regular.

We were marched back to the billets with instructions to try the kit on, and anything that did not fit should be brought with you to take to the tailor for adjustment in half an hour. We had been told that this was the Air Force, not the Army, and we had to look smart and be well fitted. Half and hour later most of the platoon was being marched back to the tailor –

Kent again in front of me, he had a pair of trousers that he put on when we got there, with a waist wide enough to hold someone else as well. In turn, he marched up smartly to the tailor, holding the gap out in front of him. When the tailor slapped his hand on the back of his trousers pulling the trousers tight at the front and remarking – "perfect fit" as his fingers felt the front waistband. My tunic had a slight pucker which I had to take back and fix myself. Most of the platoon looked a great deal smarter after a 48-hour spell at home, before being posted to ITU (Initial Training Unit).

There were several platoons in the area housed in the new blocks of buildings being readied at the time as flats, and we were marched to the zoo three times a day for breakfast, lunch and high-tea, and in between we were taught the rudiments of drill and taken to the medics for multiple injections. Again Kent was ahead of me in the line and very talkative and lively, chatting about how there is nothing to this as each man moved forward with his sleeve rolled up towards the doctor and when Kent's turn came, he marched up and promptly fainted before the doctor could touch him – the doctor dragged him out of the line and stabbed him with all the jabs while he was out and before resuscitation.

Having completed all the initiations into the service, we then had a weekend off before setting out to train at number 5 ITU at the Majestic Hotel up the hill at Torquay. We were taught to drill and were marched up and down the hill at 140 paces per minute and thus became very fit. We attended lectures in service law, navigation, gunnery etc., and in about six weeks, my course was posted to Rhodesia for flying training, but I was left behind. Squadron Leader Kyle, the well-known golfer, called me in to tell me that the Air Ministry had instructed him to hold me in the country for flying training, as I was a colonial from Trinidad. I protested, saying that I was in the country three years working as a local and had made friends on the course. He explained that he had no choice in the matter and had to obey instructions.

I became one of a small, awkward squad called 'X' flight, with a different routine to the new intake, which included all kinds of chores, as in the service one was not allowed to be spare. I was allowed to watch another course move through and then another and was getting rather frustrated, while the "brass" searched for a flying school for me in England to attend.

A young chap named Woodward, who was in a similar hold back, and I were given an attic room together and chummed up. Squadron Leader Kyle called us in one day in December 1941 to say that they were still searching for schools for us, and he realised how we must be feeling and said he would give us a week off chores and we could go off anywhere and do what we liked for the whole day after attending 8.00 am parade outside the hotel, but make sure we were not picked up by the service police. The holiday was welcomed and after we paraded, we went back to our attic and prepared to go off for the day. We would walk down the stairs, quietly creep past the administrative office, get out to the top gate and bend down to hide behind the wall while passing in front of the building and scamper down the hill. A rather unseemly performance for a trained airman of 27 years of age.

We wandered all over Torquay and walked past the bay to Cockington, a small village with a nice new small hotel, The Drum Inn, built on the site of what was previously Cockington Forge, which had been busy in its day shoeing horses. We would sit by the log fire and have a second breakfast, all very nice and cosy, but we had fits of guilt when we thought of the war in progress somewhere outside.

We went to the local cinema in the afternoon and saw the Pathe newsreels, which kept us up to date with what was going on in the world. At one time, the film "Dangerous Moonlight" was shown, about a great Polish music composer who had escaped to England to fight back for his country's release as a fighter pilot, and we all wished we could become fighter pilots then.

I was at that ITU when Christmas arrived, and felt very homesick. I took myself down to the waterfront on Boxing Day and plunged in for a swim and received a shock – it was a severe winter and the water unsuspectingly cold and of course, no one else about. My whole body felt numb, so I hurried out. A few days later I awoke from sleep in our attic room and felt quite ill with fever and itching. I called to Woodward in the bed opposite and he roused himself to look at me and said "what the hell is wrong with you boy, you are covered in spots". I got another shock when I looked in the mirror. I asked him to call the corporal and when he came I told him to inform the doctor to come and see me. He had not heard of such a request before and said that I would have to get dressed and go to sick parade, which was held in another building down the road. I told him that was out of the question.

He went downstairs and phoned the doctor who came to me after sick parade. The doctor took one look at me saying "good God, what is this," asked a few questions and disappeared in a hurry. About half an hour later he returned with a tall older gentleman in a long dark coat and a bowler hat in his hand and I thought he had brought the undertaker to measure me. This gentleman turned out to be the specialist consultant in the city of Torquay. He asked me a few questions, examined my face and decided it was chicken pox, and not small pox as the young MD had first suspected. He told me to collect my belongings and prepare to go to a hospital and sent an ambulance for me.

I was taken to Mount Tryon Nursing Home up a hill and laid on the floor in a large hall on a stretcher. A nursing sister came up and took one look at me and exclaimed "good God, what have we got here!" The attendant told her "it's all right, sister, the M.O. knows all about it". I was ushered in front of the M.O. who wrote down some particulars and told me to go into the adjoining room and strip off all clothing. I stood there starkers when an orderly arrived with a bucket of calamine lotion, a white-washing brush and painted me all over with the stuff, just slapping it on. That was a wonderful feeling as it was cool and stopped the itching. He threw me a pair of flannelette pyjamas and led me to the quarantine ward at the end of the corridor. My clothes were taken to be sterilised. I was put into a clean bed and got between the lovely white sheets and settled down. It felt wonderful after what I had had to endure in the past few months.

I had just about dozed off when I realised that someone had come into the room and was by the bed. I opened my eyes to see Peggy Wheeler, a nursing sister, who was staring at me making tut-tut tutting noises and asked "why don't you people's mothers let you have these things as kids and get them over with?" I said to her – "if that is all you have to say to me, sister, you can leave the room". We became fast friends while I stayed there in quarantine and she told me that the dressing down I gave to her was the first time that an LAC (Leading Air Craftsman) had spoken to her like that. She was truly a lovely girl and we became good friends.

In the services, once you are allowed out of bed, you are expected to help, and so I was given various chores to do. There was a nice young doctor who was friendly, and when he heard I had been engineering in Bristol, sought my aid to build a small water distilling plant for him. I did a sort of Heath Robinson contraption, but it worked. Then he asked if I knew anything about cars and engines. I explained that I had overhauled my own car and he asked if I would look at his, which was an old Austin or Morris, I can't remember which right now. I pulled the engine down and cleaned it out, ground the valves in etc. When he came to me with the plea to get it finished as his wife had been taken to hospital in childbirth and he needed transportation badly, I hurriedly reassembled it and it worked, so all was well. I got better and returned to my attic room at the Majestic. Woodward had gone and at long last they found me a place at The Elementary Flying Training School at Cliffe Pypard near Swindon. I was taken at 7.30 pm on the 12th February 1942 by car to the railway station and sent on my way, and eventually arrived at Swindon by daybreak.

There was one other cadet with me named Street, yes, Street. We two stood at the cold station, and as we saw an RAF jitney arrive, we made to jump in the back. Street got on first and promptly jumped off – there were two coffins in the jitney to be offloaded and be put on the train to London. I must say, that did give me a turn, but it affected Street a lot worse, and when he got to camp asked if he could get out of the RAF. Somehow, we never thought of being killed at that stage. He had to receive counselling and psychiatric treatment before he could start flying, but I never heard what happened to him. The course I joined was split into halves. One half going to flying and the other to link training in the morning, then changing over in the afternoon.

My first spell was on the link trainer and when I got to the flight line, I was interviewed by the flight commander, who seemed to hear that I was a cousin of Peter Huggins, who was an instructor at another unit. He said that he would like to take me on as his pupil and we went off for my very first flight in the RAF. I had flown privately, trained in a Hornet Moth with a cabin so that I flew in normal clothing, but now I was all dressed up like a spaceman with an inner cotton overall covered by the gabardine overalls, three pairs of gloves: silk, cotton and gauntlets, and a helmet and goggles as we were to fly in open cockpit aircraft. We took off, communicating through a voice tube, and I was told to hold the controls and follow what was going on.

I was shown the stall condition and various exercises, then we returned to the field at 2,000 feet. We entered the circuit at that height and Flight Lieutenant Davis asked if I could see the field. I could and he said right then, when you think you can land on it, position yourself, throttle back and take it in.

At what I thought to be the appropriate time and distance, I turned across the wind, closed the throttle and then turned into wind and we went fluffing down towards the field. Davis followed me on the joystick saying "back a bit, hold it there, now back a bit and now fully back" and the wheels were rolling on the ground.

We turned to the office and went inside to discuss the lesson and he asked whether I knew at the time I had throttled back that I would make it to the field and I replied "I thought so, that was why I throttled back at that time" and he shook his head and said "remarkable judgement". Mind you, I had held a private pilot's licence since 1939, but had flown a different type of aeroplane and my hours were low as the war stopped my flying some two and a half years earlier, but I was pleased to know that I had retained some of the skill I had learned so long ago. Davis looked on me as a prize pupil and when I had done about two and a half hours, he called me to say that in his view I was ready to go solo, but he dare not send me off so early as the C.O. would have his guts for garters and asked me to bear with him until I had done five hours. I acquiesced but it bothered him and he spoke about it with one of his instructors named Richardson, who was a small man with a bit of a hunched back, the result of a racing driver's accident at Brooklands Circuit. He was an absolute wizard at flying the Tiger Moth.

Richardson approached me the next session and said that Mr Davis had asked him to take me as he was busy, and we went off together. I was flying it and as we climbed out of the field he pulled the throttle closed and I thought – engine failure, and pushed the stick forward gently to stop the climb and Richardson shouted "push it forward more and get flying speed back". He then opened the throttle and climbed away rebuking me for being too slow about the recovery action. He asked what speed did I think the aircraft stalled at and I said "forty miles per hour" he said "no, it does not" and told me to observe the slats on the top wing as he accelerated to seventy miles per hour and suddenly pulled the stick back when the slats changed position and opened up and he explained that the stall could occur at higher speeds if the aircraft was flown at greater 'G' forces. He asked if I could get that and I answered "yes" and we went round the circuit, with me doing the flying and he told me to take it in and land it. I thought he was disappointed in my performance and was cutting short the lesson. He told me to taxi to the office and he got out, closed his door and told me to do one circuit and bring it back to him. I did that and we had a long discussion about flying and it gradually dawned on me that he was told to send me solo if I had satisfied him that it was safe to do so. I had soloed in the RAF after only two and three quarter hours of instructions.

I became the blue-eyed boy of the course until the day we progressed to planning a three-legged trip away from and back to the airfield. I worked out my flight-plan carefully and set off in the area of Swindon. The two earlier legs were completed so well and I got too confident, and on the home run I just sat back and flew my course singing and enjoying myself and when the estimated time of arrival was approaching, I looked out and suddenly realised I could not see the airfield. I twisted and turned in the cockpit while holding course and mild panic set in. I looked at the petrol gauge and it seemed low, so I looked around for somewhere to land, saw runways below with no activity so landed on the one most into wind and taxied to the tower. I climbed the steps to the office and entered the control room asking where I was, I was taken to the map on the wall and shown. I had landed at Harwell, several miles west of my home field, and realised that the wind was stronger than I had expected and had blown me past Cliffe Pypard before I had looked out. I asked for a fill-up of petrol to go home and was told that I would not be allowed to do that and the controller phoned my home base to have someone to come for me. I felt such a ninny. Davis himself came with another pilot and scolded me like a silly child, put me in the front and said nothing to me for about a fortnight. I had been sent to Coventry. That was perhaps the most unhappy time spent in the RAF up to that time.

Marguerite, Eddie & self with young Spanish, Juan Ignacio Pombo

Cuban navy pilots: Menendez stooping with Gustavo Novo, Eddie & self.

Myself, Centeno, Waterman and Norman Tang on the "Cordillera".

Left to right: Karl, a friend, Nita from Curaçao, Friedle from Venezuela, Willie - engineer cadet, and a naval officer cadet.

With Bruce & Joyce at Weston Supermare.

My instructor Riley Sawdon at Western Aero Club.

With the Hornet Moth after getting my license in 1939

Wedding of Bruce & Joyce Bleach.

Bruce Bleach, my friend at Bristol and designerof the "Concorde" cockpit.

The de Havilland "Hornet Moth", a side-by-side two-seater, on which I got my flying license in the spring of 1939.

Garth

To Canada for Training

I tried hard to regain favour and got top marks for my ground schooling and had almost completed my course schedule when we were told we would be sent to Canada to train further.

The chaps coming back from North America with their wings were not coping with flying over England and were getting lost soon after being airborne, so the fields we used were given over to an Advanced Training Course for them. I thought what a waste of time it was holding me back from going to Rhodesia with my initial course.

We packed our belongings and journeyed to Liverpool to sail to Canada and arrived at Moncton, and within a couple of days I was taken to hospital with a case of mumps. There were several of us in there and we followed the plays on the radio with great interest, especially one about a pilot who had been forced down with engine failure, who had landed on a mid-western farm and met the farmer's daughter. The theme song introducing the episode was hummed by all of us. I was cleared for flying in due course and sent west to Neepawa in Manitoba to No. 35 EFTS. We were interviewed separately by the Chief of Flying and Chief of Ground School together and I protested being there to do another Elementary Flying Course, saying that I had all but completed one in England – a lot of the chaps had only done a grading spell of ten to twelve hours and I explained I had done some fifty-six hours. They then enquired whether I had failed the Ground School, and I said I had topped the course. They looked into my records and decided to send me to a course that was finishing soon for a few hours of refresher flying. The instructor took me up in the Canadian Tiger, which had a Perspex hood over the two cockpits and a steerable tail wheel, which were improvements on the English version.

We flew around for half an hour and did a couple of circuits and landings, when he said I could take it for an hour and do whatever I wanted. I found a field about ten miles away, which I decided would be good to land in case of emergency and practised some aerobatics enjoying myself. I was checked occasionally but went solo most of the time and did about thirty hours. I finally had a check ride with a senior officer who told me I was finished and would have to wait a few days for a posting to an advanced school (SFTS). I got bored and begged to be allowed one more flight to enjoy myself and eventually they gave me an aircraft and I flew to my chosen spot and indulged in aerobatics.

Suddenly after a slow roll the engine started to splutter and I thought it was gas starvation and tried everything to get the engine going properly, but to no avail and realised I had a failure. I had a lot of height and circled the field I had chosen for such an eventuality and approached with some excess speed to make sure I reached it, but only when I was committed and low down that I realised that the field was divided into two by a thin barbed-wire fence. I was now too fast to land within one half, so as I approached the fence I bounced the wheels on the ground, jumped over the fence and landed on the other side safely. A farmer soon approached and I begged the use of his phone in the house nearby and called base.

Flight Lieutenant Underwood, who had checked me out a couple of days earlier, arrived in his car with an engineer and was annoyed as hell. I explained what had happened and he rebuked me for not getting the engine going – it must have been just a gas starvation. He would go back and come in another aircraft with a spare pilot to fly it back. He put me in the car and was driving back, complaining that it was just inexperience and lack of airmanship.

I protested strongly and said that it could not be flown back as the engine had failed. We turned back to open up the engine and discovered that the valve rocker gear on one cylinder had failed. The aircraft had to be returned by truck. The next day we were called for posting instructions and one of the admin staff addressed us saying "would the airmen now named please line up on this side of the corridor and the next set of named airmen on the other side" and when the list was completed he pointed to one side and said "you chaps are going to Moosejaw on singles" and to the other side "you lot are going to Carberry on twins".

I suddenly realised I was on the single side and started to get agitated as I wanted to be on the twins. Opposite me was a chap named Sharples, who was serious about not being on twins, so I grabbed him and we went to see the flight commander protesting loudly, he argued against any change and we protested until he agreed to a swap, but told us to go back and stand in the lines we had been called to as he did not want all and sundry to come in to change. The two of us went back after we were dismissed to make sure that the swap had taken place and eventually got our individual choices.

I was transported to Carberry, Manitoba, to number 5 SFTS to commence what I had hoped for all my life, larger aeroplanes to fly, and duly introduced to my instructor Flt. Sergeant Norgrove. I was delighted to be cranking up the two engines of an Anson and we set off on my first flight of a larger aeroplane.

Norgrove introduced me to several exercises and to what the aircraft could do and what to look for, and then told me to turn for home. I pointed it in the direction of the airfield and once he established I knew where to go he broke off and said, "by the way let me show you something else". Turning and twisting he sai, "OK, let's go homem" and again I turned in the right direction. He did this a third time, and when each time I had turned towards home he enquired, "do you never get lost?" I told him "yes, once" and I made up my mind never again, and told him about my experience at Cliffe Pypard. We got on like a house on fire, he was such a nice youngster doing his first posting as an instructor.

We had two marks of Anson at Carberry, the English version and the Canadian version with two American Jacobs radials of 260 h.p. each. I dreamed of going on to even larger aircraft and hoped eventually I would get on to flying boats.

This was autumn, with winter fast approaching, and the snow started to fall. In the mid-west the weather could get quite cold, and at times the temperature dropped to −45° but dry. On one occasion, I walked from the dining hall to the hangar a short distance away without my great coat, but never again as my ears started to freeze and my uniform tunic became stiff like cardboard. The Canadians have mastered the cold and their wooden buildings are well heated, and so one is very comfortable inside, looking out onto the snow-covered ground and trees covered with ice. The aircraft were housed in well heated hangars and wheeled out one at a time closing the doors behind. If you did not get the engine started within about two minutes you would have to push it back inside.

I made some good friends at Carberry and when we had a week's leave mid-term, I took Norman Wilkinson and Wallace to New York with me to stay with the Guthrie family in New Jersey. Mr Guthrie was the son of Mrs Guthrie, whom I mentioned earlier, from St. James in Trinidad. He had studied dentistry in New York and settled in America, marrying a lovely person named Marguerite, and had three children. The eldest of them, Connie, had visited her grandmother in Trinidad some years earlier when I was there. I had kept in touch and they had invited me down. We had a wonderful holiday with them before going to Carberry.

We were supposed to do about one hundred and fifty hours each at SFTS, but due to the severe weather, we were falling behind, and so one hundred and thirty-five hours was the new target. But the only way to achieve that was for the pilots who had completed their night flying training to use the aircraft at night solo on circuits and bumps, two nights for two hours each – an extra four hours each. The first night I was detailed to fly, I met the other five and suggested that we should engage in a cross-country flight, three at a time in formation, going off for an hour, while the other three would keep the ACP aerodrome control pilot busy by whizzing around the circuits in quick succession so that he would think there were six.

I planned the trip to fly from Carberry to Neepawa, to Brandon, and back to Carberry exactly one hour and lead the formation the first leg, then switched to number three position while number two moved into the lead and number three into number two position and on the last leg, number two would move forward to lead so that each one got the experience of being in each position. We found this to be possible because the winter nights were so clear, especially when the moon was full, and with the clear skies and snow on the ground we could see the other aircraft quite clearly. Well, we set off for the cross-country and everything went remarkably well to plan, and as we approached

Carberry airfield from Brandon, the other three were setting course and we took over the circuits. We were elated that it had all gone so well. The next night was Boxing Night, but I did not plan anything as the others were not really interested and I was faced with two hours of circuits and bumps.

The aircraft I was given had a duff battery and to keep the lights going, I had to keep the engines revving higher than normal, and using the brakes to slow down etc. The tail kept lifting so I was afraid I would tip up and damage the props or do some damage and I just could not risk that happening. So I got airborne again and circled wondering what to do and noticed the lights of Portage La Prairie in the distance and flew to them. Then far ahead the lights of Winnipeg beckoned and off I went, irresistibly as a moth drawn to a flame, and I reached Winnipeg and flew up and down Portage Avenue enjoying the Christmas lights and domestic fireworks at the various homes and thoroughly enjoyed myself, singing White Christmas etc., and then I turned for home. Portage La Prairie seemed to be taking a long time to reach, so I put up the power and when abreast of Portage, a quick calculation indicated I was quite late so I opened the taps some more and had the two Jacob engines whirring away.

I got to where I thought the field was, but there was no flare path so I went into a circle and identified the place by the barrack blocks and hangars and noticed there was a truck on the snow-covered field taking up the last flare. I turned into the direction, which the flare path had been laid and made a slow precautionary approach and landed. I taxied and parked the aircraft up against the hangar and shouted for the ground crew to take it in immediately as the lights had gone. My spine was tingling now as I had to sign in and what was I to say. I crept into the building and gingerly entered the office, which was vacant, and signed the book, which was open on the desk.

I had just signed it when I heard footsteps and whistling and the sergeant came in breezily from the cookhouse, threw his cap which caught a peg and hung there swinging, and I said "sorry serg, I had forgotten to sign in" and had come back from my barracks to do so and he said "that's all right cock, have a good night" and off I sped. I then went to the dining hall for supper and a couple of ground crew chaps sat on the bench beside me asking anxiously where I had been. I said "for goodness sake, don't pass this on or I could get into a lot of trouble" and they promised not to tell, so I told them I had gone to Winnipeg. They exclaimed "Winnipeg!" I begged them to keep it quiet and they repeated "oh gawd, Winnipeg".

The next morning I went to the hangar and Norgrove, my instructor, came up with a rather worried look on his face and asked "where did you get to last night Lyder?" I said "I was doing circuits and bumps", striking the palm of his left hand with his microphone he repeated earnestly "where did you get to last night Lyder?" and I said "Winnipeg". He looked at me and said "that was a silly thing to do, my star pupil and you could have got into so much trouble, anything could have happened and so far away". I hurriedly explained about the duff battery and why I could not continue circuits and bumps, so I went to Portage and then saw the lights of Winnipeg and I was drawn there, I just couldn't resist the temptation. It then struck me, all the things that could have gone wrong, and I worried that the C.O. would hear about it and I could be refused my wings. However, no more was said and I kept very quiet about it and I prayed to have my wings.

On 29th December we had a Passing Out Parade in the hangar and on my name being called, I went forward to have my wings pinned on by the C.O., as Pilot Officer Lyder. I thought: if only my mother could see this, after all she had been through to bring us to adulthood. I also felt happy for one of the course named Eames, who had done quite well in flying but was unfortunate enough to have both engines fail on one of the nights he was doing his extra four hours just as he was returning to the airfield from Neepawa, and got his plane onto the field in a belly landing with the wheels up as to put them down would have prevented him from reaching the field, and very little damage was done.

The C.O. was furious and threatened to make an example of him, not obeying orders and not giving him his wings. We pleaded with our flight commander to intervene, explaining that he had shown great skill and initiative and was worth his wings, especially as he was honest enough to say that he had been away from the circuit. I thought then, but for the grace of God go I.

We all went to Winnipeg for a few days off and had a wonderful New Year celebration. Those of us who were commissioned as officers went to the large store named Eatons to be kitted out with Pilot Officers' uniforms off the peg and returned as ready-made officers, feeling somewhat self-conscious.

Nassau and a Visit Home

The Flight Commander called us in to his office to tell us individually where we would be posted to from there, and I was told I was to go on an instructor's course as I had done so well.

I was horrified, as I was looking forward to going back to England to take part in operations, and I pleaded with him to let me go. He argued that I was older than the average cadet and more mature and most suitable. I argued as I had done only once before, when I had applied for a job at Bristol, and said that there were lots of others who would like to stay in Canada, but I had to get back to England. It was then that he said, "we don't want them, we want you as an instructor as you have graduated with the highest marks for flying at Carberry since the station has been open". I begged him not to do me this and he asked, "well, what do you want to do?"

I told him I would love to get into Coastal Command and onto flying boats especially, and he put me on a course at Charlottetown, Prince Edward Island. I had become intrigued with flying boats ever since the visit of the Loening amphibians to Trinidad and also Pan American Airways. I loved boating and now flying and thought it would be wonderful to marry the two. I also remembered the days in Torquay, seeing the newsreels in the cinema of the plight of so many gallant seamen trying to survive in the Atlantic Ocean after being torpedoed, and longed to be of some help to such unfortunates.

I duly arrived at Charlottetown Coastal Command School after the ice-breaker ship taking us to the island had fought its way through the frozen sea. We flew as navigators on Ansons flown by staff pilots and learned to send messages in code, decode others, and all about identifying ships and flags of every nation and especially the war ships of the enemy: the war ships of Germany, Italy and Japan. We were taught to estimate the tonnage of all ships as well, and had to identify models of them on a platform, made to look like the oceans under conditions of subdued lighting. From there I was posted to Nassau in the Bahamas to train on Mitchells (B25s) as a stepping stone to Liberators (B24s), as there were no flying boat postings available. I was disappointed but progressing towards my goal.

At Nassau, I met a variety of airmen, pilots, navigators, wireless operators and straight air-gunners, and we lived together for us to make friends and chose our own teams as crews. I was posted as a co-pilot and agreed to partner pilot Alcock as his first officer, he having done so much more flying than I as a staff pilot previously. We collected a team after a couple of weeks and then trained together as a crew, each pilot taking a turn to operate the controls. The scheme was that on completion of training, the captain of each crew would join a squadron as the co-pilot to an experienced captain, taking his crew with him, and the dispossessed co-pilots waiting for vacancies.

I enjoyed my stay in the Bahamas, flying over the sea of a wide range of colours due to the varying depths of the water, and flying the Mitchell for approximately 75 hours. We moved from Oaksfield to the Ferry Field on the other side of the islands to train on Liberators for a few hours before being posted to a squadron or a pool in England. The Ferry Field was built by the Americans as a staging post for ferrying aircraft through the Caribbean and onward via Natal and the South Atlantic to North Africa for the battles raging there.

While in Nassau, I seemed to have upset the C.O. when acting as C.O. for the station one day as part of our training as General Duties Officers. It appears that we were not intended to take the job too seriously, but unfortunately I was drilled by my upbringing to do everything thoroughly and so I did this one fully and visited the airfield at about 9.00 pm where night flying was in progress, to ask if all was well and was faced with a deputation from the ground crew that they had been refused night flying suppers. I took two of them in the car with me to the cook house to try to sort things out, and asked for the sergeant in charge to come to see me. He had shut up shop and retired to his billet and resented this intrusion. He had told me that he had refused the request for night flying suppers because his food stocks were low. I asked what was all that on the shelves and he said that was for breakfast. I said "never mind breakfast, get busy preparing something for these crews to eat" as they were entitled to. He looked at my narrow ribbon of Pilot Officer and attempted to cheek me off, and I hurriedly warned him not to be insolent to me as insubordination was a serious charge. He bit his tongue and set to the task of preparing a meal. The following morning, the C.O. sent for me and asked for an explanation, as the sergeant had reported me to him. I told him precisely what had occurred and reluctantly he dismissed me, but I suspected he was not happy about my actions.

There was very little for us to do in Nassau but go to the one cinema, which was shared with the locals and our cousins the Americans, but the Greek owner seemed to favour the Yanks as they spent more freely than we impecunious British and played mainly and if not exclusively American marches over the address system (the tannoy) before and during intermissions, of which "Off we go into the wide blue yonder nothing can stop the army air corps" was the favourite. This got on the nerves of the RAF, unknown to me. I was present one night when it boiled over and a strong group of our boys, who had had enough of this nonsense, whilst the Americans singing lustily "nothing can stop the army air corps", they shouted "except the RAF" and waded into the Americans with vigour. Quite a battle took place and I struggled my way out having received a few blows myself and returned to my billet. The following day the C.O. called us all to the hall and tore us off a strip for bringing the service into disrepute, and called for a collection to reimburse the Greek for his broken chairs. At least that put a stop to that particular march being played again.

At that time, the Duke of Windsor had been appointed Governor of the islands, and we saw a lot of him and Mrs Simpson, who busied herself with service to the troops. On one occasion, they turned up at the very nice hotel where I had been billeted for the evening's dancing. When the drum rolled, indicating that the national anthem was about to be played, everyone stood to attention and they (the Duke & Duchess) stood no more than ten feet from me. My mind went back to the time he visited us in Trinidad as the young Prince of Wales. I was a pupil of Tranquility School at the time and Mr Padmore, our teacher, who also did music, had hurriedly taught us a song to sing as he (the Prince) and his entourage slowly passed, outside of the Prince's Building on the Queen's Park Savannah. I think I can remember some of the song, even today, I hope I have it right.

"Beyond the highest mountains
And over the hills and dales
Oh let the prairies echo
God bless the Prince of Wales."

We had on board as an intelligence officer the son of the famous American philanthropist, Mr Pulitzer, who was a friend of the Duke and was a Flight Lieutenant in the RAF. He arranged an exercise of submarine bombing between ourselves and the US Navy, which entailed our flying to the Gulf of Mexico and liaising with submarines that were training in the area by radio, and we would drop a stick of pine logs in lieu of depth charges on them if we could, but they would dive at the precise moment of attack to avoid damage.

Well, my crew with Flight Lieutenant Sleep, our instructor, on board, went off on such an exercise, which was proving to be quite useful training, and made contact by radio to engage the submarine. Alcock was flying the Mitchell and I was the bomb aimer and we approached the sub on the surface and the radio gave us the go ahead, so Alcock went in with me lining up the target on the bomb sight. As we got closer I called to the instructor to say that the sub was making no attempt to dive and he replied "you carry on, he will" and as the time was ready I pressed the button and the pine logs were away. Alcock did the prescribed turn away and all hell let loose on the radio, with the shouting of expletives, and out of the noise came the news that we had attacked the wrong sub, which was moving to the yard for refitting after service, and the pine logs had inflicted damage to the coning tower.

We set course for base with all sorts of noise over the radio and we were met by Flight Lieutenant Pulitzer, who was furious. He had a blind eye and wore a black patch over it which made him look more frightening. Again we were summoned by the C.O. to muster in the hall and were told that the exercise had been discontinued, and he reprimanded us for not taking more care. I did not feel guilty, nor did I accept responsibility, because I had reported to the instructor that the submarine was not diving. The C.O. dismissed us after that telling off, and as we got up to go, he turned and said "by the way, chaps, bloody good bombing".

I had finished my training on the Liberator, which was only a few hours, and the course members were being sent on a fortnights' leave. I went to the C.O. for permission to go to my home in Trinidad and he refused, in spite of the fact that the rest were going to all sorts of places in America, even as far as San Francisco. I did not understand his refusal and he said, "just find yourself back here on a certain date or you will be on a charge". I could not fathom him. Perhaps he thought I would get home and not return. Anyway, I had been away from home for five years by that time and was determined to get there before going on to operational flying. I went to the dispatcher at Ferry Field and asked, "can you get me to Trinidad?" He said "sure" and looking at his movement sheets said "tomorrow 6.00 am". I said "not so fast, I have to clear the station"; we had to get a form signed by each department before we could leave a station. He said "Ok, the next day same time".

I hurriedly sent a cable home to say that I would arrive on that day and got clearance from the station and was at Ferry Field bright and early. I was to get a ride on a DC3 with a Captain Shearer to whom I was introduced and was so excited, home at last after five years, difficult to grasp. On that morning, in addition to the DC3, there were two Baltimore bombers to be ferried to the war scene. While training on the Liberator, I had seen about three burnt-out airframes of the Baltimores on the sides of the runway, and had learned that they were bombers which had their bomb doors opened, a huge petrol tank fitted and a closing fabric closed them in. The tanks had too few buffers inside and the takeoff had to be done very carefully as the fuel would surge badly enough to cause the aircraft to become directionally unstable.

When everything was ready, we got into the DC3 and started it up and taxied out, and suddenly the aircraft came to a halt and the engines stopped. I ran up front to ask what was wrong and Shearer said the controls were jammed. The control column was fully back and he had to push his chair back and climb out from behind it. We walked back to the building to await a report from the engineers. I thought this was really bad luck.

The dispatcher asked if I would like to get on the Baltimore; one had already left, but the other was still on the ground and he could get me on it. I was surely tempted, but having heard of their problem and seen burnt-out shells besides the runway, I decided to wait for the DC3 and went out to try to find the problem. The ground crews had taken up the floor boards to follow the control runs to the elevator but could see no faults and so I went into the cockpit following the runs right up the control column to discover that the column had been forced back past a bracket riveted to the side wall of the aircraft as a stop to its travel. I called the engineer to see, and with a huge screwdriver he prised the column back past the bracket and the thing was free. I hurried in to tell Shearer and left the chaps replacing the floor-boards.

Shearer had taxied past the back of the Baltimore which was running its engine to high power, checking the magnetos, and the blast from the slipstream had blown his elevator up to force it past the stop.

As soon as the DC3 was ready we set off from Ferry Field and set course for Puerto Rico. We landed on an airfield at the western end of the island and Shearer decided to stay there overnight, as to continue would mean arriving in Trinidad at dusk and he said he would prefer to be there in full daylight.

I was very disappointed, but had to accept that, and sent another message to my family saying that I would arrive at approximately midday the following day. The airport at Piarco was the very one that I had flown off with Mikey Cipriani, but now had runways of tarmac and was busy with aircraft being ferried as well as a base for the English Fleet Air Arm training navigators and wireless operators looking for German submarines.

Trinidad was named so by Christopher Columbus who had approached it from the east, where he noticed the three ranges of hills, which he termed 'the Trinity'. I was in the cockpit with Shearer and his co-pilot as we approached the Northern Range which we had to cross, not high, around 2,000 feet at that point, but with a peak called "El Tucuche" at 3,100 feet approximately. It was a wonderful sight and my spine just tingled with delight and with a lump in my throat I anticipated a meeting with my family after five long and troubled years. When we came to a halt, I got out to find a Fleet Air Arm officer named Lieutenant Commander Alec Blair who introduced himself and said that he had come to meet me on behalf of the family who were in the building waiting. It is difficult to describe the first embrace by my mother as she hugged me for a while, my elder sister and younger brother Eddie having taken the day off from work. Eddie drove us home to "Sunnyside".

Alec Blair, amongst others, had become a good friend of the family and made this his second home from Scotland. I was delighted to be home, we had so much to talk about that had taken place in those past five years. I met a number of the Fleet Air Arm officers who were camped at Golden Grove, several of whom made friends with my family and would call at "Sunnyside" when passing or for social visits. Two of them, Lieutenant Commander Alec Blair and Lieutenant Angus MacDevit, made it their home from home and never made it back to their real homes in Scotland. They died in Trinidad in separate crashes in their aeroplanes and are buried in the Military Cemetery on Long Circular Road. I could never understand the high accident rate there.

Fighting the War in the Air

The fortnight's leave went by so quickly and I was flown back to Nassau on a Liberator, which took the ferry crews back to Canada to start again.

I spent about one week in Nassau, preparing to be taken back to England via Liberator to Montreal where I overnighted and continued on from there by flying boat, which I thoroughly enjoyed. We took off from the Hudson River at Lachine with Captain Luck in command and crossed the Atlantic at night, arriving at Largs in Scotland the following morning. That was a wonderful experience and brought home to me what I was missing by not having been trained on my first love – flying boats.

From Largs I was taken by train to Harrowgate and installed in a hotel there, awaiting a posting to a Coastal Command Station. I had been there about three weeks when I was sent to Sidmouth in Devon to do an army assault course. We were kept very busy indeed there and had to dress for a pukka dinner every night, after which we just fell into bed.

I met Paul Gibb, the then English Cricket Team wicketkeeper, and while chatting one day, he asked me what I wanted to do and I said "get on to flying boats" and he said "what, those big lumbering things". He said he would like to get on to fast lively twins and when I was at last posted from Harrogate, I found myself at Finmere in Oxfordshire back on Mitchells. When I heard from him, he was in the Orkneys on flying boats. I was rather upset and next morning went to see the Squadron Leader Dennis to complain. I told him that I had spent a great deal of time training for Coastal Command only to end up at Tactical Airforce.

He said that if I was not happy to be there, he did not want me as it was very demanding work, and called me next morning to tell me that Air Ministry were well aware of where I was trained, but Coastal Command had no vacancies, but Tactical Air Force was losing men and the only source of Mitchell-trained pilots was from Nassau. He suggested that I settle down and make the best of it. I then promised I would and he took me into an adjoining room to introduce me to my crew. They were all Canadians who had been left over from different units for one reason or another, they were my navigator Flying Officer Tommy Good from Toronto; Flying Officer Charlie Walkden from Winnipeg, the air-gunner and W/O Roy Walker from Calgary the wireless-operator/airgunner. That was the team: no choice or ifs or buts.

We spent a while getting to know one another and started to train for the new job in Second Tactical Airforce. Finmere, like many other airfields, was out in the sticks near the town of Buckingham, and we spent a few weeks there learning the new job. We had one ENSA group come to entertain us there, which included a comedian who I thought quite funny, especially with his north country accent. In one part of his act, he raised quite a laugh when he said "what a lovely town we have nearby", referring to Buckingham. He was planning to come back next year for the illuminations when the Mayor would light 'tuther lamp'.

We completed the course and I came first and Ken Cullen, a Canadian, second, and we and our crews were posted to 180 Squadron, 139 Wing, Dunsfold, Surrey. The two crews travelled by train to London and then on to Guildford. Where we were met by a jitney and taken to the camp at Dunsfold Aerodrome. We arrived at the mess about 7.00 pm on a cold winter's night and entered the hall of the nissen-type building which housed the dining room, and hung about for a couple of minutes feeling strange, when the door flew open and an officer burst in, looking a lot like what I had remembered of my father and enquired "new crews?" I said "yes sir." He then asked "which one is Lyder?" and I said "I was" and he offered his hand to shake, saying he was the Wing Commander Johnny Castle of 180 Squadron.

He then asked for Cullen, and I introduced Ken who was near to me, and then he said he ran a very tight ship here and knew all about us. He did not wait for his Ministry to send him recruits but had been to Bicester, the parent station of Finmere, the satellite to choose us. "You Lyder for A flight and you Cullen for B flight". He suggested we came in for dinner and would be shown our billets after. He went to the front of the hall to sit with the other seniors and we took seats at the back. Presently, the Padre, Squadron Leader Tom Warner, who had been up front, came back to introduce himself asking "new boys?" I said "yes, sticks out like a sore thumb, doesn't it?" and he said that he too was new, on the station only three weeks. We chatted and felt more at ease then. We were intrigued because he wore the Air Gunner Half-Wing on his tunic, but more of that later. We were shown our billet and fell into bed after a tiring day, and next morning went to the disposal units, I and my team to A flight, and Ken Cullen to B flight, where I met Roy, who had come from the W/O's mess.

We met our flight commander, Squadron Leader Carey, and the other crews and gradually settled in at last on an operational station after so much waiting around. It felt good, but the atmosphere was electric and I wondered what the future held for me. There were three squadrons on the station: 98 Squadron, 320 Dutch Squadron and our 180 Squadron, each with two flights of six Mitchells, and each flight led by a Squadron Leader. I was called to have a formation flight-check with Flight Lieutenant Pike and told to fly in number two position, which was on the right of the leader, and an Australian, named O'Hallaran, who had preceded me from Finmere some three weeks before, would fly in number three. When I got to the changing room, O'Hallaran said that he should be number two as he was senior to me, and I told him that he could have number two and I would take number three, which turned out to be the more difficult as one had to look past the space where the co-pilot sat and through his window towards the lead aircraft, whereas in number two one had the lead aircraft outside the pilot's window. We took off and followed the leader round the countryside for about an hour, twisting and turning, climbing and descending, then we returned to base. When we got down, Flight Lieutenant Pike sent for me and said "I thought I told you to fly in number two position?" I said "yes sir, but O'Hallaran said he was my senior and that he should have number two and I accepted that". He then said, "in future, do as you are told, you are in the service now" and informed me that I was fit for operations, but O'Hallaran would need further training. I apologised, saying I would in future and left. He then called O'Hallaran in and administered a right rollocking to him.

Later that day, there was a briefing for an operation taking place in the ops room, with all windows tightly shut, and I felt the tension of the moment. When the crews poured out with anxious expressions on their faces, I felt a tinge of fright. I joined the others who were not going at the top of the runway to give them the thumbs up and wished them a safe return. As the Mitchells poured into the sky in quick succession, I felt a cold tremor up and down my spine; I would soon find out myself what this was all about.

The next day, I was introduced to a Spitfire fighter-pilot who gave me a course to follow, out and back to base, while he tried to shoot me down in mock attacks and I should try to avoid them. He made several attacks from the rear and sides and I did my best to avoid him. He called off the exercise early and told me to return to base. On returning to the crew room after landing, he came in and, throwing his helmet and goggles on the settee, he exclaimed "is that the way you treat a heavy aircraft, throwing it about like that?" I retorted that he told me to avoid being shot down and he said "yes, but such drastic measures are unnecessary" and told me what was to be done to avoid being shot. I learned a great deal from that.

I was reported fit for operations and waited a couple of days before being put on the battle order. I joined other crews lining the runway to give our chaps the thumbs up as they set off on a sortie, and at last my turn had come. We were briefed on a raid on a marshalling yard in France and had precise timetable for kitting up, checking the aircraft, starting the engines and taxiing onto the perimeter track in correct sequence. Six to a box to take off, circle the field for the box leader to collect his other five and set course over-heading the field. Everything had to be done to the split second if we were to converge with our fighter escort that would meet us off the coast of France.

The aircraft came from a number of stations around the perimeter of the airfield and the whole exercise was one of precision and punctuality. I started the right engine OK but the left refused to start and after trying everything I know, I called to the ground crew to enquire whether there was a back-up aircraft available to which he replied "yes sir, that one marked H over there", and I enquired whether it was fuelled, bombed up etc. and he said "yes sir, ready to go". So I told the crew to go to aircraft H quickly and the navigator Tommy Good said to me "look, Garth, let's not be hasty" and I shouted "get into that aeroplane". We ran across, did the necessary checks, started up and were away, but had lost a bit of time and the last aeroplane had already gone.

I hurried to the take off point at the top of the runway and momentarily stopped for instructions from the tower by an Aldis lamp, for we could not use radio contact as the enemy were listening at all times and it would give them information of our movements. I was given a green light so tore down the runway and climbed into the sky after asking the navigator for a course direct to Hastings, which was the spot we were to set course for France.

We climbed a little higher than had been planned for the Channel crossing so that we could see better what was ahead, and after a short while saw a box of five and dived to join them in number six position and we were on our way.

After crossing the coast of France for some distance, we still had not met our fighter escort, and Squadron Leader Carey turned back for home base. After landing and getting off our flying kit, I went to the mess. Carey was already there with the top brass around the log fire at the top of the room, talking to the C.O. and other senior officers. Several of them gave me the thumbs up and shouted "well done, Lyder". To this day, I do not know why I was given the green light to take off, as I was the new boy on the block doing his first operational sortie and they could not have known what I had intended to do, except of course join the box, but how? That was the only trip I did in number six position. I was in number five the second and third, and on the fourth trip I was put in number four position to lead the second 'V' of three. This was a vital position in the formation, as one was charged with leading the number five and six to position them on final approach on return to base, as it took several minutes to land a box of six, one at a time when anyone could be needing to get home quickly because of damage or injury.

On the noticeboard, Wing Commander Johnny Castle sent for me and asked if I had seen the battle order for that afternoon and I said "yes sir". He then said " I have put you in number four position, give it a try and if you find we are pushing you too quickly, just say so, and we will give you more time in number five" but he thought that I was the man for that job. Well, I always relished a challenge and willingly accepted it. We did a raid on Cherbourg on that occasion and the Germans threw everything they had at us and we struggled through it and returned home frightened and battered, though not losing anyone from our Squadron, but others suffered loss and there was great grief among the seniors whose friend, a Squadron

Leader Wheeler, who I did not know, was among others who had been killed. Apparently he was one of the star operators of Tactical Air Force. On return to base I got out and inspected the damage. There were some 32 holes in our aircraft, and the engineer checking inside the cockpit called me to see an ugly jagged piece of shrapnel that was stuck in the small circular leather-covered fibre pad which acted as a headrest behind my seat. I was leaning well forward peering at the lead plane at the time it had struck, or I would have been hit in the head and obviously killed.

Well, I wrote to my mother that evening, saying that was how rough it got. I did not dare to think how long I would survive. I soldiered on and gained in skill and confidence and was promoted to be leader of my own box of six Mitchells on my 12th sortie. Padre Tom Warner had become fast friends with me and flew with us frequently as an extra pair of eyes, and it is time I mentioned something about him – at least it gave me the feeling that I had the Good Lord on my side. He was an Irishman from County Cork, an Anglican priest who, as all Irishmen, felt that wherever there was a fight, it was incumbent of them to join. So he found himself in the queue in Kingsway, volunteering for aircrew in the RAF, and was trained as an Air Gunner, obtained his wings and had done some operational trips on a Squadron when he was summoned to the C.O.

He marched in, in his usually exuberant manner, calling out his rank – Flight Sergeant – and the last three numbers of his service number in true fashion. His

C.O. then told him that he had had a communication from the Air Ministry suggesting that he was a trained cleric in holy orders – "is this correct?" He replied "yes sir" and the C.O. rebuked him, asking "what the hell are you doing as an Air Gunner?" It was improper according to the Geneva Convention for a priest to be carrying a gun, besides which they were short of priests, and he told him to go to the orderly room and collect his orders to go to Bush House in London to see the RAF authorities there.

He duly reported at Bush House, was demobbed as an operational gunner, sent to another room where he was re-categorised and emerged onto the street as a Squadron Leader. He would now often chasten me for being a Flying Officer doing a Squadron Leader's job, telling me to get some in, an RAF admonishment to do something about my rank. Look at him, one move from Flight Sergeant to Squadron Leader.

Unfortunately, it was not up to me and I had to wait on the Air Ministry to rectify that, but it was not happening. Squadron Leader Carey had been posted for a rest as he had completed his quota of thirty operational trips and I was holding down the job, awaiting the arrival of the new Squadron Leader of substantive rank.

On most operational stations, promotions would take place from those suitable on the station, but it did not happen like that on our station for some unknown reason. In time, the new one arrived in the name of

Peter Ford, who had had experience on Blenheims in North Africa, albeit unlike what our specific job was in Tactical Air Force, but I had to teach him the job.

He was a young, energetic, flamboyant ex-public school boy and did not relish being trained by a Flying Officer, and after two trips took over the flight. He wanted to be friendly with me in his own style, joining him at the "Compass Inn" close to the aerodrome, jugging up and getting sloshed, which is not my style, having been brought up as a strict Methodist and not indulging in such behaviour, and he found a ready-made friend in O'Hallaran, the Australian, who kept pushing his claim for seniority over me. I happened into the Compass Inn on odd occasions with others, to see the two of them sloshed, caps askew, arms interlinked, dancing around and encouraging all to drink and be merry, for tomorrow we die.

I had become known to the W/O in charge of maintenance through my experience of building aircraft at Bristol to treat aircraft with respect, and he called on me to speak to Squadron Leader Ford to obey the instructions for flying the Mitchell and adhere to the prescribed speeds for extending the flaps, undercarriage etc., as his aeroplane was being damaged through misuse. I told him I could not do that and he undertook to approach Ford himself and suggested that he should have a chat with me about these things, which infuriated Ford to ask him "who the hell was Lyder to teach him anything!" That made the relationship even worse than it had been. I went to the Wing Commander when it got that bad and asked for a change on to heavies. I should have mentioned earlier that the W/O in charge of maintenance had become friendly with me because of my engineering background and had taken to asking me to ferry patched-up aircraft that had severe damage that he could not fix further to Hartford Bridge and bring back the new ones.

But I was not allowed to go alone. I had to take my navigator and at least one air-gunner on all trips, so I would have to call Tommy and one of the others whenever I was asked to do such a job. Tommy liked playing cards and cribbage and could always be found at it. And when I approached him saying "we have a job to do", he knew what I meant and would say "not another one of those dicey jobs again, why do you keep sticking my neck out?" But he was proud to do it.

I had had a personality problem with Tommy early in our association, and the other two crew members had approached me and said they were aware of the clash between us and they would support me if I asked for a change. I thanked them for their support but said that I hoped it would not come to that and I would win him over, and eventually I did, mainly because of my reputation on the station as a pilot, and he could suffer a lot worse with a change.

Tommy was a real extravert where I was the opposite. He loved being the centre of attention and hated that the crews were called or referred to by naming the pilot.

He had tried for piloting, but did not make the grade and was trained as a navigator/bomb aimer instead. It did not bother him that much, as he seemed to accept it, but he would have been happier if the navigator had been referred to as the captain of the crew. I discovered that he had trained at Brandon, the airfield I mentioned earlier, not far from Carberry where I had got my wings, and asked him if he knew of an officer there named Kelshall and he said "yes", "he was the officer who lectured them on current events and his lectures were always popular and we looked forward to them as a relief from the academic subjects". I explained that he was my cousin and he remarked, "what a small world".

Jack Kelshall was my first cousin the son of my mother's sister, Jesse. His father was a prominent solicitor in San Fernando and as children we visited and played with him and his brother in San Fernando on occasion. Jack was a bright student and joined his father's law practice and went to Canada some time after I had left Trinidad, and I had not heard that he had gone to Canada to join the Air Force after war was declared.

I had nearly finished my training at Carberry when my instructor Norgrove came to ask me to fly him to Brandon as he had to do something there. We landed and went to the officers' mess and Norgrove asked me to wait for him in the lounge, and as I walked down the corridor, an officer with pilot wings approached from the other end. To my surprise it was my cousin

Jack. We stopped briefly to have a chat and he asked what my intentions were and I told him to go back to the UK and take up the fight. He said "good, see you over there", but he never came. I wrote home to tell my family of the incident. It was nice to hear that Tommy appreciated his lectures, but it was only when I arrived back in Trinidad that I learned that Jack had been inducted into the ideology that was communism while in Canada and had become the legal advisor to the Oil Field Workers' Trade Union.

I had met chaps in London who had trained with me and who were now Flight Lieutenants and one a Squadron Leader, because promotion was made from inside the Squadron as and when a vacancy arose. The Wing Commander admitted that he had been aware of the feud between Ford and myself, as his navigator was friendly with mine and hoped we could sort ourselves out. He did not want me to leave as I had made a great contribution to this work, which was appreciated at Air Ministry, where my reputation was high, and asked if I would go to B flight, but I did not like the idea. W/C Castle had chosen me for A flight and I had grown into it; I would rather go elsewhere and start again. He spoke to Squadron Leader Fisher at B flight over the phone, and Fisher told him he would have the officer if it was Lyder, but no one else.

There was quite a strong feeling between the two flights, although we were one squadron. The W/C then suggested that I take my aircraft and crew to Swanton Morley in Norfolk, do a blind-bombing course and return to this station, but to 'B' flight. I did go to Swanton Morley but was unhappy about joining any other than my beloved A flight. I had nearly finished my blind-bombing course there when Padre Warner phoned to say "come home Garth, Ford was shot down and killed today," and he was sad to say this, but most people on the station were relieved, as he had upset them so much.

I completed the blind-bombing course at Swanton Morley and then returned to take charge of 'A' flight, but was still not given the rank of Squadron Leader. Soon the new Squadron Leader arrived and he was as green as grass. He had been in training command all the time so far and had seen nothing of the sharp end of operations. He was Robert Wood, who spent three trips with me learning the job and wanted a fourth. I told him he would have to go on his own now or never. Once you go out and return safely you will gain in confidence. I had taught him all that I knew. We never flew in the same box after that. He led one and I the other.

When we were given the job to lead the box of six, we were watched with interest by the senior officers. We planned a picnic one afternoon to the nearest village (town) of Cranley to watch a cricket match on the green and the Senior Air Controller Squadron Leader Dutton asked if he could join us, and while there, he addressed me and said "the C.O. Group Captain Dunlap considered you his blue-eyed boy, you know," and told how he stands on the gallery of the control tower with his clipboard in his hand, checking each box as it circles and sets course overhead, and on the day we led for the first time, he watched with greater interest when my box set course bang on time, looked at Dutton with a tilt of his head and said "that's my boy".

Our operations were usually carried out under fair weather conditions, as we needed to fly in formation and also to see the targets clearly and at times they were obscured by cloud. Being the only crew on the station that had done the course on blind-bombing, we were chosen to lead a formation of three boxes of six aircraft, when the C.O. decided to try out this new system, which, if successful, could increase and improve our performance. My navigator was replaced by the chief navigator on the station a New Zealander, Squadron Leader Reece.

The weather was particularly foul and we were briefed to take off at intervals to avoid collision and give the chaps time to join their leaders above the clouds at 5,000 feet. I took off climbing straight ahead and made a wide circling turn to allow my box to get together, and when I had collected six, I set course, hoping the others would follow. I enjoyed a challenge and was hoping we would make a success of it and pressed on even when we realised we were only one box.

We crossed the Channel and were now flying over France. We could not see any escorting aircraft. I was getting quite anxious and wondered what I should do in the circumstances. We were one box of six instead of three, with no escort over France in an absolutely clear sky, and I considered the possibility of making a name for myself if I bombed the target successfully – then the alternative, we could be mauled by German fighters and the whole box shot down, besides which one box could do little damage and we would have removed the element of surprise of ever going to that target in future.

I was in quite a quandary and asked Squadron Leader Reece "what should we do" and he replied "you are in command, you make the decision," and remembering our very first operation when Carey had turned back when he found himself without any escort, I said "OK, will you please give me a course for home" and commenced a turn towards base. When we got back, we discovered that the box I had collected was a mixture of aircraft from three squadrons and was told that the exercise was a complete shambles and the operation called off.

When I had changed and got to the mess, Buddy Reece was already there and explained what we had done to the senior officers assembled around the log fire, and they commended me for my decision to return. Our station was in effect a Commonwealth effort, with crews from a variety of the members from Canada, Australia, New Zealand, Rhodesia and two of us from Trinidad, myself and a navigator in 98 Squadron named Laurent de Verteuil, whose brother was a pilot on fighters, one Indian named Reddy, one American named Samuelson, who was reclaimed by the 9th Air Force when the American unit arrived in England, and a whole squadron of Dutch men from the Netherlands and Indonesia – virtually a cross-section of the world fighting the German, Japanese, Italian axis.

The war was progressing towards the invasion of Europe and we had a visit from Air Commodore Basil Embury, who gave us a pep talk about our eventual transfer to the continent and how to take care of ourselves if shot down. He had himself been shot down and made his way out through to Switzerland, having had to kill a German soldier, who stood on the bridge between himself and freedom on the other side, with his bare hands. The parting advice was that the only good German is a dead one, so go out and kill them.

We also had a visit from one of our chaps who had escaped from prison camp and got home. Information which was useful to my crew when we did suffer the same fate. Also we had a visit from a famous night fighter pilot to advise us when we were about to change to night flying. He suggested that the pilot should keep the crew members awake and alert at all times, as a night fighter is anxious to keep alive and will break off if given a burst or two of tracer fire from a vigilant crew and will look for someone else who might be asleep, and lastly a visit from Air Marshall Cunningham, to ask us to continue on squadron to complete two tours of 50 sorties concurrently as the work was coming up fast and furious and efficiency was being spoilt with the changing of experienced crews at 30 operations as had been the case. On completion of 50 sorties, we would not be asked to do any more for the rest of the war, as there was a large pool of trained pilots waiting to take over from us.

While acting as leader of 'A' flight, awaiting a new Squadron Leader, I was in the flight office and had just finished preparing the battle order for that afternoon when one of our navigators, a Flying Officer, knocked on my door, approached my desk going down on his knees to beg me to leave him off the battle order that afternoon.

I was shaken by this and got him up and into a chair, where he pleaded urgently, and I told him I just could not do that, as one of the crews coming home soon would be required to go back out, and I definitely could not ask that of them, when he was available. He begged and explained how he was tortured by bad dreams of his wife being called to the door to receive a telegram that he had been killed.

I told him, he must control himself, we were all scared but had to soldier on. Then he told me, he had little confidence in his pilot, that if he were on my crew he would not be frightened like this as I would never get shot down. I tried to dissuade him of such a notion, saying that we all run that risk as German flak was no respector of persons. He continued to beg and I explained, I would have no option other than to send him to the M/O and realising that, that would mean he could be discharged and his papers stamped LMF

(Lacking in Moral Fibre). He then said "oh god sir, I couldn't go home to my wife like that" and I said "that is the spirit boy. I will be leading that box and will do my best to take care of you". When the time came for us to get kitted up, I passed by his locker to give him a punch in the stomach to reassure him. I told only the Wing Commander of this episode and he nursed him up to 40 trips and thought that was enough and took him off operations and posted him away as an instructor. We were in the dining area of the large marquee when this Flying Officer rushed in throwing his cap in the air and hugged me saying that he had been screened. I was very pleased for him and wished him the best of luck for the future.

When we first heard that we were to withdraw to Swanton Morley to do night training, the dining tent was humming with discussion and I came in to join Tommy and Charlie, my airgunner, chatting with one of the Dutch pilots who seemed to be anxious about the prospect and Tommy said to him "my old man likes night flying" and the Dutchman turned to me and questioned that earnestly. "You like night flying?" and I replied "yes, I do" he retorted "only owls and fools fly at night and owls limit themselves to circuits and bumps".

We all enjoyed a hearty laugh, after which Charlie, who was my best friend on the crew, turned to me and said that he did not care for night flying much, but if he had to do it there was no one else he would have as his pilot. I thanked him for such an expression of confidence in me. A notice appeared on the board soon after this, asking for anyone with experience of formation flying at night to report to the Group Captain. I went to see Group Captain Dunlap and asked if I could speak off the record and he agreed, so I explained that while at SFTS at Carberry, I had indulged in a short spell of night formation flying, but the atmosphere there was very clear on a wintery, moonlit night and I did not feel that those conditions existed over here.

He asked me to set up a trip by night with another crew when we got to Swanton Morley and write a report to the Wing Commander who would be in charge. I did that the very night we arrived, getting a crew to fly around a prepared route and formatted on him and frightened myself out of my wits, as the conditions over the UK were absolutely foul. I managed to make it back by the grace of God and reported that night formation was impossible over the UK, and this was accepted by the Air Command.

I had, as Flight Commander of our 'A' flight, to brief the crew for night flying and was doing this when a young Sergeant Pilot, ex-public school and new to the squadron, wandered around the room with a bored expression with his hands in his pockets. I got tired of this and called him to me and ordered him for a start to take his hands out of his pockets and told him off for such a display of insubordination. If even he thought I could not teach him anything new, service discipline demanded he pay attention.

I was sad to report that that very night he killed himself and crew on take-off from Swanton Morley when he failed to tighten the knob which held the throttles forward, and the right hand throttle fell backwards and the aircraft slid into the ground.

We duly returned to Dunsfold having completed our training, and a couple of nights later, we were being briefed by the Group Captain for our very first night operation. He explained that the long-awaited invasion was due to take place soon and until then, we would be going out each night to prepare the ground for the assault. We were each to be given individual targets and. . . "Lyder, yours will be a viaduct to bomb and destroy to delay No. 23 Panzer Division in reaching the coast. "

We were to fly in at 4,000 feet, to which I squealed a protest that that seemed like suicide, but he explained that darkness was a great ally in night insurgence. I accepted that rather half-heartedly after having been subjected to the hammering we got regularly at 12,000–14,000 feet. Padre Tom Warner sat with me during briefing and asked me to take him, and I accepted him willingly saying "we could use an extra pair of eyes".

We duly set out and Tommy found the target and bombed it, feeling sure we had hit it, and we headed for home. On the way back over the Channel, we were engaged in our individual thoughts, when Padre broke the silence with "Garth, look over the side" and when I did, I saw what looked like hundreds of ships. I asked

Padre what was going on and he was as astonished as I was, saying "it must be one hell of an exercise". This was about 4.30 am. We got back to base and stated what we had seen when being debriefed, and went to bed in our respective tents. I had gone fast asleep when one of our pilots, named Jimmy Leadle, an Australian, ran through the tent lines waking us up, shouting that we had just taken part in the invasion of Europe. Dawn was just opening and the tannoy public address system announced that we were not going to be required to fly that day and could go to the mess for drinks or coffee.

My navigator stuck his head out of his tent opposite and said to me "we made it, chum". I got dressed and went to the mess tent to see Padre regaling the Group Captain with our exploits that night. We listened intently during the day to any news we could find, and prayed for the poor soldiers who would be taking an awful beating. The next day, we put up a magnificent show by pouring nine boxes of six aircraft into the sky, we thrilled to the job with adrenalin flowing freely. As a rule, Tommy, my navigator, would alert me as we neared the French coast by saying "enemy coast ahead, skipper get weaving" but this day, the 7th June 1944, his message was "coast ahead but you need not weave today, it is our coast now" with great pride, but we were to learn later at what cost in lives – brave men's lives. Years later I visited Normandy with my wife June and daughter Jenny, and was astounded by the task those soldiers had been asked to do and their bravery and determination to make a success of it. The cost in pain and loss of life was horrendous. The citizens of Europe owe them a debt of gratitude.

The next two night flights we did were to carry bundles of parachute flares, each bundle with a million-candle power, and cruise around at 4,000 feet and await requests from other crews to illuminate any area that they perceived had something worth attacking. We were called "Red 1 etc." and the bombers mainly Mosquitoes were "Cherry 1 etc." We cruised down the coast by the Bay of Biscay, and Tommy called to me to turn left towards St. Malo and I replied "no can do" he shouted again "left on to 090" and I advised him to look outside and he exclaimed "holy toledo" as he saw a box of molten metal being pumped into the sky about two or three miles square.

He found me another way in and we got a call from Cherry 1 and replied. A raw Australian voice asked if we could flare position and gave co-ordinates so Tommy wrote down the co-ordinates, fixed the position on the map and he replied we could.

Next question was how long before we got there, and Tommy replied about 10 minutes, and the Aussie begged us to hurry up. We headed for the position putting the speed up, but with repeated requests for a progress report and admonishments to get a move on. We eventually got there and told Cherry 1 when about to drop the flares. Bomb doors open, flares gone and suddenly the surrounding sky was as bright as daylight. I had never experienced anything like this before and felt naked and thought fighter attack was imminent. I opened the throttles wide and climbed for height, turning this way then that and asked Tommy for a course for home. Meanwhile, I could hear the Aussie shouting "wacko here we go" and another Aussie calling "are you finished cobber" to which the reply was "naa, now having another go" and the retort "hurry up for Christ's sake, I want to have a go". I thought to myself, is it only the Commonwealth boys doing the fighting. On the way back to base, we were caught in a searchlight over Alderney and I threw the aeroplane about to get out of it.

The war was getting to a crucial stage, with Hitler becoming desperate, being beaten back by Russia on the eastern front, together with the 24-hour bombing we were giving him. The Germans produced a threatening weapon called the doodle-bug by the countryfolk here. It was an unmanned flying bomb, which very nearly devastated London.

Our reconnaissance aircraft noticed small sites like pock-marks all appearing over the French west countryside, which were eventually recognised as launching pads for these flying bombs. They were small targets, just launching ramps and a shed to house the bomb, which had short wings and a small jet engine with fuel carefully metered for range and once the fuel was exhausted the device would fall to earth.

We, the Tactical Airforce, as specialist daylight bombers, were called up to deal with this menace and destroyed a great number of them, only just in time. They were very small targets and we attacked them in boxes of six Mitchells at a time. We were missing them from altitude as they were defended by mobile guns surrounding them and the lapse of a split second between calling "bombs gone" to other bomb aimers in the box and their reaction to this call. So my navigator Tommy devised a method of getting the box of six to release their bombs simultaneously, which proved very successful.

He briefed the navigators on our flight that he would call 'bomb doors open' then he would plan to broadcast a maximum of two statements 'bombing, bombing' and to ensure the next one would be 'bombs gone' he would raise the inflexion of his voice so that everyone knew the very next thing to come would be 'bombs gone' and the release buttons were all pressed together allowing all six loads of bombs to straddle the target. This was adopted throughout the three squadrons and our destruction rate improved considerably.

Our crew grew in reputation and popularity and on one occasion, there was an important target that Air Ministry said we simply had to hit and we had missed it twice, due to it being heavily defended. We had gone the evening before and again this day and the photographs taken by a camera in each box proved we had missed. My crew was on the second attempt.

The Wing Commander Lynne, who was co-ordinator in charge of operations between the squadrons, called a meeting of all crews to address us and said how important that target was and if we delayed another day, the flak would become increasingly worse as they would move in even more mobile guns to defend it, as they had done overnight. He had asked for and obtained permission to take one box of six and go back immediately – he was an outstanding leader, with a considerable number of sorties, and said, "this is the six I have chosen, I shall lead and Lyder you will be number two" and named the four others. We got kitted up and set out.

Our crew was flattered to have been chosen from among others with greater seniority and service, but was humbled by such approval that we were determined to acquit ourselves and rode into battle with relish. Approaching the target, W/C Lynne made a long and descending attack and the flak was frightening, so much so that Tommy, sitting in the glass nose, shouted "flak, flak, weave" but I stuck with Lynne as though the two aircraft were tied together, and called on Tommy to concentrate on his bombsight.

We bombed and did a steep turn away. I asked Tommy to keep looking at the target and soon he shouted, "we have hit it, we hit it". I told him that that was what we came to do and stuck in close formation while the flak pursued us, but tailed off. Over the Channel, we got into tight formation on Lynne, with our left wing behind his and number three matched us. We were feeling so chuffed.

Lynne's Gunner in the top mid-ship turret got worried and called Lynne's attention to it. Lynne looked out at us and made as though he was biting his nails, looked the other side and did the same, then gave us the thumbs up and said over the radio "OK, brown box, open to half a span and relax". This was overheard at base, and as everything said over the air was logged, I was told that this was added to the 'line shoot' book.

Our crew had become very respected and as a result, we grew in confidence. Every few months we were sent on a week's leave, returning usually on a Sunday, and on each such return we became frightened again as we were told of the changes that had occurred to personnel and tactics, so one could never become blasé and had to adjust quickly to new methods of survival. It was a perpetual learning curve. We were gradually approaching our target of 50 sorties and had to think of what we would do next. The rest of the crew were making plans to leave, but I felt it would be an anti-climax as I would like to be active, to be there, when we won. I was feeling that good.

The crew begged me to retire gracefully as they were planning, but I just felt that I wanted to continue and went to Group Captain Dunlap to ask to stay on. He said that he could not make that decision and would have to refer that request to Air Ministry. He called me the next day and reported that Air Ministry had considered my request and were pleased that I had offered, as we were short of leaders and welcomed my volunteering. He said "we shall have to look for a new crew for you" when I told him that my crew were looking forward to leaving. I then told him that I would like full charge of 'A' flight, meaning a promotion in rank to Squadron Leader, and he promised that would be done. We had done 48 trips by this time, and I was preparing to say my farewells to my crew who had given me such support.

I was invited to dinner at the friends I had made at nearby Loxwood Farm, the Spantons'. Mr Spanton was a businessman in Woking and like many others had bought a farm in Surrey, and Mrs Spanton improved the property and then they sold it to Alex Quigg, the Personnel Director of ICI, and bought Loxwood Farm, near to Dunsfold, and had improved buildings there.

Mrs Spanton gave my navigator and self a lift to Guildford one morning while we were waiting for a bus. She was in her WVS uniform on her way to the Guildford office and handed me her card with an invitation to visit the farm. Tommy had his WAFF girlfriend and was not keen, so I contacted Mrs Spanton, who had me to dinner, and I became friendly with the family.

It was at one of such dinners, the evening of 8th August 1944, that I enjoyed and returned to my tent which I shared with my Gunner Charles Walkden and a Norwegian named Gronmark, who was senior to me on the squadron and was a very private person and older than me, who did not socialise with the rest of the chaps but kept himself very much to himself. We had a lot in common, the two of us. So when we had to move into tents, he asked to share mine. He was a big fellow, who had worked in the forestry department in Canada, but he never conversed much, so I did not find out a lot about him. He was just anxious to operate and take the fight to the Germans and became a very senior officer in the Norwegian Air Force after the war. Squadron Leader Carey had told me how Gronmark waited to see the battle order on the noticeboard and if his name was not on it, he would knock on his door, come in, bend over him at his desk and demand to be put on the battle order. He just lived for that and may have been driven to it by some personal loss due to German action. When I returned to England after being a POW in Germany and recovered my belongings, I noticed that my log book had been signed off by a Wing Commander Gronmark.

Shot Down

To continue my story from where I mentioned the dinner party on 8th August 1944, I arrived back in my tent at approximately 11.30 pm to find Charlie awake, waiting up to tell me that we were flying in the morning.

I told him "no, Robert Wood, the Squadron Leader was leading the box" and he said "yes, but we are down as his number two". I was stunned for a minute and thought I would call someone else to take our place, as this was a waste of one of my trips as leader, but considered the consequences of waking some other crew as well as Robert Wood. To tell them at that hour would cause complete confusion and be an act of madness, as they may even be much the worse from drink and unprepared. At least I was rested and sober.

We went to bed and as good airmen obeyed instructions and never said a word to anyone in the morning. I thought of speaking to Squadron Leader Wood when we returned from the operation, but that never took place. We had been given the job of attacking a large ammunition storage in a wooded area in France and set off.

All went well until we were fired on by German guns and Robert Wood seemed to be not himself and not really coping in avoiding the flak. We arrived in the target area and the flak became very heavy indeed and suddenly all hell was let loose. The box had received a direct hit, with the leader falling out of the sky and we with heavy damage, together with the starboard engine on fire.

I turned away and tried to assess what we had left of our airplane, but was having great difficulty in holding it as it was shaking so badly, and with Roy Walker, the Rear Gunner, shouting to me "Garth, let us get out of this thing, it is going to explode" as the flames were streaking past him. I decided that he was right and reluctantly ordered the crew to bail out.

Bomber crews, at least on our station, wore the parachute harnesses, but not the chutes, which were hung on quick release hooks on the sides of the fuselage, and Roy had his off and hooked to his chest very quickly. Taking Charlie's off its hook, he placed it on the floor near to the escape hatch, which was jettisoned for exit. He shouted to Charlie, who was getting out of the mid-upper gun turret, "here is your chute Charlie" and dived out the hatch.

In the meantime, Tommy had crawled back from his position in the nose to appear in the well behind the cockpit and Doug Hogarth, an Australian, was in the co-pilot's seat waiting to get out, while I fought furiously with the wounded bird, trying to hold it under enough control for them to get out and then I could follow. I should add here that Doug Hogarth was an extra gunner who was separated from his crew as they had completed their quota of ops and had finished, but he had not as he had joined that crew as a replacement member and now went around the squadron asking crews for the opportunity to ride with them to complete his quota.

Suddenly I heard a shout from Charlie "Garth, I have no parachute". For a split second I was frozen with fear and then shouted back "I will stay with you, the rest of you get out". Tommy was now standing in the well behind the cockpit and asked "what about Charlie?" and I shouted "get out, I am staying with him".

He reluctantly pulled the lever that jettisoned the escape hatch near his feet and looked through it to see the starboard engine fall off the aeroplane in a ball of fire and shouted to me "the engine's gone" to which I replied, as he recalled later "oh, good show" and he shouted back "good show hell, the engine has fallen off".

I discovered that with the engine gone, so was most of the fire and what was more, I had more control as the bucking had stopped. I then said to Tommy "I can fly it now, get up front and give me a course for home, but avoid Dieppe", which was a nest of guns. I had to fly the thing purely by feel as we had considerable damage, one engine and a ruddy great expanse of engine bulkhead to drag through the air. There was also very little left of my instrument panel for information from the dashboard regarding speed etc. as the lot was in my lap in broken pieces, while the altimeter was unwinding its readings of height at a furious rate. I had hoped to get out to sea where I would ditch, but the main thing was to keep flying speed or we would fall like a stone.

Soon I realised we were not going to reach the coast as the horizon was rapidly coming up to meet us, and I asked Tommy for the surface wind. He shouted back "south-west about 15 knots" and I looked at a clearing between two areas of wood and manoeuvred into the wind and prayed "please help me father, I cannot do this alone".

Tommy had come back and sat up on the cockpit deck and braced himself against the back of my chair, looking over his shoulder and carrying on a running commentary of our progress with Charlie in the rear of the aircraft. The bomb bay separated him from us. As I slowed down, the aircraft tended to turn to the right with the left engine pulling and depleted control, as our right fin and rudder were badly damaged.

I observed a Frenchman in the field with his horse and cart and became concerned about running into him and had my left rudder and aileron hard over to that side to keep the aircraft reasonably straight. We had a further problem in that the right leg of the undercarriage had fallen off with the engine and the left leg had fallen down freely and locked due to total loss of hydraulic oil.

As we got closer, I observed that the field was rough with potato beds running across our path and I tipped the aircraft to the left, hit a mound and broke the left leg off. The aeroplane made a dive for the ground, but I was able to pull the control back hard and arrest the dive. I switched off the master electric switch on the overhead panel and crash-landed flat on the belly with the perspex roof over the cockpit breaking up and the aircraft coming to a hurried stop.

To my great surprise, both Tommy and myself were intact, but Doug was curled up against the dashboard and very still for a second or so, but when I shouted "get out", he was out through the broken roof like a jack out of a box. I had to unplug his headset from the wall to release him.

Tommy followed Doug, while I climbed out my side and ran to the rear of the aircraft calling for Charlie, but got no reply, so I pushed in the side window and climbed in to find him in a heap on the floor. He had been tossed about as there was nothing to hold on to and would have been far better off in his turret. He had been stunned, but was slowly coming round, complaining "my leg, my leg". I realised it was broken from the way it was bent under his body. I told him to stay still, while checking him for other damage as something like broken ribs could do him harm when lifting him up. I looked out and shouted to Tommy "bring me the crash axe from the cockpit". He did so and at the same time put his navigator bag on the fire on the right wing, which was catching the dry scrub alight. As he handed the axe to me, I could hear the German soldiers grabbing him. I found the axe of little use inside the restricted fuselage and climbed out into the arms of the Germans. I tried to chop an opening from outside, but the Germans tried to pull me away and I swung the axe about, shouting "camarade in there" and they left me to it, apart from tugging at my revolver which was in a webbing pouch attached to my waist with the lanyard around my neck.

I unhooked the lanyard from around my neck and threw it at them saying "take the bloody thing". The fire was now building up and I shouted to Charlie to drag himself to the window, and Tommy came to help me pull Charlie through. By this time, the fire was raging and the belts of 0.5 calibre ammunition, which we carried, started to explode like a fireworks display and the Germans ran some distance away.

I told Charlie "come on chap, one last heave", and with that he pushed himself with his last ounce of energy whilst we tugged his injured body out of the window in the fuselage and on to the ground. We dragged him whilst cowering low to a safe distance from the inferno. I did not think at that time we would survive, but the bible tells us that he who lays down his life for his friend shall be saved, and we proved that, that early afternoon on the 9th August 1944 in a field near Amiens.

We lay Charlie on his back and straightened his right leg with the broken femur as comfortably as we could make him, while the Germans hung around. At times, he appeared to be fainting and I patted his face and begged him to stay with us, when an older soldier came up, probably from the 1st World War, and sympathetically said "oh, Kamerad kaputt". I spoke to him saying "yes, camarade sick, go get a doctor, get doctor" and he walked away. We just did not know what to do next.

Then a young Feldwebel (Sergeant to you) came up and asked his men why they did not take us away, and they obviously replied that we would not move. I had squatted on Charlie's left and Tommy lay off on his right side. The Sergeant took his pistol, a nasty looking weapon, out of his holster and, opening the safety catch, pointed it at my head and shouted "raus".

I patted Charlie on his chest and told him that we were going to have to leave but that I would see he was taken care of. A promise I made with my tongue in my cheek, as I had no idea how I would achieve that. They marched us away in single file with a gun at each of our backs, while the French farmer we had nearly killed hovered around, obviously hoping he could help. The soldiers kept shooing him away but he followed us.

We were marched through the village of Woincourt, I think this is how it was spelt, and I carried myself upright and with pride as I had nothing to be ashamed about. I remembered as a young boy, reading about one Englishman named Caradoch who was captured by the Romans, taken prisoner and paraded through the streets of Rome, who had impressed the Emperor with his fine bearing. The villagers lined the street and a number of the old generation bowed and greeted us with "bonjour monsieur" and I replied "bonjour". But the youngsters who were standing with their German soldier friends spat and swore at us as though we were vermin. I thought then how ungrateful they were to us, we who were risking our lives to achieve their freedom.

We were taken to a spot where we were set down and a German officer called us over one at a time to be interrogated. Tommy first, because he looked more willing to speak. I watched as he repeatedly shook his head and his ears became redder and redder. Then I was called and recited the usual – name, rank and number and refused to say any more.

There was a change in the watch and now a Sergeant appeared, who seemed more friendly and offered me a handful of very poor boiled sweets with what sounded like an apology, explaining they were part of his ration. I thought it was a very nice gesture and took one. I asked him as best I could in broken English/French/German to go and ask the Lieutenant what had happened about my camarade. He came back to report in gestures that camarade was in the hospital with his leg in splints or plaster and we were greatly relieved – the old soldier had gone to his camp and got help to take Charlie on a push cart to the dressing station.

This was a lovely summer afternoon, and suddenly I realised our position and made to get up and walk away, to get home, and the Sergeant jumped up and pointed his gun at us. It dawned on me then that we weren't getting back to England for a while. We were put in a sheltered dug-out for the night and I took the opportunity to slit the lining of my battledress top and carefully insert a nylon map each side. Tommy had a small sewing kit in his pocket, with which I stitched up the lining. I told Tommy and Doug that if we were to get away and get home, we would have to do that before we were taken into Germany.

The next morning a Frenchman with a cab and horse were brought to take us away and we whispered between us as how we might tackle the guards to escape as the cabby gave us looks indicating he was ready to help, but we decided against any attempt as a German sat on each side of us, while another with his gun at the ready followed on foot. I felt sorry for the poor horse as it was struggling with the load. We were taken, of all places, to a camp near Dieppe, which was the place that was raided in 1942 by our Commandoes who suffered severe losses, a sort of dummy run for the subsequent invasion of Europe. The Germans there still remembered that assault and were most antagonistic.

We were searched by a rough officer who took my battledress top and carefully felt it and asked me "vat is dis?" and I replied "lining". He called for a knife and cut it open one side and then the other and removed the two maps that I had hoped to use on an escape while shouting "lining, lining" derisively before throwing it back at me in a fit of temper, pushing me away and kicking me in the backside as I turned to go.

Our pockets had been emptied and the contents placed in a brown paper bag with our names on each, and it was only when we were sent out of Dulag Luft after the interrogation to a POW camp, that I discovered that my cherished Parker Duofold fountain pen had been replaced by a cheap broken German pen. This did upset me as the pen and pencil set had been a 21st birthday present from my mother years earlier. I was in the habit of leaving that pen at base on setting out on all operations, but I had forgotten to do so on this occasion. When I got back to England and was debriefed and was asked if there was anyone in particular who I wanted to report as being nasty to me while a POW, that officer was the only one that I mentioned and with such a feeling of bitterness that the officer debriefing me said, "leave it to us, we will get the bastard".

After being dismissed with a kick we were put into a cellar, down in the bowels of the brick camp of Dieppe, with a small claustrophobic area to sleep, and I thought we were about to be murdered. That night all sorts of things passed through my mind and I dozed off in pure mental exhaustion. The following morning, we were transported by jeep to a small ex-police station in the small village of Poix. This building had very thick walls and three cells. We (Tommy, Doug and myself) were placed in the middle cell and heard noises of movement next door. Tommy took his boot off and tapped on the wall and got a tap in reply. We tried to communicate, but could not use morse as there was no means of tapping dashes, so Tommy called for the guard to take him to the toilet, and once our door was opened, I stuck myself in it and the guard pushed me in the chest saying "nein,nein" but I refused to be pushed inside. Tommy then asked to go to the friend next door saying "camarade" and pointing in gestures that we needed to see our camarades. He eventually relented and we were let into the neighbouring cell to find some Aussies stripped to their jock-straps because of the heat and looking like pictures of old films of pirates in ships' holds.

We talked about trying to escape and I mentioned that I had attempted to cut through one of the iron bars in the window, high in the outside wall, with a 6 inch hacksaw blade hidden in the bottom of my trousers and only succeeded in polishing it, as it was so tough. One Aussie asked the other "shall we show them?" and they agreed to show us, and by my standing on Tommy's shoulders as I had done to try to cut the bar in our cell whilst singing to cover the sound.

The Aussies had dug away at the cement and made a channel in the sill of the window at the bottom of the iron rods and loosened the holes at the top so that the bars could be moved sideways at the bottom and pulled out of the top. This was achieved by using the metal arm from the water tank high above the toilet pan, which, when pulled by the chain, emptied it into the pan. They had broken it off and hidden it under one of the palliasses of straw used for beds. The iron bars were standing upright in position ready to be pulled out, but they had discovered that a guard had been placed outside that wall day and night. We went back to our cell to join Doug and wondered what would happen to us next. Late that afternoon, we heard movement like more prisoners being brought into the cell on the other side of us, and Tommy got down on his knees and peered through the small hole into that cell, where a brick had been removed for a four-inch pipe to feed hot air into it from a heater once placed in the corner of our cell, but now removed.

Tommy could get one eye to it and said there is someone in there who looks like Roy, our Wireless Operator, who had bailed out. I pushed Tommy aside and shouted "Roy, Roy" and presently an eye appeared on the other side and a voice asked "that you, Garth?" and I knew it was him. He said the rumour was that we were moving out tonight. That proved to be correct when about 7 pm, the three cells were emptied under heavy guard to board an open truck with boards across as benches, and I positioned myself next to Roy so that we could chat. I learnt that he had been fired upon when descending by parachute, but had pulled vigorously on the guy-ropes to set up a swaying motion and had not been shot. He had hit the ground fairly hard, but with no bones broken.

A gunner named Flintoff from Squadron Leader Woods' crew descended not far from him and was badly burned, hands and face, and Roy helped him as they were taken away by the Germans. Roy asked what had happened to us and I recounted our experiences.

He then remarked "you fellas been in some funny places eh, we have been in the Bastille". We were driven through the night to a railway station in Paris and on the way there driven through the L'Arc de Triomphe as a cynical gesture by the Germans.

We were put aboard a train, which moved out eventually on a fitful journey into Germany. Progress was slow due to the line having been cut in several places, and at one spot we had to walk about ¼ mile to board another train. We arrived at Mannheim Ludwigshafen station eventually to change trains for Frankfurt and be put into solitary confinement in Dulag Luft, where all flying crew prisoners were brought for interrogation.

In the German Prison Camp

We were housed in cubicles, ten feet by six, each with a single palliasse of straw to sleep on as furnishing. On the door was a one-foot length of angle-iron hinged at one end and held horizontal by a pin through a hole in the door, this was for calling attention if you needed to go to the toilet.

We would push the pin out, hung by a bit of string and the iron bar would drop to a vertical position to be noticed by the guards. Every time you received attention and were put back in your cell, the bar would be reset. I soon discovered that one had to wait until one heard someone moving about to hear the bar drop or one could wait a long time before it was observed.

I was locked in my cell late that evening and roused at dawn with a guard handing me a sort of broom made of twigs and motioned that I should sweep the room. I took it quietly and made to do just that in all humility, and in disgust he took it away and passed on to the next cell. I thought about this experience and concluded that this was a psychological ploy to discover who was going to be co-operative or belligerent.

We were served some horrible gruel for breakfast at about 8 am, just guessing, as my watch had been taken away from me. My cell was opened by a small man in a pin-striped suit who called me out and took me to an office where he told me he was from the Red Cross Society in Geneva – nothing to do with the Third Reich. He gave me a form, asking me to sit at the desk and fill it in – all very friendly like.

It started off with the usual: name, rank and number, which I wrote down and noticed him toying with his hands and smiling and then came squadron, where based, C.O's name etc. etc. I drew three long lines across the form and he jumped up shouting "vot are you doing, you are destroying Reich property". I replied "a short few minutes ago you had told me, you were nothing to do with the Reich". He shouted "you either give me that information or I shall treat you as a spy and take you to the Gestapo". I got up and said "OK, let's go to the Gestapo", to which he shouted with his arms flailing saying "you are crazy, you are crazy".

He then took me back and put me into a different and larger cell with another fellow lying on a palliasse, who quietly motioned with his finger over his lips for me not to say anything. He pointed to a place on the wall where the paper was not stuck down and I went across to it and tapped it with my finger and heard a noise like a microphone. I never found out who he was as a few minutes later I was removed and was taken to a single room once more.

Later that day, I was taken across the driveway to a block of offices where my interrogation began. There was a white corridor with interrogating rooms on the side adjacent to the driveway and clerical offices on the other. I was ushered into this room with a jackbooted SS officer sitting at his desk and he stood up to invite me to take a seat opposite him, producing the same form I had seen earlier, and I wrote my name, rank and number and told him that was all I was allowed to say.

He tried different tactics to draw me into conversation and said "I can see you are going to be bloody awkward" and opened a drawer in his desk and took out a packet of cigarettes and, selecting one, carefully lit it and leaned back in his swivel chair, blowing the exhaled smoke into the air with a grand flourish. Whilst enjoying his smoke, he suddenly pulled himself up, apologising profusely for being so ill-mannered at not offering me one, and explaining that unfortunately we Germans were not as well bred as the British – to which I silently concurred, and offering me one I politely refused, and he continued to persuade me. But I did not smoke, so there was no hardship in my refusing, but I did not tell him that. I left him to grovel. Not having got anywhere with me, he rang the buzzer and the guard came to take me back to my cell.

There were lots of names and ranks of officers who had preceded me scribbled on the wall – one with the admonishment, in pig latin *'nil desperandum, bastada carborundum'* – don't let the bastards grind you down. I was buoyed up by this, which increased my resolve to stick it out. There were three meals, if that is what they were called, per day and I tried my best to get some of it down to keep my body functioning, if for no other reason, and had a lot of time to reminisce about Trinidad and family and longed to tell them that I was OK. Up to that time, I knew I would be reported missing, but there was nothing to let them know how I fared. I decided to keep a calendar as I was beginning to wonder what day it was, especially after falling asleep. I had nothing to make any mark with so managed to remove a screw from a heater at the head of my palliasse with my fingernails and used that to mark the wall down by the skirting.

The interrogation went on day after day with different officers, each trying to make a breakthrough. On one occasion, the officer got fed up and ranted at me, "what the hell is wrong with you?", "are you dumb, are you an imbecile?" to which I replied "I was", and told him that my name, rank and number was all I was going to tell him and nothing more, and if he continued to ask he would be wasting his time as well as mine. He listened intently until I had finished and, leaning back in his swivel chair, said "a very pretty speech, Mr Lyder, they must have told you to say that when you were in England," and leaning forward suddenly he pounded the desk, frightening me and with his eyes wide opened continued "but this is Germany now!" With that he pressed the buzzer for the guard who came in promptly, handed him a note, the officer shouted "take him away" and I left.

The treatment meted out to me in there gave the guard the feeling that he could humiliate me, and as we walked down the corridor, he kicked me twice on the back of my flying boot and shoved me forward with his hand. That told me that the first was not an accident, and in a fury I turned on him with a clenched fist and shouted "keep your filthy hands off me, if you do that again, I shall knock your teeth down your ruddy throat, don't you dare touch me again, I know where I have to go". The second part of my tirade was for the benefit of the staff, women and men, who hurriedly opened doors to see what the commotion was.

I returned to my cell and, to recover some of the authority he thought was his, he opened the door, gave me a push in the back, and hurriedly closed it. That night it got gradually hotter in my cell and I stripped off garments, one at a time at intervals, until I was in my underpants, and suddenly I thought, this just cannot be due solely to the August weather, and realised that the heater was on. It must have been written on the slip of paper the officer had handed to the guard 'heat treatment'.

I started to worry what next, but presently how to deal with this one. There was no way I could turn off the heat, nowhere in that cell, and I wondered how long I could stand it. It was stiflingly hot and no air could get in, as the only window was a small, shallow one in the top of the outside wall, but it was locked down and there was no means of reaching it as there was nothing to stand on.

My mind was in turmoil as a short while before I was shot down, the Germans had shot some fifty of my fellow men in cold blood, just for trying to escape. No one yet knew in England what had happened to us; they would very easily dispose of us as having been killed in the crash. They were mad at being beaten back at that time, added to which I could hear while lying in my cell, prisoners being taken out for questioning and a short while later a gunshot was heard and I presumed they had been shot and killed.

I became exhausted and fell asleep, later to wake up shivering with cold and nothing to wrap up with. I prayed and wondered what the future would hold, but worried more whether there was a future. I was now becoming ill with my mouth very sore. I had had a tooth pulled out from my lower jaw a couple of days before being shot down, which had haemorrhaged badly and now, without frequent washing, was getting infected, especially as I got such rubbish as food.

I was at a very low state of resistance and planned to abuse the interrogator when next I was taken out, so that he would shoot me and get it over with. I wept over this as I thought of my family back home and begged their forgiveness. I got all my clothes on and eventually got back to sleep. The next day I stood on the radiator and managed to pry the window open and see out.

I could see a window open in a cell across the yard and stared out hoping to see someone. It was quite a while before I saw some movement in there and waved until I got the occupant's attention. He waved back energetically and through sign language, I gathered his name was Fleming and he had been on a Mosquito type of aeroplane. I was feeling a lot better for that and made signs to him to hold fast and not give away any information.

Later that day I was taken before a new officer and when ushered into his office, I stood in front of him instead of sitting down and off-loaded a volley of abuse at him. My jaw was so bad that it was even painful to speak and I asked him what sort of uncivilised animals were they to keep me rotting in a cell like that.

His eyes went small and mad with rage. He had a swipe at my face but I pulled back and his hand just brushed my uniform and he shouted "you, you call me uncivilised, when you RAF killed some 10,000 of my people, bombing them to death in Frankfurt in two nights and you dare to call us uncivilised!" "You can go back and rot, I don't care."

With some relief that I had not been shot, I had a renewed wish to live. He told me to sit down and composed himself before he started to ask anything. He pointed to a picture on the wall behind him of a Mosquito aeroplane and said that that was the best aeroplane in the whole war, and when he said that to an American airman he had in that chair a while ago, he went mad. I had to smile and that broke the ice. He slowly started and I asked him "for God's sake send me somewhere to get attention for my mouth", and he then explained the facts of life to me, he would very much like to send me out tonight, but it was conditional on my giving some information about myself. I asked "what sort of information?" and he said "for instance, where were you trained". I asked "was that all?" and he said "well yes". I saw no harm in that and said "I obtained my wings in Canada" and he said "oh yes, I knew you were commissioned in Canada because of your officer number". I then told him it was at 5 SFTS in Carberry and he replied "oh, Manitoba, we knew quite a lot about Carberry, who was the C.O. there when you qualified?" I stood up and said "I thought you said that was all you wanted, you are not a man of your word and I am going back to my cell". He begged me to sit down and cool off. He really would like to help me but he had to place me before I would be released.

He said he could not place my accent and I told him I was born in Trinidad and he said "why did you not tell Hauptmann Sommer that, his father is a priest and travels all over South America." Hauptmann is the German rank of Captain, and he had interrogated me earlier. I learnt later that he was my cousin, because his father, Bishop Sommer, came to Cambridge University to study theology and married my mother's aunt. I learned all of this when Bishop Sommer got up to speak at a conference in Bristol.

I sat down again and he asked, "would I like to go with my crew?" – up to that time I had not let on that I had a crew or that I was a bomber or fighter pilot and thought surely some information must have accompanied my arrival there, as to my having been shot down on a Mitchell. He asked again "do you want to go with your crew, yes or no?" I looked at him and said "you are pretty smart, aren't you", he said "not particularly, but I need to know as I have two parties to send out tonight". I had to say yes, because I was dying to know how Tommy and Doug had fared, and said "yes". He then said "very well, you will be going to Sagan" and made the necessary note on his form. He stood up and came to a map on the wall and asked "what was my target the day I was shot down?" and I pointed to an area saying "an ammunition dump in that wood". He offered his hand and I automatically shook it while he said "you have been a good soldier, for you the war is now over".

I went back to my cell-block where I was given an old razor blade and soap and taken to the washroom to clean up. Some chaps went past the door and I saw one who might have been Tommy and who turned back to satisfy me that it was, saying "hi chum, you going out?" and I said "yes". He said "me too, see you when you come out". He was waiting for me to join a queue and explained that we must join this. We did and at the end of it, we were given the brown paper bags with the articles taken off us in Dieppe. It was then that I discovered my favourite Parker fountain pen was missing, but the number of things was correct, my pen having been replaced by an old German one.

We joined a number of others, including Doug Hogarth, and were put into a holding room for the night in preparation for moving out in the morning. I looked around for Fleming, the chap I had signalled to through my cell window, but he was not among us. Early next morning, we were herded to stand outside the building with a couple of soldiers to guard us. An officer came up with a clipboard and held a roll call. He then explained that we were to be marched to the railway station and taken to Vetslau, where we would have facilities to clean up and a good meal, then taken on a long journey to POW camp, Luft 3, and for us the war was over, but first starting at this end, he needed each man to sign next to his name on this clipboard to the effect he will not attempt to escape en-route.

Well, I have always agreed that unity is strength and all of us buoyed up by the mass of us gave him a voluble rumble of abuse, telling him in no uncertain terms that we were refusing. He then tried to regain control by taking his pistol out and shouting "be quiet". He proceeded to tell us, while pointing to the two sad sacks of guards, that we had to obey every instruction of theirs as "the most junior of our forces is now your superior".

Well, that raised another and worse outburst of derision of the Germans and their Third Reich, details of which I prefer not to mention in writing. He had more trouble that time, obtaining silence only by waving his pistol and firing a couple of shots in the air.

When we had settled down, we were marched to the station by those two sad sacks, with civilians staring at us as we shuffled past. One woman was at a door just ajar and I called Tommy's attention to her antics of sticking her tongue out at us, she saw me tell Tommy and gave us a special encore to which Tommy replied with an appropriate salute. We arrived at Vetslau in due course and had to walk some distance to the camp. We were individually recorded and each issued with a fibre suitcase of clothing items from the Red Cross Association and told to go to the showers and clean up, after which we were taken to the canteen and fed a fairly decent meal for a change and returned to our billets.

The next day we waited there for another batch of approximately fifty chaps to join us, and I saw one who looked like Fleming in that batch. When we got back from the canteen, I verified that it was him and introduced myself, and we sat together for a long chat. He was in a very sorry state of mind and I did my best to console him. He was a 27-year old auctioneer from New Zealand and had been on a Mosquito squadron, which had co-operated with us when we did the flaring, first nights over France. He kept murmuring that he was going to be court marshalled when he got back because he had to give some information, as he was at breaking point to get out of Dulag Luft.

I tried to relieve his fears, by asking "what sort of information?" and he said that he had to tell them where he trained in Australia. I asked "is that all?" and he nodded and I told him to forget it, "I had to say that I had been trained in Canada and there was no harm in that, as it was made plain to me in the last interview, that I would never get out of there without some sort of surrender as we were bucking the authority of the Third Reich and they had to win that battle at least". He felt a lot better after that and seemed happier on the train to Sagan. When we arrived there, I asked to be sent to the same room as Fleming, but they explained their system of adding one only to each existing room. I was the 11th in the room to which I was assigned, and he to another. This was for the purpose of easy integration into the workings of the camp, as we each learnt from the experienced other members.

To move forward a bit here on Fleming. I visited him a few times in his block, but things were regimented and visiting hours limited to three hours in the evenings. He seemed to be falling back into a state of depression, and the padre had visited him and charged his room-mates with never leaving him alone. One early afternoon I came upon a commotion outside a dugout cellar where foodstuffs, potatoes and mangel wurzels were kept because it was cooler, and I learnt that Fleming had got away in there and had hacked at his throat with a pair of scissors. He was taken to hospital but I never heard how he had fared after that.

The next day at Sagan I was interrogated by a group of our own officers responsible for our own security in the camp and found it distasteful, as they were anything but friendly, until I asked "what the hell is this, do you belong to the same RAF as I do?" and objected to the way I was being treated.

The mood hurriedly changed and they explained that my Trinidad accent gave them to thinking that I might just be a plant (spy), put into the camp to obtain information on subversive activity. I felt a trifle better but not fully recovered, I learned that there were other West Indians in that camp. There was a pilot officer Bourne from Barbados, whom I last saw before I left Trinidad, where his family were living at the time, as a college boy helping a friend of mine repair his motor-cycle.

Then there was Flying Officer Mike Gilfoyle from Jamaica and a Flying Officer May, who asked to meet me. He had been to Trinidad on a visit to his uncle and family, the then Chief of Police, Colonel May. That was interesting, as Deryck and myself used to frequently go to the police barracks and the Mays' quarters to play with their sons Peter and Tony and the family of Major Carr, whose eldest boy, Sonny, eventually became Chief of Police there, and so did Tony May in the passing of time. I think I am right in saying that Sonny Carr was the first local boy to be commissioned in the Trinidad Constabulary. Previously all recruits were imported from England and most had gained experience through serving in Palestine. His youngest sister Jean Carr, who married one of our British West Indian Airways pilots, Johnny Purchase, who came from Jamaica, still lives on Newbury Hill near to our home there, but Johnny passed on many years ago.

I saw my navigator Tommy Good frequently on the exercise circuit around the camp compound, but Doug

Hogarth had asked for a transfer to North Camp, where his brother was held, and I never heard any more of him. My wireless operator/air gunner Roy Walker was a Warrant Officer and unfortunately separated from us after arrival at Dulag Luft, more of him later. Our room complement had one more added to it with the arrival of Flying Officer Dinty Moore, to make it a dozen a short while later. He came in on the same (purge) batch of new prisoners as the Dutch navigator from one of the crews of the Dutch Squadron 320, which operated with us from Dunsfold. He was the chap who at Bicester had protested vigorously the evening we arrived there in transit to Finmere's O.T.U., when an open truck was brought in to take us to Finmere. The transport officer apologised for it, but he was unable to get anything else at that time.

We were all quite happy that the chap had done his best and we boarded the truck, but this Dutchman insisted he was an officer and wanted better treatment than this. When he refused in spite of all explanation, Tommy, who was a big man, and others physically bundled him on board and we were driven to Finmere, the satellite airfield. Whenever a new purge was due, the camp would hear in advance and congregate in a crescent around the main gate to see who was coming in.

Presently, this Dutchman passed through the gate and I said to Tommy, "look who is here" and he said "shit, not him again". As he saw us, he shouted "Tommy!" and approached us as long-lost friends.

I must have heard from Tommy how he had been shot down, but cannot remember now. In our room, Dinty Moore told us that he was the bomb aimer on a Lancaster on Pathfinder duties, who had mistakenly marked the wrong place with a flare, that the heavies had bombed and written off a French village and for his sins, they were sent to attack a nest of V1 sites, which we Tactical Air Force had asked for as we were losing so many crews in daylight. His father ran a pub in Southall and he regaled us with the things that went on in running a pub, for instance, like opening a water tap which was poised over the main tank of beer when they were running a bit low on the demand for more beer.

While on the subject, in our room we had one Paddy Leydon who had been shot down in 1940, on Fairey Battles over France. Among other characteristics, he snored like a lorry offloading gravel, and was ordered to take his bed every evening to the room at the end of the building, which was used as a lecture room, so that the rest of the room could get some sleep. Well, Paddy sold his 1/12 share of his so-called Christmas cake to Dinty Moore for a promissory note to give him five bottles of whiskey from his father's pub, the White Swan, when they were returned to the UK. I never heard what happened, but can imagine the father's language, if and when Paddy ever presented that cheque.

When we were eventually overrun by the Russians and being evacuated, Paddy was quite unhappy over this disturbance of the daily routine he had grown into. The camp was very well organised and run as close to a normal RAF station at home and lectures were offered on all sorts of subjects. I was offered one on learning the German language and I rejected that, saying that when I got out of there, I would decree it a dead language and insist on all Germans speaking English. There was a lecture by a Canadian who had lived with the eskimos for two years, another by Wing Commander Collard on the Constitution of Britain, or more correctly the lack of one, etc.

There was a library with quite interesting books and the map on the wall with pins holding threads of different colours depicting the perceived positions of the lines of the various forces, which were amended daily from information or rumours received. When I first got there, I was besieged by many enquiring when the war would end, and I was at that time convinced it would be over by Christmas and told them why I thought that.

The Gerrys were retreating from parts of France at that time, though I did not know then that Charlie, my injured gunner, had been taken back to a hospital in Brussels, which was overrun by a Canadian force, and he was flown to the army hospital near Horsham. But Hitler had got his rockets (V2) operational that autumn, in addition to the doodlebugs that were pounding away at London, and he thought that one more push by the army through the Ardennes would reverse this situation and turn the tide and win the war. That is how the war was extended into 1945.

Our camp was very depressed, but Christmas was coming. It was traditional to put on a pantomime show and would-be theatrical directors started to book the available talent and planned the show. Meanwhile, Russia had turned their tide and was pushing the Germans back on the eastern front. I was worried that my family had still not heard what had happened to me and as staunch a Christian as my mother was, she must be going through hell. I did not know that Charlie had got back to the UK, flown there by Dakota hospital aeroplane just a month after being shot down, and had asked an orderly to send a message to Padre Warner at Dunsfold. Tom Warner received that message as he came for lunch and got into his car and tore down to Horsham to see him and hear his story. He rushed back to camp to report shouting "VC for Lyder" and then the letters of appreciation started to flow to my family in Trinidad. I had earned a fair reputation for good work on the Squadron, and Padre wrote to my mother saying that it was being said on the station that they had lost the best Mitchell pilot they had had the day I was shot down.

Luft III was a hive of activity, due now to the prisoner of war parcels that were reaching us and the tins being hammered into utensils for drinking etc. The noise was ear-piercing in the daylight hours. The Gerrys perceived we were getting information from somewhere and suddenly locked us out of our billets for half a day, and we were standing around on the parade ground after 8.00 am appell (roll-call), while a swarm of what we call ferrets in dark blue overalls and huge screw-drivers descended on the camp, ripping up floor boards etc., but finding nothing. We stood around chatting or cursing the goons, and suddenly a lone swan came into view and went into a circuit around the field, once, then twice, then three times, and one of our lads standing with his overcoat collar up and hands in his pockets and looking fed up shouted "for Christ sake someone give him a green", meaning a green light to land as was the practice on Squadron, but then it had satisfied itself that there was no water there and pushed off. That relieved our boredom for a short while.

I had asked about Wing Commander Bader, our legless pilot, who had been shot down sometime before me and was, as I thought, in that camp. I was told he had been moved to Colditz Castle a while ago, much to the relief of the old-timers, as they thought him a bloody nuisance with his bating of the goons and their reactions of penalties imposed on the whole camp as a result. But there were some anecdotes of his stay at Dulag Luft, such as sitting on the floor with his legs taken away as he annoyed them with his repeated stomping down the yard and when asked where do you think you are going, the Wing Commander would retort "back to England, you idiot, I am fed up with this place".

Well, this day he saw one of the German officers go past the door and recognised him as Eberhardt and shouted "come here, Mr Eberhardt", who approached him with a click of the boot heels and an outstretched arm in a Nazi salute saying "heil Hitler". Bader asked him "tell me, Mr Eberhardt, what do you chaps see in this bastard Hitler". Eberhardt pulled himself up to his full height and looked around to see if anyone else had heard and said "Wing Commander Bader, you must not speak of our Führer like that" and Bader retorted "I can say what I like, but you can't, because you are just a bloody foreigner".

Also, when he was being taken to Colditz Castle on the train and it stopped to take on water, he shouted for the guard and handed him his billy can, telling him to take this to the engine driver with the Wing Commander's compliments and ask him for some hot water, I want to shave. At that time, the war had not got so bad for the Germans, so they were inclined to pay deference to persons such as he. Now the war had turned against them and they had shot some fifty of our officers in cold blood, just for having escaped from Luft III.

The time came for the Christmas show to get on the road and each block was sent tickets for the show, which was scheduled to take place each evening for a week. The thing was advertised as though one was going to Drury Lane and started promptly on time etc., and was a great success.

The German officers were given front row seats and treated like royalty. I remember in particular Aiden Crawley, who entered politics on his return to the UK later, in the role of a guard. A tall man with huge feet, as one of the guards in a skit about everyday life in the camp, who went past a billet window, tossing a box of matches into the billets, while his other hand collected a packet of Camel cigarettes strategically placed on the window sill. The German officers laughed their heads off as though that was preposterous and could not happen in their camp, but in fact that happened quite regularly. We got cigarettes in our food parcels, but were never allowed matches and when approached, the guards would protest vehemently but eventually succumbed to the bribery with cigarettes. This way we were able to obtain many things from outside to keep our spirits up and the escape committee supplied with material to make facsimiles of documents such as passports, workmen's passes, paints, dyes and material to copy uniforms etc.

We maintained an office near the main gate, which a team of our chaps would man every day to log all movements in and out of the camp, so that the senior British officers would know the status of the camp at all times. I was thrilled to serve on that roster for a while and learned a great deal from it. We knew every guard by name or nickname and the goons were aware of our purpose there; for instance, there was one guard who looked very much like Jimmy Durante, the American actor, with a huge prominent nose, who was nicknamed Schnozzle. He tapped on the window sill as he passed the window and shouted "Schnozzle coming in".

In each room the chores were divided between the members (occupants), and every month a list of the jobs was produced and we were invited to volunteer for them. Being the last one in, except when Dinty Moore joined us, I never volunteered but took what was left. One fellow, Peter Stead, got the cook's job almost every month without challenge, but there was very little to cook except a few potatoes and mangel wurzels – a large, root-type vegetable like a hard cabbage and mauve in colour, which used to be fed chopped up to pigs and cows. Peter had to adhere to a rostered time on the kitchen stove, which tied him down at midday, after which he was free. I shall try to recall who occupied our room.

There was Eric Templar, a navigator who had been a jeweller at Hatton Garden; Robert, an ex-policeman; Angus Turnbull, Fleet Air Arm; Bob Pailey, a Polish fighter pilot; Peter Stead, a pilot; Paddy Leydon, Irishman, pilot; Reds from Kenya, a pilot; Dinty Moore, navigator, and self from Trinidad. I can't remember the others, sorry.

With Christmas approaching, Peter Stead, the cook, put a few ingredients together supplied from our food parcels to make what was called a kreegie (creigie) cake. It was put into an oblong pan about 14″ x 9″ x 2″ deep. There was no raising element in the mixture, so it was pressed down with a fork to get rid of all the bubbles and baked. It was then divided into twelve sections by one of the chaps who was told he would have to take the last piece. This ensured that each piece was exactly the same size as any other. An ingenious system, which worked well in view of our state of starvation.

I used to hear many complaints about our lack of food and how we should be reporting the Germans for not adhering to the Geneva Convention, but I took the pragmatic view – so long as I was given enough to survive and was allowed home safely in the end, I was satisfied. After all, we had been engaged in killing Germans, and they could have killed us in return. The kreegie cake referring to prisoners was shared out and it was this share that Paddy Leydon gave to Dinty Moore in return for the promise of five bottles of whiskey from his father's pub the White Swan in Southall. We sang Christmas carols and tried to be as happy as possible, while thinking of the folks back home.

The Russians were pushing the Germans back, and the war was going so badly for the Gerrys that Hitler issued orders to liquidate all prisoners as they had now become a severe liability, but the German army officers refused to do that and decided to move us west, and we were told to prepare to leave and take only essentials.

The seniors in our room called a meeting to inform us that we would split up, each man looking after himself. We were marched out of the camp heading west and using secondary roads to avoid traffic, the camp of Americans next door to us was first on their way. It was bitterly cold, in fact freezing winter weather, and we made slow progress on the rough, snow-covered roads.

We stopped to rest at intervals, and after the first stop we had been warned not to lie down as one American had died doing so. Death crept up without pain and warning, when freezing to death in sleep. We trudged on to a village where we stopped for the night. The Americans had secured possession of the school-house and we had to put up in an open barn on a farm. The farm folk got cans of hot water for the first few and it became evident that the solo individual was at a severe disadvantage as he missed the water queue, missed the choice of a comfortable spot to settle etc.

The senior old sweats had experience of these marches before and formed groups of three or four, and the juniors, like myself, were caught out. So Dinty Moore, Reds the Kenyan and myself teamed up, but not for long, as we fell out over the purchase of a sled from a German kid on the way. A lot of the chaps had bought sleds off the kids to drag their stuff instead of humping it and were doing better that way. So the three of us pooled our resources to buy the sled that had to be paid for in cigarettes, and I was told to do so with my cigarettes that I had saved from my food parcels, while they had already smoked theirs. Their argument was that I did not smoke so I should pay up.

Such selfishness and lack of reason appalled me, so we were singles again, at least I was. This selfish attitude was rife in prison camp and it upset me terribly as I had come from a large family and a part of the world where team spirit was imperative, all for one and one for all.

I forgot to mention that we had in our camp a naval man with a huge red beard, something like the one Uncle Albert in *Only Fools and Horses* wore, and a handsome, dark-haired chap called Charlie Bay, who grew a long beard. They teamed up together with a sled being dragged between them, in clothes that looked as if they were from a jumble sale, and as they approached the Americans ensconced in the school-house, who were looking at us over the fence, I heard one American shout "look out the Russians are here". The naval chap was nicknamed 'Bungee' because he would reach out to all parts of the camp to collect rumours, then snap back with what information he could find.

It was at one of these overnight stops that I noticed two other Trinidadians on moving out. They had come from north camp and I had not met them in prison camp before. In fact, I did not know they had been prisoners. First there was Edgell Carrington, the son of a Barbadian dentist who had a practice in Dere Street, Port-of-Spain. Edgell had still been at Alstons & Co. when I left in 1938. Soon afterwards I saw Arnold Kelshall, brother of Phil and the son of Joe Kelshall, our family solicitor. I called out in turn to each of them and they waved in passing, but could not stop to talk. I met Arnold Kelshall in Luckenwalde Camp at the end of our journey about 30 miles south of Berlin and had several chats with him there, but never saw Edgell until I got back to Trinidad. Those two had trained at the Light Aeroplane Club, formed after I had left Trinidad, which was turned into an elementary flying school for the RAF, and I had not met them in England, so did not even know they were this side of the world.

We continued the march to a glass factory at Spremburg where we put up for the night before boarding the train. We were crowded into carriages about 60 or 70 to each carriage and had a most uncomfortable journey to Luckenwalde where we were piled in, sitting with legs over one another, and the tin cup would be passed around at intervals for the chaps to pee in and then back to someone near a porthole to have it emptied outside.

We arrived at Luckenwalde at night and had a long wait in line before each was admitted after being searched. This had been a workmen's camp for farmers brought in for slave labour. I was suffering with sciatica in my left leg and could not find the position in which to stand to find relief. My spirits were so low that when an air raid warning was sounded, I wished the RAF would come and bomb us all to smithereens.

At long last we were shown into a building with a huge nest of three-tiered bunk beds, crude as could possibly be, on one side, and with sitting and manoeuvring space adjoining. I was given a bottom bunk and the only other member of our room at Luft III, Eric Templar, an adjacent one, head to head with mine. I do not know what happened to the others, but did not come across them there.

We were virtually starved when there for about six weeks. All we got was 1/10th of a loaf of bread

(4 slices) and a cup of some sort of green bush tea or acorn coffee morning and evening. At least it was warm, brought from the cookhouse in a large tub. No Red Cross parcels were reaching us; it was rumoured that the Germans were using them to feed their own soldiers, things had become so bad.

I made a couple of friends there, one in particular named Jim Crampton, who was indeed a kindred spirit. I found we had a lot in common. He started a small joy-riding air business when he returned to the UK and eventually East Anglian Airways operating out of Norfolk. I was then back in Trinidad flying for BWIA, a fully-owned subsidiary of BOAC My first trip back to England after leaving in 1950 was in 1954 and I contacted him at Clacton-on-Sea where he camped for the summer, joyriding in Austers. I visited him there one day and within minutes I was piloting one of the planes for him.

In an adjacent block, my friend from Trinidad, Arnold Kelshall, was housed; he had been at Sagan as well, in the north camp. Arnold was the son of our family solicitor and when I eventually got back to Trinidad, he was already back there and his brother Phil, who also served in the RAF, was already flying with BWIA.

There was an Australian called Joe lying on the bottom bunk on my left, who groaned at nights and when I enquired what was the matter, he explained he was shot up on Lancasters and ordered the crew to bail out. He held the aircraft until he thought all the crew had gone. When he got out of his seat, he was distracted by the wireless operator beating flames out with his gauntlet, and Joe went to him to tell him to go as he had not heard the order to bail out. Joe had not yet put his parachute on, and suddenly there was an explosion and they were in the open air. Joe grabbed at the feet of the wireless operator close by and hung on for his life. The wireless operator opened his chute and was floating down in the darkness shouting "anyone else around?" and of course Joe shouted back "yes me". He then asked "where are you?" and Joe replied "hanging on to your feet, you dozy bugger". The wireless operator shouted back, "we must be descending at a hell of a rate, when we get close to the ground let go" and Joe shouted back "to hell with that" and the wireless operator fell on top of him and broke some of his ribs, which had repaired, but were very painful still.

There were many extraordinary and miraculous tales to be heard in these camps. Some time later, a party of some 600 American soldiers arrived to join us. These had been taken prisoner in the last push of the German army in the Ardennes in an attempt to recover their position of authority before they were finally beaten.

At last, after some six weeks of near starvation, a train load of food parcels arrived at Luckenwalde railway station and we were paid a visit by the camp medical officer in the night about 9.00 pm and asked to wake anyone asleep next to us, as he had an important message to convey. We got very excited and he reported that this train had arrived and they would be bringing the Red Cross parcels of food in the morning, and asked that each and every one of us should show self discipline and restraint in the use of the food. The C.O. had wanted to share one parcel among four persons, then two, but the doctor pleaded that the chaps had been starved for so long that even if we did not get another train load for a long time, we should have a whole parcel for each man now to repair the damage, and he won the argument. "So for God's sake, eat the food slowly and make it last a week," and hopefully there would be another parcel next week. I regret to report that in spite of this warning, a few chaps finished their boxes in a day or two and made themselves sick and lost a lot of that food, because their stomachs could not take the shock.

For the first time we were exposed to the spectacle of the American business ethic, as some of them had run strings through their boxes, which they hung around their necks with the boxes resting on their chests, and moving through the camp exchanging items of food for others that some chaps preferred, and using the cigarettes that each box contained as currency. In many cases, if not most, they seemed to come out on top.

I managed to ration mine so that it lasted the week. I saved up my ration of black bread, 1/10th of a loaf per day, remember, for about three days and grated it with my homemade grater into a reasonable fine state, soaked some prunes until very soft and falling apart, added powdered milk, margarine and sugar and whipped up the lot to make a cake mix and filled a small tin I had among my makeshift utensils. I took it down to the fence outside the cookhouse and called for one of the chaps to put it in the oven for me, and waited anxiously in the hope of getting it back. When I was asked why I was standing around in the cold, I explained and the questioner left with wishes of good luck, which did not help my composure.

However, in due course the chap came back with my tin of mix, which smelt like a cake, and had even cracked on top and risen in a converse shape due to the fermented prunes. I thanked him profusely for his honesty and he said "that's ok, cock, enjoy it". It even smelt like cake. That remark indicated the amount of self control and honesty displayed by one in the ranks, compared to some of our officers who could not control themselves and bashed their food.

We had a number of NCOs who had volunteered to live in our camp and serve us instead of being sent out to work for the Germans. According to the Geneva Convention, officer prisoners were not made to go out to work. In the Norwegian officers' compound adjoining ours, there was a Russian Colonel working for them, who had stripped his uniform of rank badges and presented himself as an NCO when taken prisoner so that he was not shot, as the ruddy Germans had a practice of not taking Russian officer prisoners.

To continue, I took my cake back to my billet and as I passed Jim Crampton sitting by his bunk, he called "what have you got there, Garth?" and I said "a cake" and showed him. He exclaimed "but it does smell like a cake" so I brought him back a small piece to taste and he was amazed. I also gave a sliver to Eric Templar and he got quite angry with me for not having volunteered to cook for them when back at Sagan. The roommates there thought me to be a pampered colonial from the West Indies who never had to do anything for himself.

Templar had been a prisoner like Crampton for about 3 ½ years and I was surprised how some chaps reacted to their incarceration. Crampton was an extremely nice and balanced fellow in comparison. I had secured a large cardboard box in which I kept my utensils and food stuff, and kept it by my bed and slept with my arm over it, when Templar, tossing and turning in the night, eventually told me to do something about that bloody cake to hide the smell or he would get up and eat it.

There was a furtive movement in the building one evening with some chaps from another building coming in and asking for guards to be posted while they put together the separate pieces of a clandestine radio, and I listened to the 9 o'clock news of the BBC "this is London calling". That statement sent a gratifying surge down my spine and thrilled me to tears.

After the report on the war that day, there was a message to all British POWs to be of good cheer as it should not be long now before we should be relieved. An audible rumble of approval went through the building to whispers of quiet, quiet from the radio crew who separated the units once more into pieces and they departed. It took a long time before we got back to sleep. There was a rumour that some NCOs were due to arrive in an adjacent compound after a long trek from the east, and I wondered if by chance my wireless operator Roy Walker could be among them. I had not a clue what camp he had been sent to, but I would be most pleased to see him again.

They duly arrived and I went to the wire fence to see if I might see him, though I appreciated that it was a long shot of a hope. There was a wide space between the two sets of boundaries separating the two compounds. I stayed out a long time considering the cold, without any luck.

On the following day, I took up my position again and saw a small figure with his coat collar up and moving in the manner that seemed somewhat familiar. I took the chance to shout "Roy, is that you, Roy" and to my surprise he hurried to the fence saying "Garth, is that you?" and we enjoyed the reunion and promised to meet the same time each day at the same place, just to gawk at each other and exchange greetings. Tommy had been sent to some other camp and Doug Hogarth, who had asked for a transfer to north camp at Sagan, had not been seen since.

One day, after we had run out of words, Roy said to me "Garth, I must be off as I am on cookhouse detail" and, with a dismissing shrug of shoulders, as he turned away said "chicken again" and my stomach turned over: how like him, cheerful to the end. The same spirit I had always admired in him and that had saved him from being shot when descending by parachute over France. He had pulled on rip cords setting up a swaying motion when the Gerrys started to shoot at him and hit the ground hard, but avoided being shot.

The war was getting closer to us by the day and the evenings were spent trying to judge the distance away of the Russians firing in the east and the Americans in the west. We were hoping the Americans would reach us first and bets were taken, but soon realised that the Russians were making headway, whereas the Americans seemed to have stopped. That must have been when General Patten had been recalled from his beeline for Berlin by Eisenhower to satisfy the agreement to let the Russians get to Berlin, as they had suffered so much at the hands of the Germans. This was agreed between Stalin and Roosevelt against the wishes of Churchill at Yalta. Had Patten not been called back, we would have been relieved a lot sooner and avoided a great deal of trouble with the Russians when they did get to us.

We were told by our camp authorities that we were about to be moved again and to get prepared for this as the Russians were getting close and that morning arrived. We were called out on the parade ground and waited while the argument raged between the German commander and our senior officer as to whether we should move. It was rumoured that we were to be taken by train to Munich where we perceived that we would be held hostage as a bargaining chip for Hitler's life in his stronghold at Berchtesgaden, and we of course were resisting that while the German staff were scared of the Russians because of what might happen to them. We were eventually marched to a railway station and put on a train. There was a lot of confusion and many of us hung around outside of our carriages hoping to stall the move, preferring to wait for the Russians. Suddenly, there was panic as we could see explosions some distance down the line, followed by American Thunderbolt fighter bombers sweeping overhead. Some of us took shelter under the train as we expected our train and station would be attacked.

The aircraft disappeared without interfering with us and we heard that the railway line had been cut at Jüterbog a few miles away, and we were marched back to our camp. We were elated and overjoyed at not being moved and viewed our camp as a refuge on return to it, singing all the old army songs "a long way to Tipperaray" etc. etc., while the German guards shuffled along, depressed and showing it, as the home crowd does when Manchester United is beaten at football. From that moment, we felt freed and now in charge of our destiny, and had been warned over the radio not to move, but wait to be collected. The camp had been made ready for this and a management team was drawn up. Some to go foraging for food, while others kept order as policemen etc., and I was drafted as fire-fighter and camp security.

Russian Intermezzo

I think it was the 22nd February 1945 that I was awakened by noise outside and woke to find that the Russians had arrived. One of their tank divisions asked where "ruski camp" was and we directed them to the Russian compound nearby.

They called us out of the camp and proceeded to tear down the wire fences and guard boxes around the camp, but we stayed put as directed. A management group in the form of Russians took up offices in one compound building and invited our chaps to go with them to sack the town of Luckenwalde, but we declined, and soon tension grew between us as they perceived that we were more sympathetic to the Germans than to them. However, they accepted our orders to stay and wait for relief from our own troops, and permitted us to roam a radius of 1 kilometre from camp.

I wandered into the town square and saw a Russian soldier pulling a young woman to go with him and she was resisting and called my attention ("mein Herr, mein Herr") and I ordered the soldier to let her go, pointing to my rank and wings as an airforce officer, and he released her and moved on. I thought afterwards what a risk I had taken and hurried back to camp.

I heard that some of our senior officers were invited to join them in the town hall when they interviewed the Bürgermeister and humiliated him by making him kneel on the floor in front of them and repeat after them, "war kaputt, Germany kaputt, Hitler kaputt, alles kaputt".

On one occasion, I was out walking with Crampton and two Russian soldiers rode up on bikes, stopped us, asked a few questions and requested Crammie's watch, which was a good one sent to him by his father some time after he had been shot down and which was very treasured. He of course refused and they started to get rough and menacing and we turned for the camp but they grabbed our arms saying "Kommen Sie mit" and we shook them off by replying "no, com si mit to Colonel Medvedev" pointing to our camp and set off briskly. They followed us to a spot where the track forked and where we turned right, they rode off left and we gave a big sigh of relief.

We had saved Jim's watch and thought that we would stay within the confines of the camp after that. One morning, a couple of journalists rode in on motorcycles and asked who we were, and they said that they were following the situation into Berlin, but would report on our plight to someone.

Two days later, an American convoy of several empty trucks turned up to take us away. The Russians mounted machine guns pointed at the trucks and ordered them off the camp. We were very upset over this and now felt prisoners of the Russians. We wandered through the Russian compound to see several bodies still lying naked in a room used as a morgue and up the slope of the field, where there were two closed trenches and an open one with many bodies naked lying there. We learned that they would be stripped of clothing to supplement those who survived and the dead bodies were dragged by their own men on a cart and dumped in the trenches.

There was one huge wooden cross overlooking the area. One room of their compound was set aside as a dining hall and a huge mural of Christ and his apostles depicting the last supper painted on one of the walls. We were surprised to see this thinking of their Communist regime, which had rejected Christianity.

The Russian prisoners, when released by the spearhead of tanks, were thrown rifles and rode out of the camp on the outside of the tanks to continue the fight, although they were emaciated and unwell as the Russian dictum was that they should have died fighting rather than be taken prisoner. There was no sympathy for them and we wondered what had become of those poor chaps, thinking they must have perished soon after. We had some idea of their lack of appreciation of life when we saw those soldiers going past the camp.

One chap was riding a commandeered bicycle and waving to us, when he was hit from behind by a Russian armoured vehicle and thrown into the field. We could hear him moaning and a number of us climbed through the fence to go to his aid and were shouted at to get back and threatened with being shot, while the poor devil was left there to die.

The agony of waiting to be relieved was most trying and we did what we could to lift our spirits. We projected our thoughts to home and what we would do when we got there. A small group gathered close to my bunk one morning when I was trying to contain myself and were discussing what they should have to eat when they awoke in the mornings at home. One chap said "a huge bowl of cornflakes", another preferred rice krispies and each in turn expressed his choice of cereal, then two eggs and two rashers of bacon and another said "no, I want four" then lashings of toast and marmalade and several cups of coffee. They were writing these down and turned the page and the lead chap said "now for lunch" and another chap shouted "no, you are forgetting elevenses". With all this mention of food my stomach started growling and my rest was over.

A number of civilian British as well as would-be British found their way into our camp, begging to be taken back to the UK, and the reasons they gave were many and varied. Of course, they were mainly women or offspring of theirs who had married Germans in Britain, and had been called up to the forces in Germany when or before war was declared. The recall spread far and wide, as previously all German males were required to do military training and released on the reserve list. The very senior of our officers,

Air Marshalls and Air Commodores, had long since been removed from our midst by the Germans and Wing Commander Collard was left in charge. He had an office next door to Colonel Medvedev and was continually plied with vodka, forced on him by the inveterate drinkers that the Russians were. As a result of which, he was quite ill when he reached home, poor fellow.

Finally Free

The time eventually came when we heard that General Eisenhower had signed an agreement with General Smirnoff to swap us for Ukrainians whom the Americans had taken, and a large number of Ford trucks that were supplied by the Americans through a lend/lease arrangement as allies of ours, and we piled on, twenty-five POWs per truck, and were driven by mad Russians at speed towards the Elbe River.

I stood up at the back of the cab, hanging on for my life and full of excitement at the prospect of going home, when I heard a loud, ominous sound coming from the engine and I said "oh, oh, listen, this engine is shot, kaputt" and was shouted down as a pessimist, but it was not long before it exploded and we had to pull off the road. Panic set in now as the stream of trucks refused to stop to take us and we just stood in their way, which was very dangerous, faced with these mad drivers, and we scrambled on a few to each truck as they slowed down.

We eventually arrived at the Elbe to find that the Allies had blown up the bridge, but the Americans had laid a pontoon bridge on the water and we crossed in groups of twenty-five, checked by the Russians after they had insisted on one of their groups, which they were swapping us for, crossing first. So they would be at least one group ahead if at any time the agreement was broken.

At last on the American side, we were transported to the favourite Luftwaffe station of Herman Goering in Leipzig and after a meal, were marched in groups to the airfield where American Dakotas were operating a ferry service to Brussels. As luck would have it, my group was second in line for boarding, when the operations ceased for that day and we were marched back to the station buildings to spend the night. Delays and disappointment had bugged me throughout my career in the service and this was no surprise.

Next day, we marched back to the airfield and got off and were taken to Evere Airport, I think it was, and put up in a large building, deloused with DDT powder pumped over us, and given a good meal at last. By the time we were catalogued and ready to travel to the UK, the message broadcast over the address system was that the last aircraft had left and that we would have to wait until the next day.

We were free, if we wished, to go out on the town, but my only interest was getting back to the UK and I returned to my room disappointed once again. After a short while, the address system called again to say that two Lancasters had arrived and could take twenty-five each, and I hurried down and was put on one of them. In the narrow fuselage of the Lancaster, we sat with our knees under our chins opposite each other and arrived at Oakley Airfield in Oxfordshire at around 11.00 pm that night. As I got out of the plane, I enquired, "where was this?" and was told "Oakley, Oxfordshire" to make sure I had landed in England. "Are you sure?" I asked, and one of the crew said "yes". Only then did I feel I was back and I bent down and kissed the ground.

We were offered food and showering facilities. I went to bed, but slept little due to the excitement of being back at last. The following day, we were taken to Cosford, where we were registered and debriefed, then medically checked, and those of us who were declared fit were given rail warrants to get home. In due course, I got a train to London and then tube to Neasden, to the Reverend and Mrs Watson, my family home in England, who had served in Trinidad at the local Methodist Church. I was received with open arms, although they were grieving over the loss of their young son Donald, who was shot down and killed. I was awfully upset at this news, as he had been a mere boy in short-pants when I left Trinidad.

It was there that I learned that I had been awarded the DFC and told that my sister Pat was in the University College Hospital as a nurse. I sent a cable message to my family in Trinidad and received a reply full of joy and admonishment to get on my knees and give thanks to my God. They had had a very anxious several months after hearing that I was a POW, wondering how it would all end. I did what I could to comfort Auntie Winnie Watson, who bore her loss bravely. She was a real saint.

Her older son Bill, whom I met and cared for me when I first arrived in England, was well and unhurt. He had been in the Royal Army Service Corps.

I had been shot down weighing 164 pounds and when weighed at Cosford found to be 110 pounds and was rattling in my uniform, but feeling quite well and certainly now very relieved. The letters of good wishes started to pour in and there was a call from my friends the Spantons of Loxwood Farm, asking when I was coming, my room was ready and waiting for me.

When I had taken care of all I had to do in London, including renewing relationship with my sister Pat, I took the train to Guildford and was met there by car and driven in style to Loxwood Farm, where a huge banner "WELCOME HOME GARTH" was spread out over the front door. That was nice. I was accorded a wonderful homecoming.

I forgot to mention that whilst I was in London, I had asked the RAF to allow me to visit my Squadron, which was now in Germany at Achmer near Hannover. I was advised to go to Swindon by train and would be met there by transport to take me to Lyneham Airfield and put aboard the daily Anson Airplane commuting with Brussels. This I did and everything went smoothly.

I arrived at Helsbrook Airfield in the heart of Brussels and went to the RAF Headquarters, where on the wide marble staircase I ran into Squadron Leader Powell, who had been in my flight at Dunsfold and had taken over after Wood and myself had been shot down. He congratulated me on my award of the DFC and seeing the same ribbon on his chest, I replied "I see you have collected one as well". He dismissed that by saying "mine is only for surviving, you really earned yours". I thought it was a very nice thing to say. I got transport to Evere Airport, where the Mitchell mail plane arrived every day from Achmer, and I sat in the co-pilot's seat on the way to the station. This was now evening. I was greeted by a number of new faces and very heartily by the few old timers, but Padre was away at the time. I went to bed in a large sort of garage place and Padre came in late at night to greet me, a wonderful reunion.

The following day, he took me on a drive to heavily bombed Hannover and surrounds, and we chatted about old times. He told me how proud the whole station at Dunsfold was when they heard how I had stayed with the damaged airplane to save Charlie's life. It made me feel even better to be alive and part of such a wonderful fraternity.

After I left Trinidad, a number of citizens there formed the Light Aeroplane Club and a New Zealander named Yerex, who had been in Central America for some time. He had started an airline there and had heard about the Caribbean Islands' plight of lack of transport as the German U-boats (submarines) were busy in the area and had sunk a lot of ships that serviced the islands. The Canadian National Steamship Company, I think, had had four nice ships known as the Lady Boats, which they named after some of the wives of the maritime heroes, such as Lady Rodney and Lady Hawkins. But in a short time they had all been sunk. They used to travel from Canada, call at several of the West Indian islands, and then return to Montreal.

Yerex brought a small, twin-engined Lockheed aeroplane down with about 12 seats and started a service to Barbados in November 1940, and called the company British West Indian Airways Ltd. with headquarters in Trinidad based at Piarco Aerodrome. He brought a small team of men, headed by one Kenrick Murray, the Managing Director, who was a pilot and the first commercial trip was made to Barbados and back.

The service was used primarily for Government executives and most others resorted to travel by schooners, sailing boats between the nearby islands. My brother, the Reverend Deryck, had to resort to schooners when he returned from Jamaica an ordained Minister of the Methodist Church. When I returned to Trinidad for a quick visit in August 1943 and wanted to see him when he was then serving in St. Vincent, I managed to get a seat on the plane to Grenada and then a schooner to St. Vincent to spend a couple of days with him before going back to the UK to take part in operations.

It was a memorable reunion and I cherish that memory. We two had been very close and together had been through many very trying times, but now we were pursuing quite different careers. He spent quite some time in St. Vincent and brought out many interesting and amazing stories. He served in the main church in Kingston and later in the North East Parish at a station named Parlatuvier.

While there, he had a pirogue type boat built, which he used to travel around the coast to neighbouring villages, and named it the *John Wesley* after the leader who founded Methodism in England. My mother went by schooner to spend a holiday with him and wrote back to say "*John Wesley* rides the waves".

Methodism is an Evangelical offshoot of the English Church, which did so much good throughout the world to bring a sense of dignity and purpose to a wide section of people, and to a great extent saved England from the same fate as the French at the time of their notable Revolution.

Deryck made many friends there and eventually married one, Helen Pilgrim, whom he had met there as a graduate teacher after he was posted to Tobago. At present, she survives him, living in Barbados. She was born there of the Moravian Minister of the Church, whose brother was Grant Pilgrim, one of the tutors at Queen's Royal College in Trinidad when we were growing up, and he used to visit us at Shamrock Villa in Bournes Road. He was a great cricketer and hockey player and played on the college team for many years, eventually returning to Oxford, where he married. He gave us one of his cricket bats, which Deryck used to start his training as a batsman, and he joined the

Queen's Park Cricket Club. He played for the team against other clubs and was well thought of, and would certainly have been on the West Indian team if he had not entered the church and had to give it up for lack of time. In many ways, his career in life mirrored that of the Reverend Dick Shepherd, the English cricketer who became Bishop of Liverpool later.

Deryck became the Chairman of the Methodist District of Trinidad, Barbados, Grenada, St. Vincent and British Guyana. Deryck and Helen were very much loved in Tobago and even more so in Barbados, where he eventually retired and died. On two separate occasions, they were the Queen's guests on the Royal Yacht *Britannia* when she visited Barbados, and Deryck was awarded the CBE. It is sad to have to say that neither he nor I, who attained the highest qualifications in our respective careers, were ever appreciated or honoured in our own country of birth, Trinidad. One of the truths that are found in the Christian bible where it is stated that a prophet hath no honour in his own country.

Having chosen aviation as a career and as a pilot I set out to be the best that I could be and attained the highest qualifications possible in the profession. For my services I was awarded the Master Pilots Certificate by the Guild of Airpilots and Navigators of Great Britain among a very select few in the industry.

My instructor at S.F.T.S. (Service Flying Training School).

Garth

Our Padre - Tom Warner.

My Ford Anglia.

B-25 Mitchell Bomber in flight, like the ones used by the 180 Squadron.

Roy Walker, Tommy Good, Charlie Walkden and Garth standing in front of one of the Squadron's B-25 Bombers.

Personalkarte I: Personelle Angaben

Kriegsgefang. Lager Nr. 3 d. Lw. (Oflag Luft 3)

Erkennungsmarke Nr. 2440

Lager Krgsgef.-L.d.Lw. 3

Des Kriegsgefangenen

Name: LYDER

Vorname: E. Garth

Geburtstag und -ort: 5.1.14 Trinidad

Religion: Meth.

Vorname des Vaters:

Familienname der Mutter:

Staatsangehörigkeit: ENGLAND

Dienstgrad: F/O.

Truppenteil: RAF Kom. usw.:

Zivilberuf: Ing. Berufs-Gr.:

Matrikel Nr. (Stammrolle des Heimatstaates): 138123

Gefangennahme (Ort und Datum): Dieppe 9.8.44

Ob gesund, krank, verwundet eingeliefert:

Lichtbild

Nähere Personalbeschreibung

Grösse	Haarfarbe
1.73	d. braun

Besondere Kennzeichen:

Fingerabdruck des rechten ! Zeigefingers

Name und Anschrift der zu benachrichtigenden Person in der Heimat des Kriegsgefangenen

Rev. S. E. Watson The Manse, Neasden Lane, London N.W. 10

2440 LYDER, E.G.

Beschriftung der Erkennungsmarke Nr. Lager: Name:

Bemerkungen:

Personalbeschreibung

Figur: schlank

Größe: 1.73

Alter: 30 J.

Gesichtsform: oval

Gesichtsfarbe: gesund

Schädelform: oval

Augen: braun

Nase: gerade

Gebiß: gut

Haare: d. braun

Bart: Schnurrbart

Gewicht: 70 kg

Besondere Merkmale: Narbe a. l. Wange

Deutsche Sprachkenntnisse:

Registration card from the German prisoners of war camp.
The description reads:
Figure: slim. Height: 1.73. Age: 30 years. Shape of face: oval. Colour of face: healthy. Shape of skull: oval. Eyes: brown. Nose: straight. Teeth: good. Hair: dark brown. Beard: moustache. Weight: 70kg. Special marks: scar on left cheek.
The address given is for the next of kin.

...ager:

Strafen im Kr.-Gef.-Lager

Datum	Grund der Bestrafung	Strafmass	Verbüsst, Datum

Schutzimpfungen während der Gefangenschaft gegen

Pocken	Sonstige Impfungen (Ty., Paraty., Ruhr, Cholera usw.)	
am	am	am
Erfolg	gegen	gegen
am	am	am
Erfolg	gegen	gegen
am	am	am
Erfolg	gegen	gegen
	am	am
	gegen	gegen

Erkrankungen

Krankheit	Revier vom	Revier bis	Lazarett–Krankenhaus vom	Lazarett–Krankenhaus bis

Versetzungen

Datum	Grund der Versetzung	Neues Kr.-Gef.-Lager
[illegible].44		[illegible]
[illegible].44		Krgsgef[illegible].d.Lw. 3

Versetzungen

Datum	Grund der Versetzung	Neues Kr.-Gef.-Lager

Kommandos.

Datum	Art des Kommandos	Rückkehrdatum

Reverse of the registration card from the German prisoners of war camp.

My crew outside our Nissen hut.

Roy Walker, Garth, Tommy Good & Charles Walkden.

Rolls and chauffeur at Loxwood farm.

Exercising Blossom at Loxwood Farm.

Back in the War

Now to continue where I left off, I spent a few weeks on the farm being fed right royally and soon put flesh back on my bones with the milk, eggs, etc. that were available.

I had applied for leave to go home to Trinidad and in due course was sent a signal to report to King's Cross Railway Station, where the RTO would hand me arrangements to travel to Trinidad. I thanked the Spantons for their wonderful hospitality and took the train to London, King's Cross, where I received warrants to take the train to Largs in Scotland and board a ship to Canada.

I arrived at Largs early the next morning and was taken by launch to the *Isle de France* that was anchored in the bay. As we approached the ship, I could see hundreds of uniforms lining the deck, Canadian ex-POWs returning home, together with a few bods for the West Indies. I looked up to see if I recognised anyone and heard a familiar voice saying "shit, here comes my old man, I am getting off this ship, it is not big enough for both of us". It was my navigator Tommy Good of course, who welcomed me aboard.

We took about five days to get to Halifax and on two occasions, we saw a Liberator fly overhead and I wished

I had been on one of them. We arrived at Halifax around dusk in the evening to a tumultuous welcome with the fire boats spouting water and a flotilla of small pleasure boats to escort us into the dock, where cars lined the wharf with lights flashing and horns blowing. The North Americans do really appreciate their war veterans.

On shore, we were shepherded into a large hall with food galore and were invited to eat as much as we could and drinks flowing continuously. It did make one feel appreciated. I was then taken by train to New York and then another to Miami, where I spent a day, and then put on a Dakota aircraft with two ATS girls returning home to Guyana. We overnighted in Kingston, Jamaica, and I was invited to a large party and while chatting with a girl there, she asked my name and as soon as I mentioned it she said "Garth Lyder?" and I said "yes" and excitedly she came back with "your brother Eddie is here" and hurried off to fetch him. We had a great reunion. He was an operations officer with BWIA and was then based in Belize, but had to be in Kingston on business for a couple of days.

The next morning we continued to Trinidad and again I was met by Lieutenant Commander Alec Blair of the Fleet Air Arm on behalf of the family waiting in the lounge. It was a wonderful homecoming and I met some of the local chaps from the RAF who had already arrived on leave, including Ian Bourne, who had been in my POW camp in Sagan.

We were flown back to England via Montreal and started a term of rehabilitation at Wittering. While there, we were brought up to date with post-war arrangements in the RAF, and offered various jobs like Air Controller and Transport Officer etc., but all non-flying. I insisted being returned to flying duties and their argument was that I had been off flying for a long time and there were no vacancies, and because I was older than the average, it was most unlikely that I would get a flying job. I was then offered promotion to substantive Squadron Leader rank if I would take a two months' course and become a Paymaster. I was horrified at going from station to station weekly, handing out small brown envelopes to airmen, and rejected them all.

I was then sent to Turn Hill in Shropshire as Engineer Officer Administration, amending manuals and drawing up work schedules etc. It was a very nice permanent station and I had met two chaps who trained with me in Neepawa, Manitoba, Canada. Sharples with whom I swapped in Neepawa to get onto twin engines, he had gone on singles, and Wilkinson, who had gone with me to New York on leave with the Guthrie family. They were both instructors, training pilots on Harvards for the Fleet Air Arm.

I shared a room with an ex-operational Spitfire fighter pilot named Darley and the first day we shared experiences, and it transpired that he had escorted me over France on two occasions, having checked on our log books. He said "you fellas must have had nerves of steel, or did not give a damn, flying straight and level through all that flak". I explained that it may have appeared so, but we made calculated changes to height and direction to avoid being hit, which may not have been apparent to you chaps who were on your own and who could move around the sky at will. We had boxes of six large aircraft in close formation and were unable to do that. It was a comfortable station and a nice part of the country, which I enjoyed, but I felt frustrated as hell wasting my time there.

One day, Air Commodore Haughtry arrived to carry out an inspection of the camp and came into my office and asked "who are you and what do you do here?" I explained that I was an ex-POW now acting as Engineer Officer in a job I did not want, hoping for refresher flying. He asked his Wing Commander to take my name and request and said to me, "Lyder, I cannot promise to get you back on to flying, but will promise to have a good try". True to his word, within a few days, I got a message to report to Wheton Aston in Staffordshire for refresher flying.

I was then sent to Siford, which was their satellite airfield, and refreshed on Oxford twins. I was teamed up with Flt. Lt. Mackie and had Warrant Officer Simmonds as an instructor. I was happy again, back in the air where I belonged, and we had completed our course and been assessed. I was in the mess for dinner when Mackie came in and announced they were in the brown stuff. He and Simmonds were on low flying training detail and hit a tree returning to base with some twigs sticking out of the starboard wing. I commiserated with him and next day heard that Simmonds was suspended.

The Adjutant rang me to ask if I would act as Defence Officer for Warrant Officer Simmonds, whose court martial was due soon on the station, having hit a tree while low flying. I was taken aback and protested that I had no training in law and felt hopelessly inadequate to take on such a task that could ruin an instructor's life in the service, and asked if there was no one else more suitable. Together, we went through a number of names, but could not find anyone else who had Simmonds welfare at heart, and I accepted the task. After all, he had refreshed me in flying and was a very good instructor as well as serviceman.

I now had to get down to the task of reading through tomes, such as the King's Regulations and Air Council Instructions pertaining to Court Martials and took the whole thing very seriously. I picked through several of the severe charges to see how I could counter each one and did a lot of research on the topographical maps of the area involved, the weather conditions of the day, if inclement etc., and gradually a plan of defence was put together. The evening before the trial, I received a phonecall from one Flight Lieutenant Tyrrell from the town Stafford, who introduced himself as the Prosecuting Officer in the coming Court Martial and asked if he could come and have a drink in the mess with me. I said certainly not, as a legal officer he should know that that was not allowed, but he protested that he and the Judge Advocate were sitting in the hotel in this godforsaken place and just wanted a social chat, no mention of the case in hand. I relented under those circumstances and received them at the bar of the mess.

Tyrrell turned out to be one of the officers who had been at the Neepawa Elementary Flying School in Canada, where I had received training many years ago. So we had a lot to talk about until he broached the subject of the Court Martial, saying that he being the trained lawyer, would coach me through proceedings and hopefully get it over in quick time as they needed to get back to London etc. I immediately reminded him of the regulations, to which he said "this is an open and shut case Lyder, what defence could be put up?" and I told him there were extenuating circumstances and he asked "what circumstances?" I got upset and anxious not to pursue the argument and just then the C.O. Group Captain Harris arrived and I introduced them to him and left. That evening I went over all my arguments to make sure I could put up a fight and prayed for guidance. I felt hopelessly inadequate without any legal experience.

The next morning, before the case was called, I met Tyrrell and the Judge, I can't remember his name, and went through the documents with them. W/O Simmonds was listed as Pilot 4, which was the proposed new rank of NCO Pilot ratings instead of Flight Sergeant W/O I and II. The ranks were to become Pilot 1,2,3,4 but so far this had not come into being and I seized upon this to make my presence felt. I told them that I knew no such person as Pilot 4 Simmonds and asked what sort of badge of rank would Pilot 4 Simmonds be wearing, and that threw them into confusion as no badges had yet been decided upon. I seized this opportunity of confusion to stamp my authority on the proceedings, and with consummate cheek I told them I was there to defend one W/O Simmonds and knew no one known as Pilot 4 Simmonds and suggested that they go back to London and sort out the paperwork. I surprised myself, but could see that they were in confusion and after a few minutes, I said to them that I was prepared to leave with W/O Simmonds, but if they changed the papers to read W/O Simmonds and not the obscure Pilot 4, I would be happy to proceed.

The shock tactics worked and they humbly agreed. I, the unknown, had won the high ground and was going to do all I could to maintain it. The case was called and Tyrrell called Squadron Leader Dismore as his first prosecution witness, and after he had asked his questions told me it was my turn to cross examine. I asked Dismore quite simple questions about how long he had known W/O Simmonds, had he any complaints about him with reference to his conduct or flying ability etc., to each of which he replied favourably.

Tyrrell then called Flight Lieutenant Mackie and interrogated him and again handed over to me and so it went on, while I built up a fairly good character profile of Simmonds until the Judge said that I should call my witness. I explained that since the only persons who were present when the accident occurred were Simmonds and Mackie, there were no witnesses that I could call, so I would have to ask W/O Simmonds to take the stand. The Judge then briefed Simmonds that if he did, he would be cross examined and had the right to decline to give evidence, but warned that that might prejudice his case. I had explained all this to Simmonds beforehand and so he was prepared for it and replied he wanted to take the stand and did so.

I asked him his name, rank etc., then a pertinent question relating to the incident, and Tyrrell jumped up shouting "objection, leading the witness" that was sustained by the Judge. I put it another way and again Tyrrell shouted "objection". When this had occurred three times I told the Judge that since I was not trained in these matters I would sit down and ask Simmonds to explain what happened that afternoon and he proceeded to do so.

All this had been agreed with Simmonds beforehand, so he was composed and quietly related the events. He had properly signed the low flying book to say he was taking Flight Lieutenant Mackie on this special exercise and was maintaining the prescribed height of 250 feet around the allocated low flying training area, and at appropriate times I would interrupt to hand to the Judge exhibit one, a topographical map of the area showing the land to rise in height on the inside of the area as different from the perimeter; exhibit two, the Forest Office report showing trees 70 feet tall; exhibit three, the meteorological report showing the wind from the south west 17 knots gusting to 25 knots, and then Simmonds describing how on turning west at 4.45 pm that bright afternoon, they had become blinded by the sun and hurriedly turned away towards the middle of the area, felt a jolt as the right wing dropped in a gust and found they had touched a tree with that wing and straight away set course for home.

This set up a buzzing of comments from the bench and I got up and addressed the court saying "gentlemen, the RAF has a reputation for having the best-trained pilots in the world and do you know why? Because they have the best instructors in the world!" pointing to Simmonds "and if we are to hold the threat of Court Martial over them whenever they set out on a critical exercise, they will jib at flying to the limits and our flying training will suffer," and I sat down.

There was a discussion among those on the bench and the Judge said the court was adjourned to consider the evidence. Simmonds and I went to an adjacent office to await the result, and he was trembling so much that he had some difficulty in getting the flame of his lighter to the cigarette in his mouth. I tried to calm him saying "relax, boy, we have got them". I felt sure of that and explained that when the court was reconvened he should look first at the table to see whether the tip of the sword or hilt was pointing towards him. If it were the hilt, he was free.

In due course, the court was recalled and to our delight the hilt was towards us, so we approached with confidence. The Judge started his report and on each one of the serious charges Simmonds was exonerated, but the last one of being guilty of conduct prejudicial to discipline and good order, which we learned was always added to all charges, was left for the Air Ministry to decide and the court hearing was terminated. I left that room very satisfied and Simmonds greatly relieved for not being one of the other ranks he could have been reduced to, Corporal or even lower.

As I hurried away from the building, Tyrrell ran behind me shouting "Lyder, Lyder" and came up to shake my hand in congratulations saying "you should be on our side" to which I replied "no way, I am happy as a general duties officer". The Group Captain drove up for lunch just then and he asked what had happened and Tyrrell told him "he has got off". Harris replied "got off, got off" and, looking at me with disdain, hurried into the mess hall with me trying to speak to him. He opened the swing doors and allowed them to swing back in my face; he was furious and did not speak to me for about a fortnight. I heard afterwards that it was the C.O.'s job to call for a Court Martial after reviewing the evidence in an enquiry and that if he failed in three, he could be relieved of his command. This was the second failure for Harris, so he was duly concerned.

We went back to the parent station, Wheton Aston, and did odd bits of flying from there, waiting for a real flying job. There was a lot of transport flying taking crews back to Rhodesia, South Africa, Australia and bringing others back, but I missed out on that, which I would have enjoyed as we were returned to the UK later than most, having been held up by the Russians.

I happened to see in the mess a catalogue of light aircraft, which had been commandeered at the outbreak of war, now put up for auction at Kemble in Wiltshire. I took a day off to go and have a look after asking the C.O. Group Captain Harris if he would give me permission to bring a light plane on the station. He agreed, provided that I would take him to Shoreham airport in Hove every weekend, as the train service out of Stafford was atrocious. I agreed, so off I went for the day and enjoyed myself wandering through the hangar filled with all sorts of light planes of previous vintage that I used to read about in *Flight and Aeroplane* magazines. I put in bids for three, a Piper Cub 2-seater side by side, a Miles 18 Experimental 4-seater, and Lindberg's special Miles Mohawk, and within a short while, I was informed that I had got two of the three. I duly went down and paid for them and got a Sergeant Engineer to check out the Piper Cub there and then, finding it ready for flight. I flew it back to Wheton Aston and put it in a spare hangar to prepare it for a certificate of air worthiness, which was required before it could be used.

I worked on it whenever I could and fitted a turn and bank indicator to help, as the instrumentation was rather basic, and overhauled the engine myself with occasional help from a ground engineer. But before I could get it finished, I was posted to Padgate in Warrington to train National Service recruits as airmen. The officers there were non-flying personnel, the senior ones having served as army officers in the First World War and joined the RAF in the Second by way of a change, so had a lot of old army tradition and tricks.

Now that the war was over, there was a feeling running through the population that this service was no longer necessary, but still in force, so the RAF was replacing the old guard with new, and to give something to encourage the youngsters, were posting officers who had been operational and decorated to help and inspire the chaps. I was given a batch of 126 or so raw, unhappy youngsters, who were to be turned into smart airmen within ten weeks. I received them in the station cinema for their introduction into the service.

I explained that it was the law that they should serve, and how fortunate they were to have been chosen to join the best of the three services, the RAF, and had a rowdy, uncooperative response. They were shown to their quarters by a sergeant and two corporals and instructed in the requirements of making their beds and cleaning their floor spaces etc., and all that was required of them to graduate as airmen.

Meanwhile, the parents or persons who brought them there, hung around outside the camp for a while, wondering what was to happen to their children, and floods of letters arrived on my desk, saying that their boys were not accustomed to being away from home and they were holding us responsible for them etc. The old guard of a Wing Commander I had rang me to ask, what nonsense had I sent him on my list for church parade on Sunday, there were those listed under C. of E., Catholic and other denominations and one Sun Worshipper, and he wanted to question that one. I told him that I had interviewed the chap and he assured me that he was a druid and in this country we respected all religions and had to list him as such. He replied, "very well, I'll take care of that".

When Sunday came, the various parties paraded at their respective times but at 6.00 am, the druid himself at the guard gate with full pack was being made by the Sergeant to bend down and up worshipping the sun as it rose. Next Sunday, he became a C. of E. member. This is what previous army life can teach one. In time, this Wing Commander as other senior officers were replaced by operational ones, and our new Wing Commander arrived in the form of W.C. Braham DSO bar, DFC bar, night fighter ace at 27 years of age.

The next query from the W.C. was an offenders list, which I had not supplied, and I replied that I had none. He said "oh, come on, Lyder, this is part of their training, they must be made to do jankers as part of becoming disciplined", I explained that that may have been in the army, but I had been through the whole of my airman's stage without having done any or having any bad report and so was never required to be punished. I had lectured the chaps about staying clear of all trouble and told the NCOs that coercion rather than punishment was to be our policy and it worked. Half way through the ten-week course, the chaps were sent on 48-hour passes and when they came back, I was flooded with parent letters again, asking how we managed to transform their sons into such clean, disciplined and well-mannered persons in such a short time, whereas previously the boys lay in bed till 10.00 am or later, threw their clothes on the floor for us to pick up, had no consideration for anyone else and were now up bright and early, having made their own beds and bringing Mum a cup of tea.

They were amazed at the change and when we had open house at graduation and relatives were invited to see them march past at the end of the course parade, they queued up to speak to the officers who had wrought such a transformation in their sons. I was very sad to hear that National Service had been done away with a while later and think that it should be reintroduced, as youngsters today are growing up wild like weeds and are in severe need of some schooling in discipline. That has to be the basis of citizenship.

After training three courses, my demob number came up and I gave the C.O. notice that I would be going. At that time, I had a handlebar moustache, which was the envy of the camp. Wing Commander Braham arranged a farewell party for me at a local pub and intimated that he would have my moustache as a souvenir. When I refused to permit that, he said he would settle for half and promised that he would not give it up. They did their best to get me sloshed in order to remove it, but I held out and I had the job of putting them to bed instead. I left the station at 10.00 am on Wednesday morning in March 1947, one of the severest winters I had experienced in England, and I set out to drive to Morton in the Marsh, Gloucestershire.

The snow fall had been very heavy and whole villages were cut off and the animals in the fields were receiving food dropped to them by the RAF. I got as far as Stafford only because I had an old Wolsey 14 that stood high of the ground. I met a snow plough that had just cut a path on the road and the driver advised me not to try to go any further as the road was closing after him as fast as he cleared it.

I thought I would try in the hope that things would improve further south, but had soon to abandon the attempt and was lucky to get back to the town of Stafford. I drove into an RAF station and requested accommodation. The mess officer was called and said that he was sorry but he could not have me as he had no spare bed and insisted that I move on. I told him that I was not moving a foot further and walked into the lounge and said that I would sleep in the chair or on the floor, but I was not going anywhere else. He then quizzed me about who I was, where had I come from and found me a bed after apologising as quite recently he had a highly decorated Wing Commander spend a whole week there, who turned out to be false and had left without paying anything. I told him that I was not flattered to be looked upon in the same way. I spent two days there before I dared move on and I settled the bill to profuse apologies and left. I eventually arrived in Morton in the Marsh where my parent station had moved to from Wheton Aston at 3.00 pm on the following Sunday. The weather cock on the church steeple had twisted completely around itself with the force of the wind it had encountered. I explained that I had come to be demobbed and was accommodated.

To Cape Town and Back

 My first night in Morton in the Marsh I had a good nights' rest and appeared before Group Captain Harris bright and early.

He greeted me with "hello, Lyder, what brings you here?" I said "good morning sir, I have come to be demobbed" and he replied "demobbed, no Lyder, I cannot bring myself to do that, haven't you applied to stay on?" I said "yes sir, I applied for a permanent commission but was turned down and offered a ten-year extension instead". He then said "you cannot leave the RAF, you are an intrinsic part of it, you are the quintessential RAF Officer" and picked up a pen saying "we can do something about that" and appeared to want to make an appeal on my behalf, so I hurriedly explained that I had been away from home for nine years and had a mother and sisters to look after and decided that I must go back, besides which, my friend and I had bought an airplane and had planned a trip to Cape Town, South Africa, and back. He relaxed and asked some questions of my route etc. and said "good luck, and if you see any interesting jobs down there, send me a cable".

The formalities were duly completed and he bid me farewell and I made my way to Lytham St. Anns, where

I was sent into a large warehouse with instructions to choose two suits of clothing, a hat and a pair of shoes. I was then signed off the strength of the RAF and put on the Reserve of Officers until the age of forty-five, when I was fully released.

I went back to stay with the Spantons on the farm and continued the planning of our trip. We had bought an American Beechcraft Traveller, a five-seater bi-plane with the top and bottom wings staggered, with the bottom one forward somewhat of the top one. It was a cabin job like a luxury car, which was very popular in the U.S. as a private owners vehicle, with a 450 bhp rotary Pratt and Witney engine. It was purchased from the MOD as surplus and had been commandeered for executive transport during the war. It had been sent to Fields Aircraft Co. for refitting with a new certificate of air worthiness and eventually delivered to the Fairoaks Airfield in Woking.

With great excitement, I took Mr and Mrs Spanton and their son, fifteen year-old Gerald, who was being schooled at Charterhouse, on a short trip to White Waltham on a test run and landed on the grass there, but found the undercarriage rather hard and not spongey enough. After tea, we returned to Fairoaks and felt the same discomfort.

I wanted to explore the aeroplane to ascertain the stall speed and other flying characteristics, so told Charles Spanton that I would take it up solo the next day to be happy with it. I got up early and got airborne and, having got the feel of it, returned for a landing. I put the gear down and checked the light green as locked and made a slow, controlled approach, but for a split second I seemed to be sitting rather low over the field, and the next thing it was on its belly, coming to a quick stop. I was unhurt, but shaken and sat there trying to figure out what had happened.

When Charles and the others came running up, I looked at the undercarriage light but it was red and I could not understand as I had checked it green as locked down. It transpired that this was a common fault with that type of aircraft, with the electric motor cutting out partway in its travel, and a handle was provided to physically wind it down. The light had appeared green as there was a green convex lens protruding into the cockpit and the bright morning sun was making it appear as though it was alight. This is why the British Air Worthiness Authorities insisted that on all British aircraft, those lights should be red and inserted in the dash so that this could not occur.

I discovered later that there were two other aircraft of the same type with a similar problem in hangars in the south. A recovery crew arrived to take the aircraft back to "Fields" at Hanworth for what was minimal damage, but in raising it with an improvised block and tackle they dropped it and did more damage. Back at the workshop I complained about the hard undercarriage and it was discovered that the duo legs of the undercarriage had been filled with oil instead of oil and air.

Mr and Mrs Spanton managed to secure passages to Cape Town by the Union Castle Steamship Line and travelled out that way. When the aircraft was repaired, I took it back to Fairoaks and advertised for three passengers to Cape Town and found an engineer named Andrews, who worked at Hanworth and was planning to migrate to South Africa, and signed him up with wife and daughter of ten years. We left Fairoaks on the morning of 4th of August 1947 to fly to Lympne to clear customs and flew directly to Marseilles. It was a lovely clear day and we could see most of the countryside of France en route. I then cleared for Tunis, but was not allowed by the French to fly direct, but routed via Ajaccio in Corsica.

We overnighted in Tunis, where the temperature was extremely high and the locals were sitting out on balconies, fanning themselves with huge palm leaves. We were also warned about not using the tap water for drinking, so had to buy several bottles of water. Next morning, we flew to a small airstrip at Gabes and then on to Siddiberani and on to Cairo.

I had bought a Shell carnet to cover the payment for fuel en route. This was a letter of credit that had the cost at each stop deducted as one went along. In those days, there was no such thing as a credit card.

On landing at Cairo, I was approached by a chap who offered to clear me through immigration and customs, and I told him that I was doing my own handling, but he assured me that I would have great difficulty on my own and I employed him. The first thing he did was to go to a bank and draw a fistful of pesetas and at every desk would produce the appropriate fee.

We put up for a couple of days at the Heliopolis Palace Hotel, a fabulous place, and visited the town, the shops and the pyramids, and enjoyed it all. We then flew south to Wadi Halfa in the Sudan and overnighted there. There were a few light aircraft waiting for others with radio equipment to escort them through the Sudan, as the authorities had insisted, because of planes forced down with problems en route were costing a great deal in search and rescue.

We met a chap and pilot of a Miles twin engine Gemini, who were on their way to South Africa to set up a paint business, who asked if I would escort them through. They said they could cruise at 150 mph and we agreed. Wadi Halfa was even hotter than Tunis and we were glad to find another aircraft so quickly to go through together.

The following morning we set out and were merrily on our way when I discovered that the cylinder head temperature was getting too high and realised I would have to turn back because we were having to fly too slow at low altitude to stay with them. We did not have radio contact with them and tried to wave them to turn back, which they took as exuberance and waved back.

Things were becoming critical, so I had to turn back and they got the message and followed. Back on the ground at Wadi Halfa, I explained and they were very upset. Within a short while a BOAC crew, who had arrived in a Dakota, were walking out with their passengers following, and I asked the Captain if he would escort me and he asked what speed would I do. I told him up to 170 true airspeed, providing the temperature was normal, and he agreed to escort me through. He took off and climbed quite fast and I tried to follow him but could not keep up with him and climb at the same rate, but hoped to pull level as we progressed. I had him in sight for a long time but he was gaining on me and I was so far on the way that I continued.

On arrival at Khartoum Airport, I was met by the authorities in uniform who enquired why I had come through the Sudan out of convoy. I said I did nothing of the sort, I had come with the Dakota and pointed to it parked nearby. The chief then said, that that airplane had arrived some ten minutes before you did, and I had to think fast. I replied that the Captain of that airplane agreed to escort me and did not. If you gave your child to an adult to take somewhere, would you expect that adult to walk on and leave your child behind? He accepted that explanation and waved us inside.

We put up at the Victoria Hotel as well as the crew and their passengers, and while walking in the grounds later, the senior captain – there were two, the senior was checking out the younger one – came up and asked "what was your problem?" He had heard me say that I would cruise at 170 mph. I replied that the temperatures being experienced were extremely high and I lost way in the climb. He then said that tomorrow I should get off first and set course and they would catch up with me at altitude and I agreed, as otherwise I would have to wait in Khartoum for another plane. The mornings are light by 5.00 am there, so we were up early and off, and as planned the Dakota caught up with us and I settled down formatting on his left side.

We were getting along famously when I saw a menacing black-line squall in the distance. As we approached it, we were getting into rain, becoming heavier as we flew on. I put my navigation lights on and he did the same and I stuck with him until the rain became so heavy that at times I could not see the Dakota. I realised that a collision was imminent and so broke off to the left.

I had been having to keep my eyes glued to the Dakota and did not know where we had got to, but assumed he had maintained a track for Malakal, our destination. I calculated mentally how far we must have travelled together and tried to fix my position. I had now descended to be below the cloud and could at least see where I was going. Fortunately the River Nile bent west across my path and once I came upon that I would know how to get to Malakal. I was pleased to see the bend in the Nile and turned left to land at Malakal.

The Dakota was already there and when I was being refuelled, I asked the Shell man if any other aircraft was expected and he said that a Bristol Wayfarer was due shortly so I felt I could ask him to take me to Juba.

The Dakota crew, on arrival at Malakal, had been asked about the Beechcraft and they had replied that they had lost me in the rainstorm and feared the worst had happened, so the people at Malakal had been relieved to see us turn up. Before I had completed refuelling, the BOAC crew came up asking how much longer I would be and I told them to go on and forget me, I would find someone else.

The Wayfarer of Sky Travel out of Liverpool arrived a short while after and the passengers were in a state with cut heads and blood-soaked shirts etc. They too had come through the storm and been thrown about as some did not have their seatbelts done up. A number of these charter companies had sprung up after the war as there was a rush to emigrate to various parts of the Empire. I asked the captain of the Wayfarer, a press on Australian type named Meredith, if he would escort me as he too was going to Juba, and he agreed.

We got off and I got on his right side and we set course for Juba, but soon ran into a lot of cloud and he twisted and turned, climbed and descended until I had no idea where we were, so had to stick with him. At times we got low below the clouds and could see all manner of wild animals like wilderbeest, giraffe etc. scampering away from the noise of the airplanes. On one occasion, lightning struck the small lake just in front of us and Meredith swerved away to the right and I had to take quick action to avoid a collision. He had forgotten all about me.

We pressed on and at last, the single strip carved out of the woods, which was Juba, came into sight. I circled while the Wayfarer backtracked up the runway and then landed. The ginger-haired hostess came running up to greet us, saying she had been worried about us and had been up to the cockpit to ask Meredith about us, and he said that I would have to take care of myself. She was worried whether I had enough fuel. This is one of the reasons I had chosen the Beechcraft for this journey, it had a range of about 700 miles and I planned stops every 400 as near as I could.

We had a bit of a party with them all at the only hotel near the strip. The next morning was another very wet one and I decided to give it a day to rain off, and was having breakfast when the MET officer joined us and asked what were our intentions. I told him that I did not know much about Africa, but lived in the tropics and if we saw rain like this, we just called things off, and he thought I was wise to do so. The Wayfarer had chosen to press on. I was happy to let him go as I no longer needed to be in convoy from there on.

Next morning, as I suspected, we awoke to fine conditions and had a lovely smooth flight to Kisumu on the north east of Lake Victoria and, after refuelling, flew on to Tabora. We were having a drink with the Shell man in the grounds of the hotel when we saw the Wayfarer overhead coming in to land and the Shell man left us in a hurry to service it. When he got back, he reported that they had had another bad day getting to Entebbe, and he was surrounded by the passengers enquiring "where was the nearest railway station". They had had enough of this mad pilot.

The next day we flew on to Kasama and stayed in a rondavel, a round mud hut with a thatched roof, attached to the small hotel, and next we flew on to Ndola in Northern Rhodesia. When I went up to the control tower, the RAF Sergeant asked "why had I come there" and I said I was touring the various countries of Africa and this was supposed to be the capital of Northern Rhodesia. He invited me to come to the window and, pointing to one street with a few buildings on either, said "this is it". I then flew on to Salisbury, which was a lovely town, and enjoyed a couple of days there. To see what it has become today can hardly be termed progress.

We put up at a very nice small hotel and visited the famous Old Colonial Hotel with all its history and elegance to find that the BOAC Dakota crew, whom we had met in Juba, awaiting an engine change had reached Salisbury and were having a party, and we were embraced like long lost colleagues. I could see the effect that their celebration was having on the staid clientele and made a hasty retreat.

I tried to clear my journey in the control tower to fly direct to Johannesburg, but they insisted that I fly to Bulowayo on a dog leg and then on to Johannesburg, as the direct route was not approved due to the hostility of the native tribes there. We just refuelled at Bulowayo, so I did not see anything of that town. We arrived at Johannesburg's Germiston Airport some 6,000 feet above sea level and put up in the Carlton Hotel in the town. We met the Wayfarer crew in the town and they were staying at a small hotel, and two days later we continued to Bloomfontein, Beaufort West and finally Cape Town.

On the leg from Bloomfontein to Beaufort West I was having difficulty in map reading and landed on an open area that appeared to be an old disused airstrip to ask a local farmer where we were, and discovered that the compass was reading badly in error and, allowing roughly 15 degrees for that, arrived safely in Cape Town.

The aerodrome there was a lovely, well-kept, pretty green area and the people most friendly. I asked for the aeroplane to be thoroughly checked and they found a number of faults that should have been taken care of at Fields Aircraft at Hanworth, including the compass, which was now 19 degrees in error, and the tailwheel, whose lock was not functioning. They did a very good job, including repainting the leading edges of the wings and engine cowlings, which had been stripped of paint in the heavy rains we had flown through.

I met a friend, John Colman of the South African Airforce from POW camp Luft 3 at Sagan, who very kindly drove us along the scenic coast road around the

Cape. We did the usual sight seeing trips to the wine making area of Constantia, climbed Table Mountain etc. and thought Cape Town a very pleasant place.

My passengers Andrews asked me to take them back to Johannesburg, as he had learned that that was the real hub of business in South Africa in which to look for a job. We flew to East London with a tail wind clocking some 232 mph ground speed, where we just refuelled and continued to Port Elizabeth where we put up for the night. The next day we set out for Johannesburg but turned back having run into bad weather and waited until the following day to fly to Johannesburg. Andrews and family left me there and both he and his wife got jobs there, but were not paid what he had expected as they were in a tight recession.

I went to look for Jim Cody, the grandson of Buffalo Bill Cody, who was a friend of Jim Crampton, as Crammie had asked when I told him I was going to do that trip. Cody was also in the RAF as a technical officer on electronics and on leaving the RAF had made some quick money that had encouraged him to emigrate to South Africa, and was now in business in Johannesburg. I found him at his office and introduced myself. He took me downstairs to a busy coffee shop where I heard a voice from the table behind us that sounded familiar, so I looked round and recognised another South African ex-RAF from Luft 3. He gave me a hearty greeting but I didn't see him again. I put up at the Carlton again and spent some three weeks there, I think. I visited the shops and found several branches of the well-known shops in London, bought some presents for the family in Trinidad and posted them off. Enjoyed several visits with Cody, at his home on the road to Pretoria, the capital.

I advertised the aeroplane for sale and was invited to the Rand Flying Club at Germiston Airport for their annual party and found myself placed at the Chairman's table as a special guest from the mother country. One of the members named Stobbart was interested in buying the Beechcraft, but not at my price and was haggling, but I held firm. He was a key member of the club so I was feted to soften me up and then his sister was provided as my partner for the occasion and we had to arrive in dinner suits etc. all very pukka!

Speeches were made and I was introduced as a friend and colleague from the old country who had flown his own plane out to them, and a toast was drank to me. As I was expected to do, I took to the floor asking my partner for the first dance, during which she quizzed me about the journey and the aeroplane, saying that her brother was very anxious to buy it and why did I not sell it to him. The approach was so direct and crude, which made me more determined to hold out for my price.

In addition to covering all my accumulated expenses I also had to buy my return ticket and passage by sea or air, which were difficult to obtain at that time. My glass was never allowed to become empty and I was plied with as much drink as was necessary, and I learned from that how much it took to get me sloshed, if I truly resisted. In discussions with Cody afterwards, he told me that had I gone into attack mode instead of being on the defensive, I might have swapped it for a DC4 of South African Airways, as they were mostly members of the management board.

My money was running low and, as I mentioned earlier, there were no facilities like credit cards in those days, and I started to plan my return trip. I advertised for three passengers to take back to the UK and had several replies, all of whom were females without money who had been encouraged to come to South Africa for wonderful jobs, which had not materialised. Some heart-rending stories of abuse.

Just before I decided whom I should accept, Cody said he would come with me, as he too had spent all his money and had accepted a job with his partner an ex-army sergeant from Southampton for £10 per week. Elizabeth, his wife from Scotland, was anxious to go home and so I dropped all others and agreed to take them home to England and he would settle with me there.

I planned the departure for Saturday and was having dinner with them on the Wednesday, when Cody said that he had changed his mind and decided to stay and regain his fortune. Elizabeth begged me to take her and their daughter while Cody was on the phone and I told her, I could not do that, her place was with her husband. I left the house that evening, telling Cody that I thought he should go back to England as I did not think that he would succeed in the existing economic decline. I told him that it was too late for me to take anyone else at this stage and that the Beechcraft would be lifting off from Germiston at 9.00 am on Saturday with or without him, and bade them goodnight.

The following day he phoned to say that they would come with me. I had been trained to be punctual and at 9.00 am that Saturday morning, the Beechcraft was slithering over the fence with the Cody family and all their worldly belongings.

We set a course for Durban and enjoyed the flight, putting up there for the night. I went to visit another South African ex-POW navigator, who had been with us at Sagan. His family, parents and brother and sister, gave me a great welcome and dinner. The next day, we flew to the Victoria Falls at Livingstone and spent the night there and then on to Luxor, but could not stop as I was having to pay all expenses and my funds were running low, so we pressed on to Cairo.

After just a night's stop we continued across the desert to Tubruk for fuel and on to Castle Benito in Algiers for the night. I counted the foreign currency that I had left and discovered that I could not fund another overnight, so told Cody that we would have to get off at 2.00 am the next morning to reach England by the afternoon. I then sent a telegram to Fairoaks Control Tower to tell Mrs Spanton that we would be there at 5.00 pm on that Saturday. I learned when I got back that the Controller had phoned the message on but said "there must be a mistake, he must mean Sunday, as he is now 1550 miles away" and Mrs Spanton replied that Mr Lyder was a very responsible man and if he said Saturday, he meant Saturday, so look for him tomorrow. We got up at about 1.00 am and got off around 2.30 am and had a smooth night's flight to Tunis first.

On arrival there in the early dawn, I could not see the airport and asked the Controller to fire a green 'very-light' and immediately saw it and landed. A quick refuel and we were off to Marseilles. This time direct and another quick stop and we were on our way across the French countryside. Cody was having a snooze and when he woke he saw the white cliffs of Dover and asked "is that England?" and I replied "yes, that is Dungeness ahead" and he broke down weeping.

We landed at Lymne to clear Customs & Immigration. There was a bit of a delay as there were some light planes ahead of us, but once cleared, we hurried to Fairoaks Airfield where we landed at 5.47 that Saturday afternoon. We were met by Mrs Spanton and Cody asked about trains to London, and looking at her watch she replied that there would be one in a few minutes, but we must hurry. She drove us to Woking station where the train had just arrived and while I helped the Cody family and all their baggage on to the train, Mrs Spanton ran to the ticket office, bought the 2 ½ tickets to London and handed them to the Cody's outstretched hand as the train was moving off. Mrs Spanton explained about the doubts that the Controller had had about our arrival and she was tickled pink that she had been right to tell him to look for me on Saturday. Mr Spanton had gone back out to finalise the purchase of a hotel in Salisbury.

I had a good rest to recover from that journey and when I returned to London, I looked up Cody in his digs. Elizabeth and daughter had gone home to Scotland. Cody asked for a statement of account and I gave him one covering all his family's expenses en route, but leaving him to decide what he could pay towards passages and I am sorry to report that I never received a penny. He took me to a pub in Knightsbridge to meet some cronies of his and he introduced me to the famous Augustus John.

Saving Berlin

I had had my fling and had now to consider obtaining my commercial licences for flying and joined the very first course at Air Service Training at Hamble, known as the University of Aviation, for the new specialist navigators licence.

Previously, that had been first and second class, but with the post-war increase in the use of aeroplanes to fly passengers all over the world, a new and super licence was planned. The only trouble was that the persons who prepared the early exams went overboard and made them so tough that very few managed to pass the first time. So, as a pass mark of 70% in each subject was required, I dropped just below that on two papers, which I was allowed to resit. But if you did not pass this all within six months, you would have to take the lot again.

My trouble was that I was slow and could not get the papers finished in the allotted time. Squadron Leader Hoy, the Chief Instructor, went to the Civil Aviation Ministry to plead my case when I did not pass them all within six months, but they argued that we would soon be using fast jet aeroplanes and this was a specialist licence and I would have to get up to the speed required if I wanted the licence. Several of the senior captains of

BOAC attempted it, including the famous Captain O.P. Jones, and had difficulty. I needed to practise more, so I moved to the Southampton Navigation College at Warsash where I could go over the subjects with more time on each and pass the lot the following year.

I enjoyed my time at Warsash as it was a school especially for marine navigation, and I met a number of ship's captains working for their Masters licences. One was the harbour master of Montreal, who was given the job on the premise that he obtained the Masters certificate. We became friends when he learned that I had come from Trinidad, which was a regular port of call for him.

I shared a room with a pilot named Lord, I can't remember his first name. He was quite a character and had an old banger of a car in which he added kerosene to the fuel to extend the mileage possible with what petrol coupons we were allotted, and it moved off with bangs and jerks to everyone's amusement.

Our instructor was Vernon Canton, who had a wife and young child living on the camp and had certain domestic chores to carry out after school. He was very fond of the cinema, especially Western films, and we would invite him to join us at the bug house in Fareham, as it was called. He had first to get permission from his wife and on occasion, Lord and myself would go to beg her for him to join us, while he waited hopefully in another room. Lord had applied for the dole and went down every Saturday morning to collect and suggested that I do the same. But I could not bring myself to do that, as I had always paid my way in life. He explained that after the first few visits, while hiding his face behind the local newspaper, one met the same chaps in the queue and it became an open social gathering.

I finished the exams and went home to an aunt of mine in Bexleyheath with whom I was staying at the time. I remember the morning I picked the telegram off the mat and nervously opened it, I read it twice, no, three times, before I showed it to Aunt Lena, and she hugged me and hurried off to open the proverbial bottle for a celebration. It was a wonderful relief and now I could move on.

I studied for my R/T licence and the Auster Aeroplane technical and had a couple of hours on it in order to apply for a commercial flying licence. Once I got that, I started to look for a job. There were so many trained pilots coming out of the RAF that there would be long queues outside any office which dared to advertise any job.

I heard of the Berlin Airlift and that Air Vice-Marshall Bennett, who had been in charge of the Pathfinders in the RAF and now had his own company, was advertising for a pilot. I had applied to Skyways, who had aircraft on the airlift, and had just received a telegram from them offering me a job at £800 net and accommodation, but would prefer to work for Bennett and went off to see him at the RAF Club in Piccadilly. He received me in the lounge and we discussed the matter and my qualifications and offered to take me on at £600. I mentioned to him that I had had an offer that morning to join Skyways at £800 and thinking that I was bluffing, I suppose, he replied "in that case you should take it". I waited a minute to consider, then got up and said "very well, sir, I will" and marched off.

On my first trip with Skyways to Gatow in the Berlin area, we flew a Lancaster tanker with a huge tank in the bomb bay filled with motorcar petrol, and went to the coffee shop for a cuppa while it was offloaded. Blake, the captain, met friends in the coffee shop from Bennett & Co. and introduced me. One of Bennett's captains asked my name again, as it seemed to ring a bell, and asked whether I had applied to Bennett for a job and I said "yes". He then asked if I had seen a blonde lady in the lounge while I was being interviewed and I said "yes, there was one such lady sitting a short distance away, reading a book" and he said "well, that was Bennett's wife, who was a Director of his company, and when you walked out she told him, that was the man you should have hired". She had listened to the whole interview.

I enjoyed my time on the airlift as it gave me a feeling of doing something well worthwhile after my career on squadron was curtailed by being shot down, and that Berlin airlift was credited with preventing World War III, this time against the Russians. They had made up their minds to take over the whole of the city of Berlin and closed all access on the ground that had been agreed with the other nations: Americans, British and

French. There was an air corridor about 20 miles wide into Berlin, but they ignored that because they never thought it necessary. The Russians were far behind in the use of aeroplanes for transport and had laughed when we started the airlift to relieve the siege of Berliners. This was a bold, unprecedented exercise that they were sure would fail, but practise makes perfect and the lift went from strength to greater strength and took the wind out of their sails. They tried among other things to intimidate us by carrying out gunnery exercises at night on the sides of the corridor.

We flew almost everything into the city to keep it supplied and flew out what they produced, a fantastic undertaking for which I am proud to have served.

The Russians finally gave up their attempt and opened Checkpoint Charlie and other ground access to the city. The airlift was disbanded and my job with Skyways terminated.

When I got back to England after being a POW, I decided that I would never go back to Germany, but having worked on the Berlin Airlift and having had the opportunity to meet and speak to the residents, I felt differently. They were so kind and appreciative of what we were doing for them that we felt as though we had been fighting the wrong people. That gave me the wish to go back for a visit when the Airlift was terminated.

I took my car and drove back to Frankfurt in search of Bishop Sommer. Unfortunately, he was in Hamburg on a conference but his daughter, Mrs Junkers, would have me to tea. We had a pleasant meeting, if a bit strained, and at the end of it I asked my way to Oberursel. She told me to follow the tramcar for 12 kilometers and I would be there. She then asked what was my interest there, and I told her that I had been a POW there. She then asked how they had treated me, and I said that some of their methods had not been very nice. Pointing to a picture on the wall of her brother in S.S. uniform, she said that he had often said that he did not agree with a lot of what was done there.

So little has been written about the Berlin Airlift that I have been asked what it was like from a pilot's point of view. In short, I would say very exacting. We were briefed to be particularly accurate on approach to landings, as there was no second chance. If the first approach was missed, the load would have to be taken back to base to start again. A "Skyways" crew consisted of two pilots and a wireless operator. We flew mostly at night and in some atrocious weather at 4,000 ft, crawling from beacon to beacon. On final approach to Gatow aerodrome, the wireless operator would call out every few seconds "DOTS 1, 2 or 3" to tell the pilots if they were left of the centre line of the runway or "DASHES 1, 2 or 3" if they were off to the right, and the distance to go to the runway.

The pilots had to land and turn off at the end of the runway within two minutes for the next plane to land. Very exacting! In addition to all of this, we were always worried that the Russians would go berserk and shoot us down. It was virtually like being at war.

Becoming a Commercial Pilot

I studied more and took a test for an instrument rating for my commercial licence to upgrade it to a senior commercial pilot's licence. I then answered an advert for a job at Boston Air Transport and got the job. This was on a small improvised field just outside the town of Boston, Lincolnshire.

The company had two Miles Messengers four-seaters and an Auster and offered light aircraft transport to businessmen and farmers. There was a Director/pilot named Wilf Pearson who was in charge of the flying. Wilf started a course for an instructors endorsement at the Cambridge Flying Club at Newmarket and I would fly him there and bring him back when necessary, and on one occasion I was to take him to the school, but there was a devil of a storm taking place, so he phoned me and we delayed departure. He asked when I thought we would be able to leave and I said that I would call him back on that.

I observed the weather front move through Boston, calculated its speed roughly and worked out when I thought it would clear the airfield in Cambridge and gave him a time for departure, which would put us there soon afterwards. This was to prove my worth as a meteorologist and I was putting that to the test. We got off as planned and joined the circuit of the airfield barely a few minutes after they had been showered by the storm. Wilf was impressed and I very self satisfied. The Managing Director of our company was a Mr Moffat, who had been running a road transport system and decided to extend that into the air. A case of history repeating itself, as in the 1930's one Mr Hillman did. He had run a fleet of buses and extended that into air transport when he formed Hillman Airways and ordered a twin-engine eight-seater aeroplane from De Havilland Aircraft Factory, known as the Dragon, with square-tipped bi-plane wings, later refined to tapered wings, and named the Dragon Rapide, which was popular for light transport in those days.

A smaller five-seater built on similar lines and a larger four-engined one produced later were used for the domestic market and proved very useful. They used to land on the beach in Jersey before an aerodrome was built there. I think it was the Grosvenor House Hotel, which organised an air race from England to Australia in 1934, which caused quite a stir in our history of the air and attracted entrants from the international world of aviators who were prominent at that time. The De Havilland Company designed a sleek tandem low-wing monoplane two-seater with two gipsy six-cylinder engines a development of the Gipsy Major four-cylinder type especially for that race and called it the Comet. Both aeroplane and engine were brand new designs and proved to be a resounding success. Four Comets were built and flown in the race by Jim and

Amy Molleson; Scot and Campbell-Black; Cathcart and Jones and Coulson and others, I cannot remember their names. The Comet flown by C.W.A. Scott won the speed section of the race, with two others placing up front and most unfortunately the Mollesons retiring down the route after having left a parcel of maps and documents at Baghdad, the first controlled stop for the fast aeroplanes. They were the very first to land there and were favourites to win – very unfortunate.

I was a youngster in Trinidad in those days and followed the race with great enthusiasm as I kept in touch hour by hour with the news from the cable office where my eldest sister Glory worked. The Dutch Airline KLM, who were particularly familiar with the route as they serviced their colonies in the Far East, entered a team with Parmontier and Moll as pilots in the brand new, all metal airliner, the Douglas DC2 or 3, I am not sure without checking this, which became so popular on the airways in America and built in large numbers for use in the Second World War and known to us as the Dakota. I would have loved being at Mildenhall Aerodrome the day of the start, which must have been very exciting indeed.

One romantic moment I heard recalled was that Campbell-Black, who had been very fond of Florence Desmond, the singer and entertainer, and who had unsuccessfully asked her to marry him on two previous occasions, was kissed by her on send off with the promise that she would marry him if he won. This boosted his incentive to win and when they experienced trouble in one of the engines over the Timor Sea crossing to Darwin, pushed the engineers at Darwin to get it working enough to get it off, then shut it down and limped across Australia to Melbourne, the finishing point. They had established a handsome lead at that stage fortunately and won, got there first, but the Dutchmen were ruthlessly closing in on them, and the news of their progress hour by hour was most exciting. It was a wonderful boost for the De Havilland Company. I think the two other Comets remaining in the race came third and fifth. The period between the 1920's and 1930's was the most romantic of times for aviation and I longed to be part of it, but due to my family's impecunious state I had to be satisfied with following events from a distance.

At Boston Air Transport I tried to extend the service and wrote to several travel companies and local councils in the area suggesting we could help them and had several replies. One came from a chap in Scunthorpe, who arranged for me to visit him by landing in a farmer's field, which was being rested at the time. I sent him a wind-sock to be mounted in one corner of the field and on the appointed day arrived with the Managing Director, Moffat, and the Mayor of Boston in one of the Miles Messengers. He was there to greet us with a party of official,s including the Mayor of Scunthorpe and the press, and the occasion was duly covered in the Scunthorpe newspapers. They rather prematurely reported that Scunthorpe now had an aerodrome like London, Manchester and others from which their population could now fly to the continent and all parts of the globe. I could mention here that I had been trying to get back to Trinidad to fly for British West Indian Airways and when I did manage that, I was hired as their most junior of pilots and had to hide my light under a bushel, so to speak.

It was some time later when one of our senior captains, Phil Kelshall, who later became General Manager, was visiting his wife's family at Scunthorpe on holiday and called in at a fish and chips shop for supper. He took his meal into the car to eat out of the usual newspaper wrapping, and as he unfolded it, he was surprised to read about one ex-RAF bomber pilot Garth Lyder arriving with the Mayor of Boston to open Scunthorpe's airfield. On his return to Trinidad with that news I was paid a bit more respect.

I was eventually hired by BWIA and left Boston on Saturday 11th March to drive to London and present myself to the BOAC Personnel Manager for acceptance. Phil Kelshall and Keith Maingot had come up from Trinidad to ferry a new Vickers Viking out and I and another pilot, Gilfoyle, were to be on board. I was keen as mustard to help and in view of my qualifications was given the job to navigate them across the South Atlantic.

We flew to Lisbon where we overnighted and then next day to Dakar in West Africa and that night across the South Atlantic to Natal on the north east tip of South America. I had wished to do that solo long before and was happy to be doing this. Once we had arrived there, Kelshall said I could get some rest now, as he knew the way from there on, but I could not sleep as I was thrilled to be going home at last and enjoyed the countryside bathed in bright sunlight after the relentless gloom of England.

The Viscount I logged the most time on.

Charlie and self at his Winnipeg Home, August 1954.

With Mr. and Mrs. Walkden (Charlie's parents) at their Winnipeg home.

A BWIA Boeing 707 "Sunjet".

 # 49 Ellerslie Park, the house I built in 1953.

Coming Home

It was wonderful to be back at Piarco Aerodrome, this time to stay. I was met by my family and taken home to "Sunnyside" in Tacarigua, the house that my grandfather had built.

I was number 32, the last on the list of pilots, and at that time, with a strict seniority system in place, I was made to feel my position in spite of my extraordinary qualifications. The main consideration was that I was now at home and able to care for my mother and sisters. The house needed some repairs and decoration and I got that done.

It was now March 1950 and I had been away nearly 12 years. My brother Edwin had resigned from BWIA and returned to Barclays Bank with seniority as though he had never left. He was thought of so highly and went on to become manager of one of their branches.

A lot of time was taken up in going over the past years and recalling the dreadful experiences we had all been through, and I renewed friendships that had been forced into abeyance during those long years. There were two in particular that I would like to recall and they are Robin Forbes, who had got married and I met frequently until he left the island several years later to settle in England and eventually passed away whilst living in Maidenhead. His younger brother Gordon later qualified as a pilot and joined BWIA and became a captain with the airline flying to London. The other is John Pocock, who is still in Trinidad and now retired. His family consisted of four boys, now grown up who have their own families in Trinidad, Canada and England. Andrew, the eldest, is a diplomat in the British Civil Service, but being posted to overseas stations.

The remarkable thing about these two friends was that the passage of those 12 years was treated as though it was just a holiday abroad and they made me feel as though we had never been separated. John had married Vida Duruty, the daughter of May Duruty, whose father was the Reverend Samuel Hawthorne, known to us as Uncle Sam when we were kids. He was one of the Methodist missionaries from England and he became Chairman of the District. He had married one of the local girls of the lovely Horsford family, friends of my parents. Vida is very much involved in Church work and caring for the underprivileged and ailing. My brother, the Reverend Deryck Lyder, while Chairman of the Methodists, had a memorial church built in Barbados to commemorate Reverend Hawthorne's service to the people there.

Before I left Trinidad in 1938, our home at "Sunnyside" was a happy meeting place for youngsters seeking relief from the stress of offices at weekends as somewhere in the country to visit and show off their various rehashed old model cars. Those chaps would buy old bangers and do them up as cheaply as possible themselves and bring them for us to see. Each one had a name of course, such as Flossie, Albert, Molasses etc. and were painted exotically with ordinary house paint or varnish. One Saturday, Ronnie Fraser, the son of one of our Scottish businessmen in the city, turned up with his 'special' and when asked the name of it replied in a broad Scottish brogue, which he never gave up: "Constipation". I questioned "how could you call it such a thing?" to which he replied "well it can't pass anything".

I tried to revive the spirit of those early days, but like everything else, times had changed and life had become more serious and those youngsters had families to look after etc. I too, was away flying, including weekends, and the village was not the same, so I started to look around for a plot of land in the town to build a new home. There had been a new development of residential homes just off the Grand Savannah called Ellerslie, but had now been sold out.

I had heard about it taking place when in England and had written my eldest sister to secure a plot, but she said I might prefer one on the seafront as I had enjoyed boating before leaving. I visited Ellerslie and saw a few plots not yet built upon and wished I could get one on resale as it appeared to be the ideal move to town for my mother and sisters. As luck would have it, soon after an advert appeared in the newspaper offering one for sale and I hurried to enquire. One Mr Galt had bought two plots, one on which he built a house for himself and the other for his daughter's home, but she had married an Englishman in the Forestry Department of the Government who had been transferred to Nigeria and not likely to be back, so he put it up for sale. I enquired from a friend the price per foot that they were sold for and, allowing for a reasonable sum for his profit, made an offer.

Mr Galt then said he was looking for a better offer, but I had already stretched my funds to make such an offer because of my extremely low wage even as a highly qualified airplane pilot. I told him that I could not afford any more and if I had not heard from him by 6.00 pm on Sunday, the offer would be off and I would have to look elsewhere. This was on the Wednesday of my third visit. At 3.00 pm on Sunday, the phone rang and Mr Galt told me he would accept. I was greatly relieved because I had now been convinced that that was the plot I had really hoped for.

Now the job was to find a loan with which to buy it. My eldest sister Glory managed to obtain one from her manager where she worked and I grabbed it and paid it off within two years. We were looking for someone who would put what we required into a design and went to an architect friend of hers who asked to be considered if ever she wanted to have a house built. I went to him and showed him the plan I had envisaged and he agreed that he could do it at the price I had set. We visited his office from time to time and things seemed to be going well and eventually the design was completed, but I did not like the windows and certain features of a Guyanese-type estate house.

I took it to Ormond de Boehmler, a friend of ours who was in charge of building materials at Alstons, where I had worked previously, and asked if he thought I could afford to build such a house. It was large and he quoted a cost figure that was a long way out of my reach. I explained that it was a family home for my mother, two maiden sisters and self, and needed that size of accommodation as well as having a clause in the covenant on the plot to build an appropriate size and value of house there. He then told me how to cost a building per square foot and I went home to try to reduce the size of the house to suit my pocket.

We had to pay the architect for his services, but abandoned his design. A state of gloom had set in among the family and I had to try to remove it. We were looking around for a builder to carry out my new design and were told about a Mr Gaskin, who had recently built one for a friend, and I went to see him. I showed him what I wanted and explained all that had taken place and how I had reduced the room sizes to keep within the target price.

After having a long look at it he told me that he could build a house like the design for me at the target price without my drastic cutting in the size of rooms, because I had not taken into account the standard length of the timbers, which were imported. I had worked purely on square footage, but to cut the timbers from their standard lengths would add to the cost and so the original size of the rooms could be restored with less cost. This was music to my ears. He then made one premise and that was that he would like to work with me on a cost plus basis and immediately alarm bells started to ring in my head. He sensed that and explained that if he had to take the risk of overruns he would be forced to quote a figure to cover such an eventuality, but with me taking that responsibility off him, he would be able to keep the price down and would do his best to do so. I went home to report to the family and as soon as I mentioned a cost plus arrangement I got objections. I explained what he had said and he seemed genuine and I felt safe with him and we agreed to go ahead.

I went to the BWIA Head Office and arranged a mortgage deal for a loan over 15 years and the project was put into motion. It was an exciting if anxious time for Glory and myself who were promoting it, but after just six months we moved into our new and lovely home in Ellerslie Park. It was the prime residential area at that time and still sought after even today because of its position. The day we moved into our new home was a most memorable one. Returning to life in the city of Port-of-Spain after some 25 years of commuting the ten miles from Tacarigua, our grandparents' house, but it was there that we really grew to adulthood and where vital decisions were made that honed our lives and ultimate professions, and so I felt it appropriate to name this record of my past life "The Boy from Tacarigua".

When I was interviewed for the job at BWIA in London, another chap named Gilfoyle, a Jamaican, whom I had met in POW camp, was also hired and when I reported to BOAC for registration on the 13th March 1950 as I stated in my letter to them, Mr Stephenson asked me "what seemed to be the trouble between Captain Cash and yourself since he appeared to do his utmost to dissuade you from joining them in spite of your extraordinary qualifications", but Cash gave no coherent reply.

I told him that I did not even know the man, as that was the first time I had ever seen him. I said, however, he had been told a great deal about me by my sister Marguerite, who was the personal secretary to the Manager, one Kenrick Murray, the person who first interviewed me in 1945 when I was home on leave after being a POW. Stephenson then asked why I wanted to be hired on 13th of the month, Gilfoyle had written to say he would be available from 15th.

I did not want to appear mercenary and said that if it were more convenient to make my joining date 15th, I would accept that, not thinking of anything as mundane as a seniority list and verily, we were both hired from 15th March 1950. Had I known what was to come later, I would most certainly have held out for the 13th, as a just and proper joining date.

When we arrived in front of the Personnel Officer, Jules Hennessy, in Trinidad together the first morning, he raised the matter and called it a problem. Gilfoyle stood beside me and pronounced that he could not see any problem as Lyder was senior to him in age and certainly qualifications, and he would be quite ready to accept seniority behind me, that problem could have been resolved there and then, but no change was made and it continued to bug me until Gilfoyle left of his own volition to emigrate to Australia many years later and left aviation for a business career.

I had befriended him when we got out of POW camp and were back in London, looking for him as a fellow West Indian and helping him when I could, even mentioning his name when being interviewed by Mr Whitney-Straight, the Deputy Chairman of BOAC. Mr Whitney-Straight had said to me never mind anyone else, once he had cleared the way for me to be hired, others would be able to follow.

After I had served for two years as a junior first officer, I wrote the management requesting a review of my position, now that they had the opportunity to see what I could do. The local Board of Directors met and wrote me to say that I was told of the seniority scheme when I joined and they had seen no reason to change my position. I had never been called in to the discussion and discovered some time later that they had been misled by the management in the person of Captain Cash and Mr John Rat, who stated that there was no record on file of Lyder having ever previously applied to them for a job. I was flabbergasted as most of the senior staff knew of my interview with Kenrick Murray and subsequent requests through my letters to my sister as I upgraded my qualifications. I even had an endorsement to my licence for flying boats after studying the regulations for operating on water when I heard that BWIA was thinking of using them.

When my sister mentioned this to Captain Cash, he replied that I certainly seemed well qualified. I have no knowledge of who cleared the file of my repeated letters asking to be employed, but realised I was up against a serious conspiracy and if I pressed the matter to expose this, I would be forced out of the company and it was now imperative that I should keep the job. However, I referred the matter to the pilots association, a local branch of BALPA (British Airline Pilots Association) and the meeting went well into the night, with most of the members refusing to allow any change in the order of the date of joining, and when it got to 11.30 pm and the chaps were anxious to go home, Phil Kelshall, who was chairing the meeting, put the matter to the vote and F/O Joe Watson from Guyana said "I vote that Lyder has no case". This was carried by a majority and that was the end of that.

Watson was fired many years later, when on Viscounts as Captain, for clowning around on the job such as on one trip to Bermuda, he announced over the address system that they were lost and called upon the passengers to look out either side and help him to spot the islands. After causing panic on board, he shouted "oh, there it is" and joined the circuit. The last I saw of Joe was in Earls Court, where he had bought a delicatessen, and my wife and I went there for a meal.

I had to soldier on facing repeated attempts to get me fired. As we were a wholly-owned subsidiary of the British Government Airline BOAC, we were required to have a link with the far-flung colony of Belize and could only do so in the late afternoon when the Viking had returned to Jamaica from Miami.

There were two centres in those days for the operations of BWIA, Trinidad and Jamaica, and there had been a feud over who was the Chief Pilot of the airline, and somehow Cash was appointed in charge in Trinidad and the other contestant, David Little, was put in charge in Jamaica. To inaugurate the link with Belize, Bill Cash had written to Little to say that he would be coming up to do the first flight and that Lyder, who was on a short rotation to the Jamaican base, should be rostered with him to do that job.

To clarify matters here, I should back track a bit. Captain Cash had attempted to have Captain Little dismissed earlier on when he was on the carpet because of an accident to one of the Vikings, returning after dark from Miami with Little in command and Noel de Verteuil first officer flying it. They had hit the mound just short of the runway and damaged the airplane and Little had taken over and over-shot to return to land safely. Cash seized on this opportunity to try to get rid of Little and Little called on the association to support him.

I was influential in the association at that time and offered to take up his defence after my success in the court martial when in the RAF. I asked for a letter of appointment from the association as an observer, since no provision was allowed for Little's defence, and on the morning the case was to be held in Piarco in Little's absence, I was there. Bill Cash greeted me with "hello Lyder, what are you doing here?" I told him I had come to attend the enquiry. He said "no, you are not" and I showed him the letter; he read it and pointed out that I was only an observer and should not join in any discussion. I said that I was quite clear of my position and the case was called with Dick White, one of the senior captains, in the chair.

Bill Cash laid out his case for the dismissal of Little and de Verteuil and was floundering around when I reminded the chairman of my presence as a member of BALPA and gradually pointed out several inadequacies of the airport at Jamaica for operations at night and how he too must have been aware of these and how the end of the runway was seldom used for initial touchdown as the wind was seldom in that direction and very light 5 knots and variable when that direction was used and I got his agreement on all of these points by quietly putting them forward and won the case. Cash was furious at being thwarted again.

Dave Little asked me for a copy of the notes I had made and became a fan of mine, so when he received this letter from Cash and told me about it, he said he would roster me to Miami to be out of the way and send his most senior first officer, who was Colin Granham, a Jamaican. Cash came up as scheduled and did the trip with Granham to Belize, but was delayed there until dark, about 7.30 pm, and cancelled the departure until the morning. He reported this to John Rat on return to Trinidad and Rat sent a strong letter to Little that Cash would be returning the following week to repeat the exercise and Lyder must be rostered with him.

Little showed me the letter and said he was left no option but to send me and I accepted that. Cash arrived in due course and we flew to Belize, which was the first time for me, and we suffered the same sort of delay as the week before, but this time, with me doing the flying, Cash got out his sextant and tried to pinpoint our position while on this 600 mile water crossing with little navigational aids. He was having difficulty in doing so and asked me if that star and pointing to it was Canopus and I told him "no" and pointed to Canopus.

We went back to work and I carried on, and by this time had reached Grand Cayman, which was familiar to him as we regularly called there and he quietly returned to his seat. On arrival at Jamaica, I went to Dave Little's home where the BALPA meeting had just concluded and was cheered on entering. Captain Murray, the next most senior, offered me a lift to the boarding house at which we regularly stayed when in Jamaica. The next morning I was rostered to return to Trinidad. Gilfoyle who was going to Miami met me at the airport and said that I was in the shit again.

When I enquired what it was all about he said that Cash was furious with me for having said that he would not have found Jamaica without my being with him. I denied saying any such thing, but en route to Trinidad, Cash was particularly sour.

On the ground in Barbados I took the opportunity to ask Cash what seemed to be the matter for his sulking and he repeated what he had heard that I had said about him. I told him that I had never said anything of the sort and was a grown man and not a schoolboy, but he insisted that that was what he was told I had said. I told him that I would have said it to him in person if I had thought it. He reported the matter to the General Manager in Trinidad in another attempt to get me dismissed.

Frank Murray came down to Trinidad to report that he was at the house when I returned from Belize and had taken me to my digs and could vouch that I had never made any such statement, and the matter was closed.

I have to mention these incidents to describe the pressure I was under at all times in BWIA, all because I was perceived as a threat to certain key members' jobs. I had fallen foul of the clique of pilots surrounding the manager, who was not an aviation-trained person, and that clique started a movement to push Gilfoyle ahead of me. BOAC had sent a new man out (ex pilot) as the Head Operations Manager and he wrote me a letter saying that Gilfoyle was claiming seniority over me and would I state my case. I went to see him and explained the situation fully and he said to leave it with him being an Englishman and always ready to compromise.

Some time later he wrote to both of us to say they needed to have two more captains and called us to a meeting at which he told me that Captain Phil Kelshall would check me out and Captain Junior Farfan would check out Gilfoyle, and we started immediately. We had got rid of the Lockheed 16-seaters and replaced them with DC3s (Dakotas) and by 1.00 pm that day I had successfully completed the full range of exercises, including a circuit and landing with both engines throttled back as though failed. Phil told me to go home and get some rest as I would be scheduled to do the evening flight to Barbados and back.

This was on the 10th day of June 1955, and Gilfoyle did not complete his check until a week later, and yet he was still tied to me in seniority in spite of the paragraph in the operational manual which stated that a pilot in BWIA would take seniority as a captain from the day he first flew in command of the company's aircraft.

This was done after Captain Wood had returned to BOAC by the local clique. I should have mentioned that before this, I had been chosen by Wood by virtue of my qualifications to attend the second course in

London on the Viscount aircraft as a First Officer in the winter of 1954. BOAC had been looking for a type of new aeroplane to service Bermuda from New York and their pilots refused to accept the Viscount as being unsuitable for that operation and the job was offered to us, BWIA.

I and a few others pushed for this and the Viscount was chosen for our major services through the Caribbean islands to New York and Miami and to operate the Bermuda shuttle on contract for BOAC. The aircraft was ready to go and so we hired some crews from BEA to get the show on the road, while our pilots were being trained. I had saved up my leave through the four years and was now going on three months-long leave and would join the course at Northolt Aerodrome in 1954.

I was very excited at the prospect, as I was anxious to fly further afield, and also because the Viscount was a jet-engined turbo prop, the very latest thing at the time. I started my leave in Miami, then went to stay with an American Army friend in Little Falls, Virginia, just outside Washington D.C. His parents had entertained me in Chicago on one of my visits on leave when training in Canada and he worked at the Pentagon.

While with him, I bought a brand new Chevrolet motorcar, which I used to tour America and Canada after seeing the sights of Washington. While in Washington, I looked up a female cousin, Ivy Burkhalter, who had a daughter, Felicity, and worked in one of the government offices. Ivy was one of six children who were born in Trinidad to my father's brother Julian Lyder, who migrated to the U.S.A. when the family were young. I took them in my brand new car to the show "South Pacific" and had a most enjoyable visit. Ivy has since passed on, but I still see Felicity on her visits to the UK with her husband Bobbin Harding, also from Trinidad. They have a grown up family in Canada, but the eldest son Andrew, who was in the Army here and served in Northern Ireland, is now employed in London in a bank.

From Washington, I drove to Montreal to see my sister, Patricia, who was working as a member of ICAO after serving in the League of Nations in Geneva. She gave up nursing due to the appalling conditions and reverted to clerical jobs for which she had been trained. I called in at Toronto on the way up to visit my navigator, Tommy Goode, who was offered a university course after the war and chose electrical engineering. I found him at home lying on the sofa and as I approached he called to his wife, Betty, saying "here's my old man". It was good to see him again. Unfortunately, he died in a car park with a severe heart attack several years later.

I then stayed with my sister in Montreal for a few days and drove her and two BWIA hostesses on a grand tour west through Canada and the USA and left them in Winnipeg to their own devices, while I visited my gunner, Charlie Walkden, whom I last saw when leaving him injured in a field in France when we were shot down. That was a most memorable visit. On my planned arrival, his mother came out to the roadside to greet me, she hugged me tightly for several minutes saying how grateful she was to me for saving Charlie and that she prayed for me every night. Charlie's father was the City Engineer of Winnipeg.

I had an enjoyable stay with them and drove on alone to Calgary, Banff, Lake Louise and on to Vancouver to see my Wireless Operator, Roy Walker. He had married a girl called June from Billericay in Essex after the war. I attended that wedding, and now that he was married and needed to support a wife, he had chosen to do a shorter course and had chosen to become a licenced electrician and form his own company. I still hear from him every Christmas, when we exchange greetings and the occasional phonecall. He has a grown up family, all of whom are themselves married and have families.

I spent a few days with him and then visited Seattle to stay with an old friend from Trinidad and Grenada, Rita Hudson, now married to an ex-army chap, Simmonds, whom I had met when he was serving over here in the war. While there I took the opportunity to clean and polish the car as I intended to sell it on the west coast before travelling to the UK.

I went back to Vancouver where I drove it on to a plot with a number of cars put out for sale and went into the office to see the proprietor and asked if he would like to sell my car for me as I was going on to the UK. He came out to inspect it and a crowd soon collected around it to see a car with 6,000 miles on the clock looking as though it had just arrived from the factory. He agreed to take it on to sell and took me to his bank where he deposited the car documents and arranged that when it was sold he would deposit the money in that bank to be sent to my address in the UK.

I was anxious to get back to the UK to visit the Farnborough Airshow and caught a Greyhound bus that evening to travel all the way with it to New York. That was a most interesting exercise in well organised transportation. A fresh driver took over approximately every four hours and the bus pulled into each staging post remarkably on schedule. The passengers took those breaks to buy refreshments, but no one dared to hold up the bus beyond the scheduled departure time. I was very impressed.

On arrival in New York, I had a thorough clean up at a hotel and was on a plane to London the next evening. I rented a car to drive myself to Northolt Aerodrome, where we did a course on the technicals of the Viscount and the new engines, and having put that behind us, we moved on to the flying training at Heathrow. I was thoroughly enjoying the experience when I was suddenly stopped, having done the required hours for a First Officer. I returned to Trinidad, when soon afterwards I was checked as a Captain and flew the Dakota for a few months before taking command on Viscounts.

While in England in early 1955, I found the house that we now live in and bought it for my sister Glory, who wanted a place to come to for the family. It had recently been divided into four separate and self-contained apartments, two of which we now occupy and two rented, my wife and I in the maisonette and my daughter on the first floor.

Now on the Viscounts I was checked out on the New York to Bermuda route by the then senior captain Junior Farfan. On one trip, we had a rather heated argument about the strength and direction of the en route winds. He maintained that they were completely different to the briefing we had been given and I did not agree. So on arrival at Bermuda, he suggested we ask the two pilots of Eastern Airlines who had arrived there shortly before us. We went to their lounge where they were both reading newspapers, awaiting their time for returning to New York. Junior approached them and said "good morning gentlemen" and they both looked over their papers in surprise, as much as to ask, are you addressing us? He then asked if they had not found the winds adverse to what we were briefed and one said "hell no, we just flew the flight plan and when time was up looked over the nose and there it was".

Eastern had some of the most experienced pilots in the US east coast, having had to cope with atrocious weather at times. I used to enjoy their southern accent on the R.T. and in those days the air was not so congested as now and odd bits of good humoured banter and remarks were tolerated.

One morning, when I was on my way to Bermuda, I could hear an Eastern Airline crew calling New

York Centre, but for some reason or other they did not answer. I called New York and when they replied immediately, I told them that Eastern was calling them and Eastern came up "hey BeeWee" as we were affectionately called, "how you get to speak on this phone, you a congressman or somethin'?" New York then answered them. On another occasion at around 8.00 pm at night when the weather was truly foul, I arrived in the holding pattern over the position, Coyle, where one waited for permission to go further and the PanAm crew came up and called New York for further instructions to proceed and was told that New York was closed and had not landed an aircraft for some six hours. He shouted "what?", being as surprised as I was for such lack of information en route for some unknown reason, and then he asked "is there any other fool up here besides me?" and New York came back "yeh, BeeWee over Coyle at 20,000 feet". With that he said "bye, bye BeeWee" and was gone to his planned alternate destination.

I then asked for clearance to Friendship Airport in Baltimore. We were previously told to use Andrews, Washington, but I did not like that as it was busy enough normally and would be overcrowded on such an occasion, so I plugged for Baltimore and got in immediately. I had kept that field in mind for just such an occasion. Friendship Airport had been recently built, a few miles from Washington, to take the heat off Andrews, but we found it little used and got permission to go there from New York to shoot practice

ILS instrument approaches and I found the controllers very friendly indeed, and so on the completion of our first detail there, I thanked them very much for their co-operation and they came back "you're very welcome anytime, just come on down". I must say I enjoyed my flying, and the spirit of friendly co-operation in those days made it most enjoyable. I was devastated when I was told I had to give it up on reaching the age of 60 years young.

At BeeWee we operated the Viscount as a 48-seater with two pilots with a Loran set between us and two hostesses, and flew through the Bermuda Triangle daily without any trouble ever. Our route was from Trinidad, to Barbados, to Antigua, to Bermuda where we changed crews, to continue to New York. The Viscount was built for short-haul trips and widely used by British European Airways, but we had had an extra tank fitted to the belly to extend the range from the original 700 miles.

The leg from Antigua to Bermuda was some 930 miles with no alternative within reach, so we had to ascertain we would have two hours holding on arrival at Bermuda and that the weather was likely to allow us to land eventually. We usually made this decision crossing 27 degrees north latitude and if not satisfied, would turn back to San Juan in Puerto Rico, the distance being only slightly less. I had mentioned earlier that we had hired some BEA crews to fly our Viscounts while we got our own pilots trained. On this occasion, I had one of them as my First Officer, who had a short while previously frightened his BWIA Captain into turning back to San Juan, which had caused the passengers to doubt our pilots' proficiency. Some even got off the airplane and continued to New York on other carriers.

Well, he tried the same trick on me this day and suggested we turn back as the winds were strong. The weather was fine in Bermuda, with no problem to land and I refused as I was not satisfied that there was a problem. He kept pressuring me and about two minutes before arrival at 27 degrees north, he went back to the toilet. On returning to the cockpit he asked whether I had reported our position at 27 degrees north and I said "yes" and then he said "you are continuing then?" and I replied "of course, I see no reason to do otherwise".

He took his seat but no other part in the proceedings and when Bermuda appeared on the radar screen 180 miles away that confirmed that we were pretty safe for time, we were supposed to arrive with 600 gallons left for the two hour holding rule and after being instructed to join the circuit behind the US tanker plane on approach from the west, we landed and parked on the ramp.

The First Officer made to get out of his seat without logging the residual fuel as required and I stopped him asking for the fuel gauge readings. He tried to ignore that so I had to demand it and he totalled it to be 594 gallons and I wrote that down and said "thank you very much, Mr Wynch, you may leave".

On another occasion I had another First Officer from BEA on my rotation in New York and we flew to Bermuda from New York. I had developed the habit of making the first move and putting the seat belt sign on myself, when calling for the approach checks to be carried out and this upset this chap we shall call Dixie, and he had a right go at choking me off saying that he had been flying these things a lot longer than I had etc. etc. and knew what had to be done. I remained quiet as that statement was true.

On the return trip to New York, just 40 minutes later when climbing through about 3,000 feet, I saw him having difficulty with the pressurisation switches and he asked me to hold it down while he got it sorted out. I looked up to see that the safety valve was still open and switched open the two spills valves he had closed without having the desired effect. I just let rip on him, shouting that he had quite recently been telling me how much more he knew about the aeroplane than I and proceeded to show him. I closed the safety valve first, made sure it read closed, even waiting a few seconds to verify, and then number one spill valve and then number two when number one was shown to be closed etc. etc. and he was duly chastised.

The following day we were returning to Jamaica via Nassau in the Bahamas. This was the longest leg over which we operated, 1012 nautical miles. We had Sir Hugh Foot, later to become Lord Caradon, on board, whom I knew from his spell as Governor of Guyana and was now Governor of Jamaica, and I invited him up to the cockpit. He asked what time we should arrive at Nassau and I told him on schedule and the time. He explained that he was to meet the Governor of the Bahamas, who was then Lord Ranfurly, at the airport to brief him as to what transpired at the Commonwealth Meeting in Ottawa, as he was unable to be there.

When he had left to go back to his seat, I calculated that we were going to be early and I was consumed with being punctual and adjusted the throttles to reduce the speed slightly. Dixie exploded and said "we are now going to be late" and I said "no we are not" and stood my ground". It turned out that we had a minute or so to spare, so I extended the down-wind leg and shut the engines down on the ramp, bang on schedule. Dixie was fuming.

We overnighted in Jamaica and the following day completed our rotation to Trinidad. The next day I went to the airport to check up on things and ran into Captain Jim Farquharson, the Operations Manager, who was devastated after most unfortunately suffering an attack of polio, which had left him lame and lost him his flying licence. He was an excellent pilot and truly keen on flying. He asked me to come to his office and told me, he did not like what he had heard the chaps saying about me and on my enquiring, he said they were not enjoying flying with me. I enquired whether Dixie had been to see him and he parried answering, but when I forced a reply, he admitted it. I then explained what had transpired between us on the rotation and castigated him for accepting the tale of a First Officer before having spoken to the Captain. The trouble was that some of our senior captains with whom I had fallen out were poisoning the minds of the juniors against me.

This led to another incident with a junior First Officer Trinidadian who had an altercation with me when on the new Boeing 727s out of New York and folded his arms and read a book en route to Puerto Rico, Barbados and Trinidad. He had assumed that I would have to call for his help, but apart from his carrying out the drills for landing and take-off, I did everything myself and on arrival in Trinidad thanked him and left. He was devasted to feel so redundant and after a few months of sulking he became friendly again. The same thing applied to Dixie and it became the pattern that each in turn discovered that whatever was spread about Lyder, his ability and professionalism was never in doubt.

I was travelling on leave to New York on our service, then BOAC to London, when Dixie was the Captain and mentioned that he was having to take the flight through Bermuda and on to New York as the Captain who was to have taken it over in Bermuda had become ill. I offered to help if he needed any and a while out of Bermuda he came back and asked for my help while he got a rest. I went up front and took over. The weather in New York was foul and Dixie came up only on the descent. I made to get out of the seat and he asked if I would like to take it in as I had got the picture of what to expect and so I did. I bade him farewell at the airport,

John F. Kennedy, and continued my journey by BOAC to London. On my return from leave in New York the crew told me that I was in trouble again with the Chief Pilot, because I had flown a scheduled service to New York in civilian clothes.

There appeared to be no end to the harassment that I was being subjected to. In Trinidad I was carpeted before the Chief Pilot, who ranted and raved and I asked him to read what was stated in Volume 3 of our Operational Manual and when he claimed he knew all that was in there already and refused to refer to it, I quoted the chapter and verse and recited that crew members were expected to assist whenever called upon even when travelling on leave and I explained the circumstances and he felt a bit of a fool.

Previously, when I was on Viscounts, an aircraft that was a delight to fly but had one particular anti-social fault, which was the terrible whine of the propellers, especially when manoeuvring on the ramp. The drill was to shut down the two outboard engines and taxi in with the two inners. I did this at first, but it was upsetting to see the ground crew and those on the ramp holding their hands over their ears, and as I was in the habit of taxiing fast with enough speed, I would shut down the inners as well once I knew where I was being guided to and coasted in to the stop on the ramp. This was greatly appreciated by the ground crews and obviously I was being praised for it by them, but the senior clique could not have that, so I was carpeted by the same flight captain who had me in and lectured me on not flying according to the book and promised that if I ever missed a parking position he would have my guts for garters – one more thing on my mind to avoid happening.

Perhaps I should mention here that one of the BOAC Directors, a Major McKrindle, who had been a senior pilot with Imperial Airways in the old days and now travelling around the BOAC outstations to report on standards generally, was often in our area and had flown with me on several occasions. He was on board on one occasion when I went back to speak to the passengers and he mentioned how impressed he was at the way I handled this aeroplane and landed it so smoothly. I waved the compliment aside saying that it was so easy to fly and he replied that he had to visit BEA often and had had some bouncy landings.

On another occasion I was walking out to the aircraft in Barbados to continue my flight to Antigua and Bermuda and the Major came running to join me. We greeted each other warmly and he said I am off to New York and so would be with me to Bermuda. I said I was going all the way and he questioned this as being a long day for me and I explained that the Captain who should have been in Bermuda to take it from there had been called to Trinidad for family reasons, but that I was rested and happy to do so. Then there was the time I was taking the Chairman of BOAC, Sir George Cribbet and team of Directors, including the Major, to Trinidad for a Board meeting, and on the leg from Bermuda to Antigua I went back to have a chat with the passengers and Sir George asked me what I thought was a suitable replacement for the Viscounts and I replied that any replacement should be a jet as the major airlines were now introducing jets. He agreed and I thought among other considerations that we should have a jet. Again he agreed. Then I said there were only two now fully operational, the Comet and the Boeing 707, and as the Comet was a 70-seater and the Boeing so much larger and more expensive, I thought the Comet was the one. He slapped his thigh with his hand and replied "you have taken every argument I have made and I am offering Comets to your Management, but they are holding out for Boeings and we cannot afford those".

Well, I saw them through to Antigua, Barbados and Trinidad and when we were in the baggage area of the old and rather inadequate terminal, Sir George climbed over the baggage to thank me for such a lovely trip, saying that he had heard about me from Major McKrindle and was consumed with admiration over those four landings. Such thanks and praise I never enjoyed from my own local Board of Directors.

It was at that Board meeting in Trinidad that the replacement of our General Manager Mr Rat was called for and he left the room to call on the government for help and they sent a deputation to say they wanted to buy the airline. Sir George was taken aback and, as they were not in a position to consider that, returned to England. Our Prime Minister took a team to England to apply for this and BOAC was instructed to proceed with the sale to the Trinidad Government. When it was discovered that all they had bought for the price of 2.5 million TT dollars, I think the sum was, one Viscount and the infrastructures, they returned to England to argue this with the Colonial Office who then got BOAC to surrender the other three aircraft, which had been on lend/lease.

Trinidad had recently gone independent under management by the People's National Movement headed by Prime Minister Eric Williams and I had been chosen to fly the Princess Royal, who had come as the Queen's representative to the twin island of Tobago for the celebration there. The Captain of the Queen's flight, Wing Commander Dennis Murray, came down to vet us. I was also chosen as the first civil airline captain to lay a wreath at the local cenotaph on Remembrance Day for those who had fallen in the two World Wars.

The Viscount was the first turboprop aircraft to see service in the USA, and BWIA within BOAC had been the airline to do that. One of our jobs was to service the Bahamas Islands from Miami and we found ourselves in competition with Pan American Airways on the short trip to Nassau and back. Pan Am flew DC6-Bs in those days on their international routes and had a maintenance base in Miami where the weather was far better for around the season servicing. The aircraft used to arrive at Miami with just a few hours between major overhauls of engines left and so their crews were instructed to beat us on that route.

One day, whilst sitting in the aircraft waiting while the passengers boarded, I saw Donald Campbell, the motor boat racer, coming to us and I called the hostess and told her to invite him up to the cockpit en route. He was thrilled and after the weekend, he was on my aircraft returning to Miami. I again told the hostess to ask him up and he bounded forward saying he was hoping I would ask him but he did not want to wear out his welcome by asking. Pan Am's DC6 had taken off just ahead of us and I had caught him in the cruise and edged passed him. I told Donald that if he found me lacking in conversation it was because I had a race on with Pan Am on the left. He looked out and said "you have him to hang", but I explained that he was faster in descent and could catch up.

I heard Pan Am call Miami for descent and as he started down he was overtaking us, Donald became frantic saying "he's coming, he's overtaking, put up the power" and motioned to the throttles. I too had started our descent but my 'never to exceed red line speed' was slower than that of the DC-6 and I told him I dare not and he asked "who's to know?" Pan Am rattled over the coast with me in hot pursuit down 36th street and into the left base leg for the airport. He was given number one to land and I was close on his heels, in fact perhaps too close and expected to be sent around by the controller. I then heard the controller tell him the time of landing and also to turn off at the next right intersection and hold for the landing aircraft. I landed short and turned off left at the first intersection and parked on the ramp before Pan Am. Donald was jumping up shouting "we beat them, we beat them", like a youngster would.

There was a separate desk for aircrew in Customs, so when we were being cleared, the Pan Am crew came up with faces like thunder and I tried to make a comment, but they just ignored us. An Eastern crew then appeared having come from San Juan, Puerto Rico, and I mentioned this to them and the skipper said "oh, he just got out the wrong side of the bed last night, that's all, they are quite a friendly bunch really. I beat one crew from San Juan a couple of days ago and when he drew passed me on the ramp to park he said, for Christ's sake don't open your gills or the engines will pour out". The gills were hinged flaps at the rear of the engine cowlings for controlling cylinder head temperatures and were usually set wide open when parking to allow for quick dissipation of heat.

A BOAC captain named Bill Williams had joined BWIA as he liked the Caribbean, having flown through Barbados and Trinidad, and had met some of our senior clique of pilots, who had promised him on the quiet that they would get him an immediate captaincy and tried to inject him ahead of me on the seniority list. I strongly objected and so he was made to do a stint as First Officer on the Viscounts and rostered with the clique members while training on them. As usual, his mind had been poisoned against me, but he happened to be rostered with me on one rotation. We flew to New York and next day did a shuttle to Bermuda and on the return journey in the night, the loran set packed up and he urgently called my attention to this and asked "what do we do now?" I said "never mind, I feel sure we were reasonably on track" and he frantically asked how would we now be able to give an accurate time of arrival at Tuna.

Tuna was a position on the sea 128 miles out of New York and in the centre of a narrow corridor through which we had to position ourselves to continue to New York as a military requirement for the protection of the East Coast of America so we could be identified. This was strictly monitored and each aircraft had to be there within two minutes of the estimated time for radar identification. To add to this, the Chief BOAC Operations Officer at that time at New York Base, who was anti-BWIA crews, had instructed the control tower to report to him immediately any crews that missed that target. This eventually boomeranged against the BOAC Stratocruiser crews, as they were missing their target time more than we ever did, in spite of having large crews including a separate navigator.

Williams started to get really concerned and to ease his mind I explained my plan. We need to relax and wait for Riverhead VOR Station, which was further back of New York Airport by several miles and was used to position us on the centre of the corridor to become within range by being active. We were flying at 24,000 feet and at this height, the line of sight range of VHF equipment was some 210 miles, if I remember correctly. I used to keep a chart handy, I would take that time carefully and deduct 128 miles from 210 leaving 82 miles to Tuna and by dividing that by 3.5 miles per minute roughly as our ground speed, we would take about 24 minutes to arrive over Tuna. When Riverhead came in, we took the time and I told him to change his ETA by two minutes on that reckoning and he passed this change to New York Centre with some doubt in his mind. He anxiously waited and when that time arrived, with Riverhead radial bang in the middle and New York Centre called to say "Speedbird 406, we have you over Tuna at this time, you are now cleared to descend to cross South Island at 15,000 feet and contact the tower on 121.8", he let out a most audible sigh of relief and said "I have to hand it to you, Lyder, you always seem to have an ace up your sleeve".

The next day was a rest day and the following day we were on our way to Nassau in the Bahamas at 24,000 feet, when out to sea from Wilmington we got a call to descend to 16,000 feet, report leaving and reaching. I told him to tell them we could not comply and he couldn't bring himself to say that, so I had to insist and when he did so faultingly, Wilmington came back loudly "you are cleared immediately to 16,000 feet report reaching".

I picked up the phone shouting that I was the captain of Speedbird 401 out of New York, cleared to Nassau at this height with 52 souls on board, a turbo-prop aircraft on a flight of extreme range and would pay a heavy fuel penalty to descend to any lower altitude, therefore cannot comply. There was a "stand by" and an entirely different softer voice came back "could you change track to fly via Carp and Snapper and then direct to Nassau?", we hurriedly checked this and replied that we could and was then cleared on that route to maintain 24,000 feet. Williams was stunned. When we got to Kingston and put up at the Courtly Manor Hotel, I heard him relating this incident to the other pilots sitting around the pool and telling them "never mind what you fellows say about Lyder, I am satisfied that he is a real commander of aircraft". I delayed leaving my room until they had gone in for dinner as I did not want to let on that I had heard what he had said.

We must have been the world's worst-paid pilots of aeroplanes. I hate to mention this, feeling embarrassed about it, but at that time, we, as captains of such an advanced operation, were receiving salaries of 840 Trinidad dollars per month, equivalent to US$500 at that time. We had been paid this for flying around the islands, but now that we were flying to New York on very modern and demanding aircraft, we had written to the management repeatedly about introducing a national salary scale, which they had promised when we undertook this type of operation.

Some two years went by without any success, so the pilots of BWIA went on strike and were severely ostracised for doing so, until we made our salary differences known to the public. I had left the council of the local BALPA at this time and was taken by surprise the night I arrived in New York to be paid a few US dollars as subsistence for one night and handed a letter from the management that our jobs had been terminated and we were now on our own responsibility.

A few of us went to the British Embassy for help and it was explained that this was a very serious situation as in a few days we would be sought by the Immigration Authorities and deported to our homelands and would not be able to re-enter the USA until Congress had rescinded the order. We were told to stay put at the hotel and the matter would receive their immediate attention. We also went to the BOAC Head Office and were given the same instructions, while they sorted things out with our own Board of Directors. BOAC Management called us the next day, saying they were setting up a repatriation flight using our own aircraft and asked us who would volunteer to fly it.

Keith Maingot offered as captain and I offered my services as co-pilot and they sent a message to our Management in Trinidad to this effect, but they refused, so BOAC ordered them to come to New York immediately. The Chairman, Sir Errol dos Santos, and Legal Director, Sir Hugh Wooding, arrived via Pan Am Airways and had the riot act read to them and had to agree but rejected our volunteers and gave the job to two of their senior captains who had remained loyal to the company. The morning we were scheduled to depart, I arrived at the airport just as Sir Errol and Sir Hugh were checking in and I saw the catering officer, Mr Hackett, passing and asked him if he was catering for us or should we go and buy ourselves some sandwiches. In a loud voice he replied that he was, and that even if he had to pay for it himself, Captain Lyder would certainly be provided with a meal. On the leg to Miami, the hostesses served us our meals while Sir Errol and Sir Hugh sat in the two seats opposite to mine and took out their sandwiches.

On walking into the building in Miami, I happened to be alongside Sir Errol and he asked, why were we behaving in this manner, Lyder, and I suggested that that question should be put to the General Manager.

We then continued our journey to San Juan and then Trinidad, arriving there at night, and my family were there to greet me. My eldest sister was there in tears and as a result of this, she refused to serve as Junior Circuit Steward of Tranquility Methodist Church with the Senior Circuit Steward who was Sir Hugh Wooding. As I mentioned earlier, we were paid 840 TT dollars per month, the equivalent at that time of 500 US dollars, and the matter came into relief when I carried a young English lady from Caracas in Venezuela to Barbados on holiday and discovered that she was being paid 550 US dollars as an elementary school teacher.

Another bit of enlightenment was when, standing alongside a tall Pan Am skipper in New York one filthy night, having just arrived from Bermuda, he looked down at me and asked "who are you?" and I replied "BeeWee" and he remarked "you are a bit off track aren't you?" thinking that we confined ourselves to the Caribbean. I explained that we also carried out the Bermuda shuttle for BOAC. He then enquired, how did you cope with this sort of weather and I said "you get used to it" and he replied "I don't think I shall ever get used to this, coming in here tonight my ILS (instrument landing system) needle which is used to guide one to the centre line onto the runway behaved just like a windscreen wiper". He went on to say that he had been at the Miami Base for two years and was posted to the New York Base recently for a spell and added that he was given an additional loading of 6,000 US dollars for the move on top of his 24,000 US dollars normal salary. I was stunned, as his extra for operating out of New York amounted to my total salary.

I could not wait to get back to Trinidad to report this to the association. This brought them to their senses. Our predicament was aired in London and the Colonial Office sent out a very professional lawyer to Trinidad to hold an enquiry and BALPA Head Office sent their General Secretary, Mr Follows, to help us present our case. He was feted and treated so well by our Board of Directors and so impressed by their knighthoods that he was thoroughly softened up and held a meeting with 28 of our pilots the Sunday evening before the case was to be heard, and presented us with an inadequate pay scale suggested by Sir Hugh Wooding. As soon as I heard it I said "sorry, no good to me, we had better put it to all of the 82 pilots who voted to strike" who were now scattered to their respective homes waiting. Mr

Follows then said that Sir Hugh had put a moratorium on this offer to accept it before the case started on the morrow or it was off. I repeated that 82 pilots had voted to strike and 82 pilots had to have their say to break that. The few of us there were not empowered to do so. Unfortunately the senior clique of locals, who had given me so much trouble, were there and in a mood to accept and I insisted that we contact the others by telegram and left the meeting.

The following day I heard that the offer had been accepted and the years of poor remuneration for our services continued, if at a slightly higher figure. A friend of ours, who was in the Civil Service and was nominated to serve as the secretary to the lawyer who was sent out to hold the enquiry, sat on my porch one evening later and said that we had missed a golden opportunity in thwarting that enquiry, as that lawyer was first class and was bent on putting us on a par with the competing airlines. He mentioned how Sir Hugh had made several attempts to see him before the hearing and he refused. Sir Hugh thought he could soften him up as he had done Mr Follows, but he would have none of that. This friend also explained that Sir Hugh was quite aware of what he was doing when he tried to get us deported from the USA so that we could not fly into America with any other airline. This made my sister resign as Circuit Steward of our church.

With the introduction of jet aeroplanes spreading to all airlines, BWIA was looking to replace the aging Viscount and I started to push for the Boeing 707 so that we could fly our own services to the UK, but our management chose the Boeing 727, a shorter-range type, which meant that we could only reach New York and then under favourable conditions.

Our then Chairman, Sir Hobson, was about to go to London to meet with BOAC and I told him to raise the subject of our pilots flying the BOAC 707s and he replied "they would not allow that" and I explained the inter-tracking agreement with the London-based crews did permit such a thing. He was uncertain of this and very gingerly enquired at BOAC when he met the Board with his tongue in his cheek and was surprised when he was greeted with the affirmative, if we so wanted, and so arrangements were put into place for three crews to be trained by BOAC to fly the 707s down from New York and back. They were chosen by seniority and if they held British Airline Pilots Licences. Captains Junior and Esmond Farfan were chosen, along with Captain Grogan, a Canadian, except that Grogan did not hold a British ALTP. He was sent on the course in spite of BOAC informing the company that he would not be allowed to fly British-registered aeroplanes. It so happened that he was eventually failed and sent back and now the company were faced with his replacement and I was the next in seniority with a British ALTP, but because of the feud between us I was refused and BOAC was asked to supply a third, which was taken from their own roster, which changed from schedule to schedule. BWIA then hired a South African ex-BOAC pilot who had been dismissed after just being trained on the 707 at a salary far higher than mine on the Viscounts and I objected through the association. He was then not allowed to fly and spent many months enjoying himself swimming and sailing. He appealed to the association to be allowed to make one trip in order to maintain the 707 type on his licence and I relented. He did one trip to Barbados, Antigua and back and his First Officer was an Englishman who had come to us from BEA, who told me after that flight that he felt the pilot was so poor that he should give up. He was eventually dropped after costing us a fortune.

While on Viscounts, we used to slip crews in Bermuda en route to New York and take over the one coming up the next day. I used to enjoy that and often rented a powered bicycle to ride around the island sight-seeing. I would have lunch, listen to the weather forecast to be informed of what to expect on the way to New York. We would get to the airport by 2.15 pm for a 3.00 pm departure and on arrival there we would be presented with the flight plan made up by the BOAC Station Officer.

On one afternoon I arrived to be told by Mr Saunders that we would be in for a rather long trip today and mentioned 3 hours and 42 minutes. I thought that excessive and I questioned it. He said that he had calculated it according to the winds he was given from New York. I told him "no, nothing like that" and he asked what time I thought it would take. I thought of what I had heard on the radio and told him 3 hours and 12 minutes, provided we get straight in without having to hold. He was so confident about his calculations that he took a shilling out of his pocket and put it on the counter saying that he was not really a betting man, but would wager that his estimate was correct. I matched it and handed him my shilling to hold. I got off on time and flew quite normally and did not notice any exceptional winds and as luck would have it, got us a straight in approach.

On landing, I went to the BOAC Operations to check in and hand in the documents. I asked if an arrival message was going to be sent to Bermuda and was told, as soon as he had finished with me. The time elapsed for the flight was 3 hours and 12 minutes precisely and I was astounded myself. The next day was a rest day and the following one had me doing the return journey, but this time all the way to Trinidad. On arrival at the BOAC counter, I was greeted by Mr Saunders with a huge grin and the two shillings which he handed to me, plus a slip of paper cut out of a magazine with the sentence 'and in conclusion it has to be agreed there is really no substitute for experience'.

When we moved on to the jets, the Chief Pilot stayed as the captain in charge of the Viscount fleet. He was sent to BOAC to be checked as the examiner for instrument ratings and was away quite some time. I happened to be going on leave to London and asked if I could have my instrument rating renewed by BOAC in London and this was arranged. On presenting myself at the Operations Department, I was greeted by Captain Wallace, who had trained with me in Canada and one of the two friends I had taken to stay at the Guthrie family in New Jersey. He was assigned to my check and this was a happy reunion. We went out to a De Havilland Dove aeroplane, which I had not flown before and was shown over it. Then we set off to shoot instrument approaches at Hurn Airport in Bournemouth. On our return, the check ride was carried out with the final instrument landing at Heathrow and my rating was renewed.

My reason for mentioning this episode was to relate how I was greeted when I first met Wallace there. He asked me what kind of an outfit I had joined, as he had been given the job of preparing our Chief Pilot as an examiner for instrument ratings and he was appalled at the lack of flying ability of a Chief Pilot of an airline. He explained, he had to spend some 35 hours on the man in basic flying techniques to make a real pilot of him. I assured him that our airline was better than that, with the return of a number of RAF-trained pilots and had indeed a very good record. This episode made me appreciate more than ever why Cash was bent on keeping me out of the airline, when my sister kept telling him of my qualifications.

What upset me was that an outsider like him was given much more credit than one of their local boys, and he was also allowed to continue flying into Miami up to the age of 64, when I was cut off at the age of 60. The argument that the Americans would not allow me in there after the age of 60 was absolutely false as I know that Air Jamaica, which was formed long after

BWIA, hired Canadian pilots who were as old as 65.

A few months after our pilots' strike a friend was sitting on my porch paying a visit, and asked why we had settled for Wooding's pay agreement and had prevented the enquiry that had been set up by the Colonial Office from going ahead. He was taken off his job in the Civil Service to act as secretary to the visiting lawyer from England, who was to hold the enquiry. He thought him an excellent choice and very able. I had made excuses for Mr Wooding, saying that he could not have been aware of the serious situation he had placed us in with reference to our being deported from the USA and so depriving us from ever returning and he said "oh no, he was fully aware of what he was doing".

In the meantime, I had been sent to Seattle on a course to learn the Boeing 727, which was very new and introduced hurriedly by Boeing when the British had developed the three-engined "Trident". With the Boeing expertise it became more popular than the Trident and is still well used. Having passed the technical we went to Miami to learn to fly it, and I ran into a heap of trouble there. We had a team of Boeing instructors and I was given one who took a delight in telling filthy stories, which I disliked, and we had a personality clash. Just at that time there was, unknown to me, a clash between BWIA and Boeing Management and Boeing were seeking to prove that our pilots were difficult and not up to their standard. Aided by the clique, they were given the impression that if they failed Lyder, the other pilots would not make a fuss, so the pressure was on me when on my first check-ride I had a problem with handling the aeroplane at night on the approach after doing a Canyon Approach – a hurried and steep descent, which was included by the Americans for some unknown reason. This was at night after the aircraft had arrived on service.

I complained to my instructor that the aircraft was one wing heavy and thought an aileron or speed brake had failed, and the instructor took over and discovered the same and handed it back to me, which of course he should not have done. When I operated the thrust reversers on landing, a trolley full of bottles etc., left on board, had come rolling up the aisle and had smashed into the cockpit door. The instructor called on me to take off again for another landing and the FAA examiner overruled him, got up to check what had happened and found the cockpit door jammed and told me to take it back to the ramp.

The next day, I went to the aerodrome to enquire the reason for the control problem and heard that they had discovered that the Boeing Flight Engineer was so engaged in watching my flying that he had emptied the left wing tip tank alone and had placed the aircraft in a condition unsafe for flight. This had to be covered up by Boeing crews and so I was blamed. I had two further unsatisfactory reports, so when I had not been passed on the third attempt I said I would go back to Trinidad to find out what was going on, and when I got home, the Manager, who was now Phil Kelshall, told me of the feud between Boeing and himself and said "take a few days rest and let me know when you are ready to go back".

In a few days' time I was sent back and the Boeing Chief Check Pilot was requested to do a check on me. He was Bill Conine and again that Friday afternoon after the aircraft had arrived, we set off without the examiner, Mr Monahan, who had come to see me when he heard that I had asked to go home to find out what was going on and said "I shall be happy to do your check when you come back, Captain Lyder". He had himself thought that something unsavoury was going on.

I did the taxi out and prescribed departure procedure and a few exercises to show I could handle the aeroplane and was told to take it in to land. I did two more circuits and landings and Bill Conine asked me if I would like to do my check ride with the FAA tomorrow. I was taken aback and said "I thought I was supposed to have a problem" and he replied "I like everything you do with this aeroplane".

On landing he came back to tell me to go home for the weekend as Mr Monahan was busy, but would be happy to do it on Monday. I came back on Monday and everything went off smoothly as it should have done the very first check and the FAA signed my papers. The following day, Bill Conine route-checked me on the way back to Trinidad and I was reported fit for operations. At last I was free to explore the aeroplane and I enjoyed flying it.

When we first used the 727, Pan Am, our main competitor advertised heavily that all their aeroplanes had four engines, but as the airline business goes, they all have to be competitive and so they soon ordered some 727s themselves, and then the competition to see who would use them better was joined. I relished the challenge and had many memorable races with them and came out the winner. One of them was a trip between Barbados and Antigua our own backyard and I just had to win.

Pan Am took off from Barbados a couple of minutes before me and I took off like a scalded cat with the same equipment and, tied by the same operational limitations as laid down in the manual, I had to use my local knowledge of the area. When he veered to the west to make a long approach to the right, I cancelled my instrument flight plan for a visual one. I crossed the island at the south coast and descending called the tower giving my position over Nelson's old dockyard at English Harbour at 1,500 feet requesting approach. I was cleared to continue and report on right base leg and when in sight was cleared number one to land.

When on the ramp, talking to my Operations Officer, the Pan Am skipper, a tall, slim, grey-bearded chap, came up and asked if I was the skipper of the BeeWee 727 and I replied in the affirmative. He then asked "did you not leave Barbados after me?" and again I said "yes", he said "well then, how did you get here before me?" and I replied "I did not know", and he charged me with pushing the aeroplane outside of the prescribed speed limits and I told him I had not. He then asked "what speed were you cruising at?" and I said "mach 83", he replied "that is what I was doing". He then enquired what weight was I and I told him and he replied so was his and looked at me with a puzzled expression, shook his head and walked off.

On another occasion out of Miami to Montego Bay in Jamaica, at the same scheduled time of 3.00 pm, Pan Am called for clearance to push back from the terminal a few minutes early and I called on the traffic staff to hurry as I had a plane to catch. Eventually we got away and were cleared to taxi to runway 9 left, and on the way out I asked to use runway 12, which would put me in a short cut to my course, which was south east, but that was denied. Pan Am 727 to Montego Bay was cleared for take-off and another 727 of theirs cleared on the runway to back track, which was going to Nassau in the Bahamas. He was taxiing slowly down the runway with the obvious intention of holding us back to allow his buddy to get ahead. I was fuming as every mile that was gained ahead of me was going to take time to overhaul.

The tower called to the Nassau-bound 727 asking if there was something wrong and he said "no, why?", the tower told him that they had cleared him for take off some time ago and he replied "I have to get to the end of the runway before I can do that, haven't I?" This cheek annoyed the chap in the tower, who called me to ask if we were ready to go and I replied "yes". So he cleared me for immediate take off on runway 12, whose top end I was then approaching. I shot off again in a hurry and when on course, switched on the radar to see my competitor some 20 miles ahead. I had heard that the controllers in the Miami tower used to bet on our races and so expected they would be monitoring this one.

Since we were not allowed to exceed the prescribed speeds which were monitored by our black boxes fitted to each aeroplane, I had to use some other method and chose to fly at increased height if cleared, in order to obtain more help from the recorded winds. I gradually requested 26,000 feet then 28,000 feet, while he maintained 22,000 feet, and I climbed when cleared and started to catch him but we were still some 10 miles behind on crossing the South Cuban coastline. All we needed now was for him to call for an early descent, which he did, and I felt we had a chance then. Bruce Marquis, who was my First Officer and who is now a Captain with Qantas, having emigrated to Australia many years ago, we still keep in touch by letters, suggested that we should follow and I said "no, we shall delay our descent and dive down like a hawk at the red line speed". We did so and had some job trying to keep the warning bell from ringing.

Pan Am had got down to 4,000 feet early and was now dragging in when he called Montego Tower for landing instructions and they gave him number one position. We had now overtaken him but had to retain 1,000 feet above and called Montego Tower to say we were ahead by 3 miles and asked for number one to land. The Tower was at a loss to decide which aircraft he was talking to and I turned in line with the runway and told them that the aircraft on long high final was BeeWee and he changed his mind and gave us number one and told Pan Am he was now number two. The Pan Am First Officer handling the RT came on the air to say "hope your wings stay on", we could only conjecture what took place in Miami Tower when the arrival times were reported to them.

On one of our trips to New York, when we landed at Bermuda, the Chief Hostess came to me to ask if we were overnighting there as she had just heard that the weather in New York was so bad that both Pan Am and Eastern Airlines had decided not to return. I told her that I would make a decision after speaking to our handlers, BOAC, in New York. I phoned and was told that the weather was pretty foul and every now and then the airfield had to be closed because of being below acceptable minimums of cloud base and visibility, but that I would get in so long as I arrived with fuel to hold for two hours, so off we went.

I always tried to complete my assignment and only on three occasions in twenty-five years of flying for BeeWee failed to do this, due to closed airfields. We arrived at New York and were given an immediate approach and landed safely. I had earned quite a reputation for reliability and punctuality that I had been awarded the Master Pilot's Certificate by the prestigious British Guild of Air Pilots & Navigators.

In 1964 the company at long last decided to go in for Boeing 707s to fly direct to London, which I had been pushing for, and I went with the first group to train with Qantas, from whom we had arranged to buy two of their 100-series. We were housed in Sydney and attended lectures at their airport. On passing the technical, we went to Geelong Airfield near Melbourne to do the flying. Fred Hamer and myself were trained by Bert Smithwell and as a result of my performance, I was recommended as the one to be given charge of the 707 fleet instead of the appointed "Senior" of the group, who had trained with BOAC and flown 707s for two years previously. This was unacceptable to his brother, who was then the Chief Pilot of the company, and insisted that the appointed "Senior" retain fleet captaincy. Later, this position was handed over to Fred Hamer, to whom some of my time was given over when training at Geelong, because he was not doing as well as I. I had to put up with this state of affairs, as I needed to live in Trinidad to care for my mother and sisters and those were the only flying jobs there.

To satisfy themselves, the company asked for a Qantas training captain to come to Trinidad to check the 707 pilots and Captain Atkinson arrived, obviously briefed to change their choice of fleet captain, and I was put through an extremely rigorous check with a host of facilities being failed. So much so, that Captain Noel de Verteuil, who was sitting behind me, was heard to remark "oh no man, that is too much" and yet I coped and landed safely. On debriefing, Atkinson had some criticisms and I just stayed silent and accepted my fate. In view of the antagonism to me, I was not prepared to accept the responsibility anyway and enjoyed being my own man.

I was in my hotel room in New York a short while after this and I got a phonecall from Qantas Captain Atkinson in his hotel to come over and have dinner with him and I declined. He pressed me to come for a couple of drinks then and again I declined because I had no wish to speak with him. I often wonder what he was so anxious to say to me. I reckon he had got a rollocking from Qantas after he got back from that trip to Trinidad.

While at Geelong, we had the occasional short break and had a look around that area. Esmond Farfan and his wife journeyed to Cairns to see Mike Gilfoyle, who had emigrated to Australia and bought a shop in Cairns delivering papers and selling sweets and ice-cream to the kids there, and on their return, Esmond's wife Helene described how shocked they were to see him doing such a menial job after being a captain and said "oh god, Garth, Mike with a baseball cap on and in a T-shirt serving behind a counter", I could not resist the remark "that water has a habit of finding its own level"! On one trip to New York, I ran into a Qantas Captain Treadgold, whom we used to meet often and had not seen for some time. He was a bright and entertaining chap, so when he turned up I enquired why we had not seen him and he explained that he had been recalled to Sydney after a two-year spell based in "Frisko" and had gone back to his home in Cairns to find that his newspaper boy was an ex-BeeWee captain.

I enjoyed at long last flying into London, first on charters, but because we had the 100-series of 707 shorter range, we had to call in at Santa Maria in the Azores for refuelling, but I did not mind as it broke the journey. Five and a half hours to Santa Maria, then just three and a quarter to London made it like that to New York and Toronto. We had to watch the weather though, as the travelling lows over the Atlantic often put the Azores out of commission, so a direct flight was preferable for scheduled services.

My wife and daughter were on one direct trip to London and Captain Chown put into Santa Maria as he felt he was low on fuel, and they refused to handle him as no arrangements had been made since we had given up calling there, and after a long wait he continued to Lisbon for a short overnight before continuing to London. One of the hostesses, who had arranged a date in London with her fiancé, was furious and told my wife that this would never have happened if her husband had been flying that flight.

One night, flying into New York on a 707, I made an approach to runway 22 in the dark, and following my instruments down the glide path quite happily, when suddenly the First Officer, Salim Alishaw, shouted "pull up, pull up, Garth" and I carried out an overshoot as he explained we were too low and short of the runway. We asked the tower for another attempt and the same thing occurred again and I overshot again. My instrument was landing me down short of the runway but his appeared to be OK, but he also had the facility of looking out as well and could see lights, which should not have been under us there. The tower asked if we would like to go to an alternative airfield and I said "no" and asked for one more attempt as we had sorted out the problem. This time I followed the First Officer's instruments instead of my own glide slope and landed normally.

This incident shook me up as my wife and daughter had arrived ahead of me from London and was at our hotel waiting for me to spend Christmas there. I reported the problem to the flight captain who poo pooed the idea and termed it incompetence until the crew using the aeroplane next had the same problem and all flights below 500 feet on instruments were cancelled, while enquiries were made and Qantas admitted that they had had that problem some time before but that it had been cleared up. I mention this on purpose because of the altercation at present with the senior RAF officers insisting that the two Chinook pilots were guilty of gross negligence, they had better think again, instruments do give problems at times.

An American group bought shares in BWIA and changed handlers from BOAC to SAS and within a short while I had collected a fan club there as well. We had bought four old type 707s known as 227s to replace our new 727s and we had to rewrite the Operational Manuals because their engine consumption was something of an unknown quantity, for instance, we needed almost 10,000 pounds of fuel more to reach New York from Trinidad with the proper reserves. I was rostered to take one on a three-engined ferry to Oklahoma for an engine change and the dispatchers were in a quandary as to what figures of consumption and speed to use.

American Civil Aviation requires dispatchers to be licensed, so they have to accept responsibility for their flight plans. I was approached for advice as the dispatcher did not know what figures to use and I thought for a while what figures would be feasible. I came up with a consumption and speed based on my experience and he used those to plan my flight. He was anxious about that, but had no alternative. He was greatly relieved to get my report on landing at Oklahoma that I was down a mere 327 pounds of fuel and two minutes of time. My reputation grew from that moment and I was always very well treated and received great cooperation from that team.

On one occasion, I had to do a charter from New York to Antigua and return just before leaving on BOAC the same evening on holiday to London. On arrival at Antigua, I found a Shell Petroleum strike in effect and I did my best to persuade the chaps to refuel my aircraft without success for a long time. I pleaded with them that they had no quarrel with BeeWee and why should they penalise us. I was becoming frantic as time passed and I could see my holiday arrangements shattered when at last they relented and we got away. On approaching New York, I got on to SAS by phone and told them of my predicament and asked them to find out from BOAC if there was any later opportunity that night. When I landed, one of the staff met me in the customs hall to expedite my exit and had brought my suitcase from the office and hustled me out to the pavement, where another member, Robby, had his Volkswagen Beetle, engine running, and hurried me over to BOAC where my booked flight had been delayed sufficiently to get me on. I had to thank them profusely for such cooperation, something that I seldom got from my own people.

I may have lost seniority from being kept out of BWIA for so long, but the study and preparation I had taken advantage of in that time certainly paid off as I emerged as an extremely well-equipped captain of aircraft and enjoyed every minute of my job. I was very fortunate to enjoy good health, and in twenty-five years of service to BWIA I never missed a flight for which I had been scheduled. I carried a large number of interesting people and had the privilege of speaking with them, to mention but a few: the Princess Royal when representing the Queen at the Independence Celebrations in Trinidad & Tobago; Lady Tweedsmuir who joined me on the flightdeck of the DC-3 on a couple of occasions when visiting with a group of Parliamentarians; Doctor Garbutt, the Archbishop of York; Sir Douglas Bader; Sir Frank Whittle, the inventor of the jet engine; Donald Campbell, the motorboat racer; and Professor Oppenheimer, the inventor of the atomic bomb.

When I was first in London with Billy Watson showing me around, he took me to Tower Hill where a young Methodist Minister held meetings in the open during the lunch hour, which was being talked about quite a lot. He was Donald Soper. After the war, he changed his pitch to Hyde Park and I saw him there a few times but I never met him to speak to. Many years later, when I had returned to Trinidad and built my house in Ellerslie Park and my sisters were active in the Tranquility Church, I arrived home from a flight one night to find that the Reverend Donald Soper was installed in my mother's suite upstairs, but again I did not meet him as it was late and he had turned in and next morning I had to be off again very early.

My Life after Retirement

I was astounded when on reaching the age of 60 I was retired at the height of my production and could easily have gone on for another 10 years.

For several months I fought to be retained without success and could not think of any other career, unfortunately, so have been at home caring for my wife June and daughter Jenny. In a way, I am happy to have done this, as I have been able to compensate them for the years they had to endure being alone whilst I was away flying. This must be considered a remarkable feat when considering the conditions under which it was achieved.

We had to traverse the Bermuda Triangle frequently, which was considered risky psychologically, due to a number of ships and aircraft which were lost in the area. We used the Viscount type of aircraft which was not really designed for that route. The early ones were poorly equipped having one ADF, one VOR and one Loran set for navigational equipment and de-icing inadequacies on the surfaces and windscreens, which had to be squirted with alcohol to remove ice.

There were few navigational facilities, no satellite position fixing or computers. One had to fix position with a sextant, taking shots of the stars, but could not do much of that by virtue of having only two pilots to tend to everything else. We had to fly from daylight through dusk into the night when the Loran fixing was by guess because of its difficulties in deciding between real and ghost signals at such time and finally, when it gave up altogether and we were left to our own devices, we had to think of and use every bit of ingenuity to continue under these circumstances, and so it was not surprising that flights were aborted but I kept going by reading the stars with my eyes as I dared not leave the captain's seat. In addition to this, I would have pressure from the First Officer to abort and I had to convince him that all was not lost.

I remember one night when I arrived in Bermuda en route to San Juan, Puerto Rico, and found a member of our senior clique who was joining us there to use his sextant and fix positions in order to renew his navigators licence and he threatened in jest to lose my arse. The weather was not very good and to add to our troubles the Loran packed up, and before half way, this captain appeared from behind the curtain to announce severely that we were some 40 miles east of track and suggested that we do something about it.

The First Officer who worshipped this clique member worked himself into a frenzy when I refused, and remarked that we should act on what he said as he was doing the navigation, to which I replied "oh no he isn't, I am doing the navigation" to which he retorted "with what, the Loran is out". I had to draw on all the resources I could muster and take a lead from the stars I could see with my naked eye, while the First Officer folded his arms and started to whistle the theme song from the film 'The High and The Mighty', which depicted an airline captain who fouled up and was rescued by the timely action of the First Officer who had been demoted from captain previously for an incident. Fortunately, the senior captain in this instance did not interfere further, although he insisted that his fixing was correct, however, this turned out to be wrong.

The time arrived when we should start our descent to San Juan and I asked the First Officer to obtain clearance. He asked in a surprised manner "are you going to go down?" to which I replied "of course, we cannot stay up here until we fall down". He obtained clearance and we started down and I prayed that I was right. I gave a revised estimate of arrival and the senior gave-up and leaned forward to ask, "what was my ETA?" and I told him. He came back with his own, which was two minutes different from mine, fictitious of course because he had no real knowledge of how we got there. I had all my fingers crossed and we descended through cloud and I was greatly relieved to see the lights of San Juan appear through the broken layers of cloud.

There was an audible sigh of relief from the First Officer who now carried out his duties and developed a healthy respect for me from there on. We landed almost on the minute of my estimate and I thanked the Lord for his help.

It was the practise on our airline to allow the First Officer to have the opportunity to fly some of the legs; in fact, in the early days, when we were nearly all ex-RAF, we shared the flying equally in the captain's seat, but with graduating to more sophisticated aircraft and routes, we confined any sharing from our respective seats as laid down by the rules.

I know that I was ostracised by some First Officers for not sharing as much as other captains, but just could not afford to, in many instances of poor conditions, because of the pressures I was under. If the situation was at all doubtful, I had to do it myself as the captain always carries the can.

One evening flying to San Juan on one of the old type 707s, I allowed the First Officer to fly and he landed fast and he used the brakes a lot. When I got out of the aeroplane, the brakes were smoking badly and I spent the whole of the ground time using the air-conditioning hose to cool them down. I had a strong fear that they would explode on the ramp and do severe damage and probably kill people. The First Officer just walked off quite unconcerned.

I ordered him not to retract the undercarriage until I instructed him to after take-off as the wheels were still hot. It was not until we had climbed to 5,000 feet that I felt it safe to retract them. He wondered what all the fuss was about. I don't suppose he ever heard the quotation 'uneasy lies the head that wears the crown'. The accent this age is on youth, but youngsters do not show much responsibility until they reach their mid-30s or experience a real situation of fright. They want to go to the top with the minimum of delay. Unfortunately in aviation, they are always in a hurry to become captains, but the only real way to become a useful captain is to spend a reasonable time as a First Officer, seeing how matters are handled by the experienced pilots. The more, the better equipped they become.

I remember sitting around a swimming pool at a hotel in Miami where a variety of crews used to put up. I was sitting next to a senior captain with grey hair and he was being badgered by a young First Officer, who was saying that he should give up and allow him to proceed to be the captain and his reply was "see here son, you will not be fit to be a captain until you stop fixing your cap in the mirror". I remember when I was new on the Boeing 727 and learning all about it, I was on my way to Montego Bay from Kingston, Jamaica, at night with a rather critical First Officer and on approaching Montego Bay Airport close in to the top end of runway 07, the tower called to say that I could land on runway 25, the reverse instead, as the wind was light and variable. As one who was always anxious to save time and money for the airline, I accepted and hurriedly carried out the drills to land.

As the runway was short with possibly a light tail wind, I needed to get on the runway as early as possible. I landed with a bit of a jolt which earned me a grunt of disapproval from the First Officer. On the return journey the following day, I let him fly it from Miami to Montego Bay and waited in anticipation. This was in a bright afternoon with a good headwind and on runway 07 with an unobstructed approach from the sea. He landed with a more severe jolt than the night before and I thought to ask him, what was his excuse, but kept silent and left him with something to think about. That same First Officer was promoted to Captain on the DC-3 soon afterwards, the normal route of progression to learn on the training ground of the island airports and on his very first trip in command, he failed to land on the first island and turned back from Grenada because the hill on the normal approach at the west of the airport was cloud covered in the early morning. The usual thing to do under such circumstances was to approach from the east over the sea, even though that would be landing down-wind, but the wind could be light at that time. The aircraft would soon slow down while running uphill. I used to do it quite frequently and never missed a landing there. That abortive effort caused no end of confusion for the airline and passengers.

My sixtieth birthday was approaching and I was getting anxious about my being allowed to continue in my job. I felt that my performance was of a standard enough to convince the management that I should be allowed to continue, but soon the dreaded letter of termination arrived and I appealed against it and respectfully requested to be allowed to continue, but certain members of the management were adamant that I should leave on the contention that the Americans would not tolerate my flying into their territory after the age of sixty. I argued that this was false as Air Jamaica had Canadian pilots who were as old as sixty-five still flying in and out of their country, but I got nowhere. I tried every argument I could think of but to no avail. I left the situation in the hands of our pilots' association and joined my family in the UK for a long holiday and took the opportunity of going to the Civil Aviation Authority in London to question the matter.

I was told that I would be allowed to continue to fly aircraft of a gross weight of up to 30,000 lbs. I put the matter to the officer that here was a pilot with some 24,000 hours of flying experience, thousands of which were in command of Boeing 707s with two other licenced pilots on the flight deck on scheduled services, being debarred from continuing, but would be allowed to fly corporate business aircraft single-handedly all over Europe 'ad hoc' on strange routes and risk the lives of eight to ten business people and they were quite complacent about that. He admitted that it seemed daft to him but those were the rules.

I scanned the opportunities advertised worldwide but could not find anything suitable as a pilot, but could not think of a career to substitute and kept my licences valid for some years, just in case something turned up. Most jobs offering meant that I should be away from the family and I had had enough separation while on the airline and needed to see more of my wife and daughter. I went back to Trinidad after my long leave and was told by the Pilots' Association that the Government had stated categorically that I would not be reinstated, so I had to accept that and requested finalisation of my finances.

I then went to Barbados to relieve Barclays Bank's pilot to go on two months leave and enjoyed flying their Beechcraft King Air plane, especially as I was able to have my family with me. I then went back to Trinidad, and my wife and daughter back to the UK, where my daughter was being educated. I rented half my home to an American doctor and family while designing another house to be built for my wife on a plot of land, which I had bought for her earlier.

I then built the new home on the plot at 35 Newbury Hill, Point Cumana, complete with swimming pool and the family were happy with it. So we sold the original family home at 49 Ellerslie Park, Maraval. The family would come out to me for Easter, Summer and Christmas holidays while I kept hoping that I could get back into the airline. I just could not believe what was happening.

I was a local-born citizen with the highest qualifications in the profession, an enviable safety record, a fantastic service record, never having missed a scheduled flight in 25 years, in addition to filling in at odd times for others who went sick, and never so much as deflated a tyre or touched a wing tip as well as putting the airline on schedule. The manager in the

New York office was so incensed that he came down to speak to the management on my behalf, telling them how day after day the service would arrive late except when he saw my name on the departure message and I turned up bang on time. So incensed he was in fact that when he could not get them to agree to have me back, he signed his resignation there and then and we lost one of the best managers in the industry.

When after a fight to stay in BeeWee, the Pilots' Association were told clearly by the Government that the company had refused to reinstate me, I had to accept my fate and try something else, but I could not bring myself to accepting other jobs that would take me away from my family and decided to look after them full-time after the separations that they had put up with when I was flying. I enjoyed the job in BeeWee and the pleasure it gave me to deliver my passengers safely to all destinations. As time has shown, I could have gone on for another ten years.

I had left Trinidad in 1938 and came to England to study engineering and get a pilot's licence to go back and set up a local airline. After I left, a group there financed a Light Aeroplane Club. I got a job at Bristol Aeroplane Company in September and in the Spring of 1939, I learnt to fly at Western Aero Club owned by Mr Whitney Straight and got my private pilot's licence and was working towards my navigators' licence and for my commercial licence when war was declared. There was a great demand for help here, so I decided to stay. I had been a few months old when the first war was declared and so had been influenced by the strong feelings about the Germans as I grew up. Unfortunately, all private flying was stopped and so my flying had come to an end, but I decided to stay on as I was doing a real job of work for the war effort. I lived through the day and night bombing of Bristol and became very angry and joined the Air Force in June 1943. By that time, I had accomplished what I had set out to do on the engineering side. What happened next was laid out in this book.

I joined the RAF and as an aircraftsman and at Lords Cricket Ground, where we were initiated into the Service and sent to a building site half built opposite Regents Park. We were handed a blanket and a bolster and slept on the floor covered with cement dirt. Marched to the zoo for meals and drilled in the side streets. We were marched to a car parts warehouse and now used to stock uniforms and equipment and to a medical centre for a variety of injections. After about three weeks, we were ready for real training. We were sent to Torquay in Devon, now promoted to the rank of leading aircraftsman, a rank we held throughout our training as pilots until we earned our wings, when I was commissioned as a Pilot Officer in December 1943.

My story from here is covered in previous pages so I shall now mention what happened after I left the airline, British West Indies Airways, which has now gone out of business, due mainly to mis-management, after having had an enviable record of safety for 66 years. All that time and effort put into it by a hard-working loyal staff – nothing short of shameful.

I set out to make the most of my savings and to care for my wife and daughter while keeping an eye open to any opportunity towards a flying job, keeping my licences valid until I eventually had to give them up. I still cannot resist looking up when I hear an aeroplane overhead.

I came to England in 1986 to take up residence here, but still missing my home in Trinidad. Unfortunately, a number of my investments have let me down and I am having to be very careful with my remaining funds as I have no wish to be on benefit and beholden to anyone. I suppose I should have taken up another career but just could not accept the idea. I am now well into my 97th year of age and thank the good Lord for sparing me this time. I married later in life than I would have liked to because I had to care for my wonderful mother and sisters. They have all gone now and I am hoping to have a little longer with my devoted wife and daughter who are helping me with this book.

I am distressed about the state of this country, I am afraid Great Britain, the country I fought for and was prepared to die for, is no longer great. Everything that was good and decent about it seems to have eroded and become vulgar and unprincipled. No longer is honesty the best policy, anything goes. We are staring at the break up of our Union that served us well through two World Wars, buddies who fought alongside of me in the second, and also the loyal Commonwealth Canadians, Australians, New Zealanders and colonies; we are turning our backs to them to embrace a strange

Europe, which has caused us such pain and anguish for centuries. We must never let go of the hands of the Americans, who are our cousins and have loyally stood by us in the two great wars. One has only to visit Normandy and see the beaches on which hundreds died, and the thousands of graves of Americans and others who gave their lives to save our country. I was given the job of destroying the viaduct and road on the night of the 6th June to delay the German 23rd panzers from reaching the coast from a position east of Caen, but had no idea that the invasion was to take place later that morning.

We hear a lot of talk about the amount of trade we do with Europe, which is grossly exaggerated by the Europhiles, and a lot of that is adverse trade. We could do much better with our Commonwealth partners. But my main concern is that we shall be sleep-walking into a trap and lose our sovereignty and freedom that we won at terrible expense. The European Treaty was thought up by Chancellor Kohl who sought to win an empire without firing a shot, whereas previous German leaders had paid a dreadful price and lost. Kohl went to great extent to unify the two separate Germanies so that he could claim that Germany was the largest member of the Union. They are not interested in being in Europe, but masters of Europe. They have given voice to that quite recently. It has always been said that a leopard does not change it's spots and I have seen enough while a POW in Germany to appreciate that that statement refers to them. Haven't you wondered why England is never mentioned in the European Scheme, while Ireland, Scotland and Wales are named members? Germany is still hurting and wants to see England wiped off the face of the map and forgotten forever, and our labour government is helping them to attain their goals. The assault on our Christian faith, mass immigration, multi-naturalisation etc. etc. are all parts of a great plot to reduce us to nought. For god's sake, let's get out of this trap now or it will be too late. I was born a colonial in Trinidad, offspring of the Reverend William Fidler, a Wesleyian missionary, and my brother the Reverend Deryck Maund Lyder CBE followed in his footsteps, and it would appear that all their good work is being trodden on.

I flew a private 5-seater plane from Fairoaks Airport to Capetown and back and because of the colonial status of all the countries I traversed I found peace, order and British laws. Today, since the dismantling of the Empire, there is a complete breakdown of all that and has in its place wars, genocide. Which do you prefer? I know which one I do. I keep hoping and praying for the return of the peace and decency we enjoyed a short few years ago. Are there others out there who think like me? Please wake up and win back our beloved country.

THE END

Appendix 1

180 Squadron, R.A.F. Station, Dunsfold,
C/o G.P.O. Horsham, Sussex.
10th August 1944

Dear Mrs. Lyder,

It was with the deepest regret that I had to cable you that your son Flying Officer Ernest Garth Fidler Lyder is missing as a result of air operations over Normandy yesterday. There is every hope however that he may be safe as all parachutes were seen to open from his aircraft which appeared to be under perfect control until abandoned.

They bombed their target successfully and were on the way back when hit by a burst of flak.

We were all very depressed to find Garth was missing as his cheerful disposition and outstanding enthusiasm for everything he did made him very popular and one of our most valued pilots in the squadron. We cannot afford to lose men of Garth's personality. Although he was a Flying Officer he had several times acted as deputy for his Squadron Leader and shown marked ability as a leader.

His personal effects will be carefully packed and sent to the R.A.F. Central Depository, Colnbrook, Slough, Buckinhamshire, while we await better news.

All the crews in the squadron tender you their deepest sympathy in what will be we know an anxious and trying wait, but we are byoyed up by the strong hope that he is safe. I shall cable you immediately we hear any news.

Yours sincerely,
R.I.K. Edwards
W/Com. O.C., 180 Squadron.

The West India Committee, War Services,
40 Norfolk Street, London , W.C.2.

Dear Mrs. Lyder,

It was with deep regret that we learnt from the Air ministry that your son Flying Officer E,G.F. Lyder was reported missing as the result of air operations on August 9th, and we are writing you to offer you our sympathy in this period of anxiety. We must hope that, perhaps in time, news may come through, if by any fortunate chance he has made a safe descent, and become a prisoner of war. In that event we would, of course, immediately let you know and would be pleased to get a next of kin in this country, if you decide for the dispatch of the Red Cross quarterly parcels to perform this service for many West Indians and so have obtained a good knowledge of what may or may not be included in the parcels

Yours sincerely,

KATHLEEN HALFORD
Personal Assistant to the Chairman,
West Indian Committee

Copy of letter from Padre Warner,
dated 14th September 1944

My dear Mrs. Lyder,

What was my astonishment yesterday when I had a letter from Charlie Walkden from Bramshott Military Hospital. They were all baling out when Charlie's parachute fell down through the hole so Garth, like the gallant and good man he is, said "O.K. I'll crash-land it- Hold tight" and screamed down in the blazing aeroplane, crash-landed it and pulled Charlie out of it as he'd broken his leg. Anyone who's ever flown will tell you how wonderful a feat this was. The chances were a million to one against his getting out alive- yet he risked everything to save Charlie. Garth and Tommy were later marched off to a P.O.W.'s camp and Charlie was left behind in a hospital in Brussels. I am, I need hardly tell you, more grateful than I can say that Garth is safe.

When Charlie looked down he saw Roy baling out and to his horror he saw his own parachute falling out after him. It must have been an awful shock for poor Garth. I know Garth and I'm sure he said to himself "This is it- we've had it now" but what he said aloud was "O.K. hold tight, Ill land it"- and that in spite of his hydraulics having been shot up. The more I think of it the more amazed I am at Garth's skill. It is suicide to try and land a Mitchell on fire and doubly suicide to try and crash land a blazing Mitchell with your hydraulics shot up- yet, thank God, he did it.

I hope you have received his photo safely and my previous letter. I always knew Garth had more in him than anyone else on the squadron. And we are all so proud of Garth. Proud of his splendid heroism and courage, proud of his skill as a pilot and I am proud of his friendship. With much love- it is so wonderful to think we shall see him again all being well.

Yours
Tom.

Air Ministry (Casualty Branch)
73-77 Oxford St., London, W.1

Madam,

I am commanded by the Air Council to confirm the telegram in which you were notified that your son, Flying Officer Ernest Garth Fidler Lyder, Royal Air Force, is missing as the result of air operations on 9th August, 1944.

The telegraphic report from Allied Expeditionary Air Force Headquarters stated that your son was the pilot of a Mitchell aircraft which set out to attack a target in Northern France and was hit by enemy anti-aircraft fire near Foucarment. Four parachutes were seen to open, two landing near Senarpont, the fifth member may also have bailed out but was not observed to do so.

If your son is a prisoner of war he should be able to communicate with you in due course. Meanwhile enquiries are being made through the International Red Cross Committee, and as soon as any definite news is received you will be at once informed. If on the other hand any information regarding your son is received by you from any source you are requested to be kind enough to communicate it immediately to the Air Ministry.

It is desired to explain that the reference to publication in the Press was included in the telegram notifying you of the casualty to your son in order to avoid prejudicing his chance of escape by undue publicity, should he be at large in enemy occupied territory. This does not mean that any information about him in available, beyond that mentioned above, but is a precaution adopted in the case of all personnel reported "missing".

The Air Council desire me to express their sympathy with you in your present anxiety.

I, am, Madam
Your obedient Servant,
CHARLES EVANS.

IMMEDIATE MRS L M LYDER
SUNNYSIDE TACARIGUA TRINIDAD

FROM AIR MINISTRY 73/77
OXFORD ST LONDON W1 PC3629/9/44

INFORMATION RECEIVED THROUGH THE INTERNATIONAL RED CROSS COMMITTEE STATES THAT YOUR SON F/O ERNEST GARTH FIDLER LYDER IS A PRISONER OF WAR IN GERMAN HANDS. STOP LE TTER CONFIRMING THIS TELEGRAM FOLLOWS STOP.

First Letter from Charlie,
my injured gunner, received on my return to England
June 5th 1995

Dear Garth,

The day when I can write to you has arrived at last. This morning there was a letter from your mother with a P.S. by your sister with the good news.

With this I am not going to attempt the kind of letter I should like to write for your movements are I imagine uncertain. Anyway I hope you may be home soon. But briefly anyway I should like to express to you my very great thanks on behalf of my parents and friends for the masterful manner in which you put that aircraft down and that saved my life. I honestly believed I had had it that day. Since then much has happened. In spite of my injuries- fractured thigh and bone in foot, I suffered little pain and considered myself to have come out on top when I was deserted by the Nazis 25 days after they picked me up. I get about on crutches and brace and am at present on my first leave from hospital.

I am at Calgary at present and am renewing acquaintances all along the line. At present, Brandon, Rivers, Regina, Richardson, Swift, Current and here. Of course I was in bed for some time and am now fat as a pig and bulge out of my clothes all over.

Poor Tommy came home to tragedy. I don't know if you are in touch with him or not. I was in close contact with Mrs. Good and she too was wonderful in her faith like your mother and mine, but fate struck and took her away at just about the time Tommy landed in England. She had been in perfect health when there was a haemorrhage of the brain and never recovered. I have not heard whether Tommy has been informed. Roy lives near here so I phoned his mother today. She has got the good news too. What news of Dough Hogarth?

Now Garth, I hope you have suffered no ill effects from your experiences and I shall be interested to hear about them. I heard from Madge today. She was quite worried about you. Many thanks again. Charlie.

P.S. Your mother was wonderful in her faith, through it all and we have become quite well acquainted.

Appendix 2

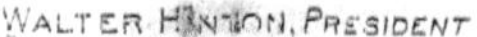

1115 Connecticut Ave.
WASHINGTON, D. C.

September 22, 1932
14136

Mr. E. G. F. Lyder
Sunnyside, Tacarigua
Trinidad, B. W. I.

TO WHOM IT MAY CONCERN:

This certifies that the bearer of this letter has satisfactorily completed a comprehensive course of study, preparatory for Aviation work and has attained high grades as a result of his efforts.

He has a workable understanding of airplane and engine construction, operation and maintenance -- he understands the basic principles of Aeronautics and has creditably passed rigid examinations designed to test his understanding of the fundamental ground work necessary in Aviation.

He has invested his money in spare time training; he has proved that he has determination and purpose by starting and creditably completing a difficult undertaking with its attendant financial obligations; he is a man who finishes what he starts and who has learned how to think as well as how to do. These personal qualities should be desirable in any employee.

Neither time nor effort has been spared to give him the best home-study training and I am confident that he will make a capable and diligent worker when given an opportunity to apply his training to practical work.

I respectfully recommend him for your consideration.

Very sincerely yours,

Walter Hinton

President.
AVIATION INSTITUTE of U. S. A., Inc.

WH:REC

CODES — A.B.C. 5TH & 6TH
BENTLEY'S · BENTLEY'S SECOND
COMMERCIAL · UNIVERSAL · SCOTT'S

CABLE ADDRESS
ALSTON
PORT OF SPAIN

PORT OF SPAIN
TRINIDAD · B·W·I

31st December 1938

GARTH LYDER joined the Office Staff of this Company as a junior employee in August 1929, on leaving school. He was transferred to our Coffee Department in May 1930 where he remained until he left in August this year to go to England. For some years he was in charge of our Coffee Hulling Mills and Warehouse, during which time he proved himself to be consistently capable and reliable. We can give him too the highest recommendation as to general character.

He has a natural mechanical bent, and handles labour well, and while we are very sorry indeed to lose his services, we feel he has done the right thing to go to England to get the practical experience which is not available to him in Trinidad.

For ALSTON & COMPANY LIMITED

CHAIRMAN.

ALL COMMUNICATIONS SHOULD BE ADDRESSED TO THE COMPANY AND NOT TO INDIVIDUALS.

LONDON OFFICE
6, ARLINGTON STREET, ST JAMES'S, S.W.1.
TELEPHONE:- REGENT 0957-8.
TELEGRAMS:
BRISTAIRCO, PICCY, LONDON.

TELEPHONE:-
BRISTOL 45051.
TELEGRAMS:-
AVIATION, BRISTOL
CODES:-
WESTERN UNION, BENTLEYS & A.B.C.
TELEX Nº BSBS. 46440.

"Bristol"

THE BRISTOL AEROPLANE COMPANY LTD

SIR G. STANLEY WHITE, BT
(MANAGING DIRECTOR.)

FILTON HOUSE,
BRISTOL, ENG.

YOUR REF.
OUR REF. AIRCRAFT/EXP/JR/ND. 4th July, 1941.

TO WHOM IT MAY CONCERN.

Mr.E.G.F.Lyder has worked in this Department as a Fitter Assembler since the 23rd November, 1938. During which time he has shown considerable aptitude and application, so that his experience of the manufacture, assembly and maintenance of aircraft is considerable.

MANAGER, EXPERIMENTAL DEPARTMENT.

UNIVERSITY COLLEGE, SOUTHAMPTON

TEMPORARY TELEPHONE LOCKS HEATH 2251

TELEGRAMS "UNINAV WARSASH"

Please address all communications to the—
DIRECTOR
and quote the following reference

SCHOOL OF NAVIGATION,
WARSASH,
NEAR SOUTHAMPTON

CWR/JH.

9th April, 1949.

STUDENT REPORT (No.769/Air)

E.G.F. LYDER

This is to CERTIFY that Mr. E.F.G. Lyder joined the School of Navigation to study for the Ministry of Civil Aviation examination for Flight Navigator's Licence on 22nd November, 1948, and has been in full time attendance since that date.

During his course of study, Mr. Lyder has shown himself to be an excellent student, and has co-operated fully with his tutors. He has worked consistently hard throughout, using his time to the utmost advantage. His work is painstakingly thorough and meticulous. He has reached a high standard of knowledge, and we have every confidence that he will pass his examination next month.

C. W. ROBERTS
Chief Air Navigation Officer and
Lecturer-in-charge Air Division.

CONTRACTORS TO H.M. GOVERNMENT

AIR SERVICE TRAINING LTD

HAMBLE
SOUTHAMPTON

DIRECTORS:
SIR FRANK SPENCER SPRIGGS, K.B.E. (CHAIRMAN)
T.O.M. SOPWITH, C.B.E., F.R.Ae.S.
GROUP CAPTAIN R.J.F. BARTON, O.B.E.

TELEPHONE .... HAMBLE 2155-6-7
TELEGRAMS .... TRAINING HAMBLE
RAILWAY STATION .... NETLEY

Our ref: CNI/26. 505/L/64.

16th June, 1949.

TO WHOM IT MAY CONCERN.

I have known Mr. E.G.F. Lyder since January 1948 until the present date, during which period he attended this School for instruction in First Class Navigation up to the standard of the International Flight Navigators Licence. On completion of his studies he was successful in achieving this technical qualification.

He proved himself to be the most methodical and painstaking student of my experience with a sincere desire never to undertake any task unless he could efficiently complete it. He has a very equable temperament and an extremely pleasant personality, and I have no hesitation in recommending him to your notice as an extremely conscientious person incapable of giving other than his best.

C.N. Hoy
C.N.Hoy.
(Squadron Leader).
Chief Navigation Instructor.

BOARDSIDES · WYBERTON
BOSTON
TELEPHONE BOSTON 2661
NIGHT 2779

DATE 28th March, 1950.

Mr. E. G. F. Lyder has been employed with the above Company for some four months and during that time has carried out his duties in a most thorough and efficient manner.

He is a most earnest and trustworthy worker and his capabilities as a pilot are of the highest order.

E W Pearson

Managing Director.

BWIA Pilot Gets Master Certificate

CAPTAIN E. G. F. Lyder, DFC., F.R.Met.S. M.I.N., has been given the high award of a Master Air Pilot Certificate. News of this award i contained in a recent news letter of the Guild o Air Pilots and Air Navigators.

Captain Lyder is the brother of the Rev. Derycl M. Lyder, chairman of the National Council of th Methodist Church in Barbados, and a Privy Councillor, and son of Edwin Hugh Lyder who was born in Christ Church, in 1876.

Captain Lyder, who is a Senior Captain with British West Indian Airways, has logged close on 17,500 flying hours of which more than 11,000 have been in command since he started flying at the age of eighteen. As a young enthusiast he did a three-year course in practical aircraft construction in the experimenta shops of the Bristol Aeroplane Company where the supersonic Concorde is no in the final stages of completion.

CAPT. LYDER

With the advent of war in Europe Captain Lyder joined the Royal Air Force and worked up to the leadership of formations on Mitchell bombers of 180 squadron of the 2nd. Tactical Air Force based at Dunsford, Surrey. On his 49th sortie he had the misfortune to be shot down and made a prisoner of war in Germany but was released by the Russians in May 1945.

Trip

When he left the servic in 1947 Captain Lyder pu in a year's light aircraft flying around Britain and Europe and also completed a trip to Cape Town, South Africa and back in his single engined Beechcraf Traveller before settling down to specialise in navigation and meteorology at Air Service Training, Hamble, Southampton. On completion of his studies he was awarded the Specialist Flight Navigator's Licence and made a Fellow of the Royal Meteorological Society.

Before joining B.W.I.A in 1950 he was engaged in charter work in Englan and on the famous Berli Airlift of 1949. He is currently flying in command of Boeing 727s on the Trinidad-New York schedule.

Extract from the Trinidad Guardian, Friday 26th January 1945

TRINIDAD AIRMAN GETS A D.F.C. AWARD

Award of the D.F.C. has been announced to Flying Officer Ernest Garth Fidler Lyder, No: 180 Squadron RAF VA. Trinidad born airman whose home is at Tacarigua. The citation accompanying the award reads:

"This officer has completed numerous operational sorties, many have been against heavily defended targets. As a pilot, he has displayed great flying ability, and his leadership in the face of danger has always been determined and reliable. On one occasion, one engine of his aircraft was set on fire as a result of enemy action and the aircraft was so badly damaged that Lyder ordered the crew to abandon it by parachute. One parachute was lost, so he decided to crash land the crippled aircraft.

Born in 1914 at Port-of-Spain, Flying Officer Lyder received his education at Pamphylian High School. After service in the ranks he was commissioned in December 1942 and he was trained in Canada."

THE GUILD OF AIR PILOTS AND AIR NAVIGATORS

MASTER AIR PILOT

Certificate number 467

AWARDED IN RECOGNITION OF SKILL, EXPERIENCE AND SERVICE IN THE PROFESSION OF AVIATION

To Ernest Garth Fidler-Lyder

On the 7th *of* March 1968

BY ORDER OF THE COURT

Philip

GRAND MASTER

Appendix 3

MY FLIGHT TO CAPETOWN

In July 1947, with some time and a small aircraft on my hands, I ran into a Mr Andrews who had sold up all his property and was seeking transport to South Africa, but was finding it very difficult. As I had always wanted to make a trip that way, I mentioned that I had an aircraft and in less time than it takes to say "Jack Robinson" we had pooled resources and decided to fly to Capetown in the Beechcraft Traveller.

With Andy in the seat beside me and his wife and daughter, aged 10, on the divan seat behind, we took off from Fairoaks Aerodrome on August Bank Holiday morning. We had to put in at Lympne Aerodrome to clear customs and at 10.15 we were setting course over Lympne for Marseilles. As we left the English coast further and further behind, I could sense that the Andrews were wondering when next they would see the old country again as they were figuratively burning their bridges behind them.

As the French coast came up, with St. Valery off the starboard bow and Le Triport a few miles down the coast, my mind went back two and a half years and I almost believed I could hear my navigator in broad Canadian saying "get weaving chum, enemy coast ahead". Then further on I spotted the little village of Poix near Amiens where we had been thrown into the dirty little jail by the 'gerries' and I recalled the names enscribed on the walls to which we had added ours, the curses, threats and even prayers, which accompanied them and the Sunday morning when, standing on my navigator's shoulders, I tried filing through the thick old iron bars to the accompaniment of hymns sung by the two flight sergeants who shared the cell next door.

It was while deep in such reminiscing and with the old twitch almost coming back that we were startled by a loud pop. Andy shot a glance at me and I at him as we thought the motor had coughed but on hearing loud peels of laughter from the rear, we looked round to find the other two in hysterics with Christine holding up a burst paper bag, which, having emptied of sweets, she had blown up and popped as school children will.

So on over Paris and down the Rhine Valley to Marseilles, where we landed at 1400 hours. We were surprised to find it so hot and made a rush for iced drinks in the airport bar. We put up at the Station Hotel, about 3 miles away, for the night and left the next morning for Ajaccio (Corsica). This was a short run, but a convenient stop for fuel and lunch. I was sorry there wasn't time enough to take in a swim as the sea looked most inviting.

At 1.15 pm we set course for Tunis, having to climb to over 9,000 feet to cross the mountains of Sardinia. How rugged it all appeared. Two and a half hours later we were on the approach to El Adina Airport, Tunis, and found the flying control officer, very proud of his English as he nattered away on the RT to me right through the whole approach and landing.

We thought we would like to see something of Tunis and so decided to spend the following day there as well. We put up at the Tunisia Palace Hotel. A heat wave was in progress at the time and we were sweltering in the heat, but the normal water supply is not fit to drink and we had to buy bottled water at 50 francs a time. Needless to say in that heat one bottle didn't go very far so quenching our thirst became rather an expensive item.

We took off from Tunis at 0500 hours on the morning of 7 August and set course for Castle Benito, Tripoli, arriving there at 0710. We refuelled there and set off again for Marble Arch, Gabes 352 st. Miles in a SE direction. This aerodrome was abandoned except for three Arabs and a few tanks of petrol maintained there by Shell. Our experience with those Arabs encouraged us to nickname them 'slow, dead slow and stop'. Still I suppose if we lived there ourselves we would fall prey to the same ailment.

At 12.25 pm we were airborne again and went up to 10,000 feet to try to avoid the hot vertical currents, which were coming off the scorching desert. We could see below the burnt out tanks and vehicles of the war in Cyrenaica and the barren wastes of sand and a greater appreciation came over us of the terrible conditions under which our troops had to fight in this area. Another 2 hours and 5 minutes and we had landed at El Adem (Tubruk) and were accommodated there for the night and tended by German prisoners who were still awaiting repatriation. We were tired and therefore turned in early but not before we had strolled in the evening air and sampled the vastness of the open desert. No wonder so many philosophers grew up there.

The following morning we were off again and set course for Cairo. The place which spells magic to countless thousands. We were all wondering what it would be like. En route we flew over Salem Siddi Barrani and El Alamein, the names which we had heard so much about only a few years before. We were thrilled to be looking down on places of such great moment but what tiny villages they seemed to be. How could so much importance be attached to them.

It took us exactly 2 3/4 hours to reach Almaza Airport, which is in the new suburb of Cairo called Heliopolis and which is by far the prettiest and cleanest sector. We saw the pyramids on the way in and decided that a visit to them would be a definite part of our program. We put up at the Heliopolis Palace Hotel, which was indeed a most imposing place and found the food very good. We spent the day doing the sights escorted by an official guide whose main task it was intended should be to protect us from being fleeced by the legion of human parasites who seemed to appear from nowhere but whose obvious intent was to do the fleecing himself. It wasn't surprising that Andy soon dubbed him the 'arch chiseller'. However, we did see most of the places of note including the bull rushes where Moses was supposed to have been found by Pharaoh's daughter.

The morning of 9th saw us setting course for Wadi Halfa, which is the first landing ground in the Sudan. We arrived in due course having flown the 563 st. miles in 3 1/2 hours. The heat there was simply terrific and seemed to take one's breath away. We were more than pleasantly surprised to be taken to a very nicely furnished hotel on the banks of the Nile, called The Nile Hotel, a real oasis in the middle of the desert.

To fly through the Sudan, one must go in convoy with another aircraft so that one aircraft can fix the position of the other if it happens to be forced down for any reason and so we arranged to fly through with two fellows in a Gemini whom we met in the Nile Hotel. After giving it a try the following day, we found that they were much too slow for us and so we came back and made arrangements with a BOAC Dakota crew. We went through to Khartoum that day and put up at the Grand Hotel on the Nile. We strolled through the streets in the evening among the 'masked marvels" who seemed to be swarming along with some intent, but the Andrews would not let me follow them to see where they were leading. We were off to bed quite early as we were scheduled to leave at 0500 hours the next morning.

We took off at 0455 and the sight of the dawn breaking over the mystic city quite thrilled us. The

Dakota was off soon after and we tucked ourselves in on her port side and we were able to carry on sign conversation with the passengers looking through the windows. Though the meteorological people had assured us that there wasn't a cloud in the sky an hour out of Khartoum we ran into drizzle which gradually developed into the worst live squall I had ever flown through. I stuck with the Dakota until at last the rain was pouring in rivers over my windscreen and I lost him from view. I waited a few seconds to see if it would clear but when it didn't I broke away as risk of collision was imminent. I then found my own way to Malakal and found that he had got in a few minutes earlier.

The Dakota went on and I waited for a Wayfarer, which came through later. That afternoon we pressed on to Juba through another bad storm and spent the night there. Juba is the one place, which really impresses you as being in the heart of Africa and no one moves outside after dark because of big game. An elephant was shot on the airstrip just before we got there and the boy told us the next morning that he had nearly speared a lion which had come nosing around our aircraft. Leopard skins were plentiful there.

Because the weather was bad, we waited a day there and set off for Kisumu on the morning of 13th covering the 407 st. miles in 2 hours 40 minutes. Kisumu is a very pretty spot on the north eastern tip of Lake Victoria. After refuelling we pressed on to Tabora in Tanganika where we arrived before midday and decided to spend the rest of the day and the night. We put up at the Park Hotel and played cards for most of the time.

Off at first light we set course for Kasama in northern Rhodesia and enjoyed the early morning ride covering the 371 st. miles in 2 hours 20 minutes. We found a very nice little hotel there about 1/2 mile from the aerodrome, run very well by an English lady who used to manage the restaurant in Bethlehem House, Waterloo Bridge. We had bacon and eggs for a second breakfast and the good silver and clean tablecloths added to the enjoyment of it. We were waved off at 0900 hours and laid course for Ndola in the copper belt. We landed there as it is the normal corridor route in order to report our progress and then set course for Lusaka which was the capital of northern Rhodesia. The next morning we took the short ride over to Salisbury, the then capital of southern Rhodesia and spent a couple of days there. This was the first English town of any size and appeared clean and fresh to us. As we strolled through the streets, little Christine kept running from shop to shop shouting 'oh mummy look at this" there were windows full of sweets and flamboyantly iced cakes just for the buying.

We left with quite a good impression of the place on 17th1 and flew over to Bulawayo where we refuelled and had some light refreshment before pressing on to Johannesburg. We spent four days in Johannesburg seeing the place, treating ourselves to the pictures and various outings as well as feasting our eyes on all the lovely things in the shops. The place seemed to be flooded with American stuff especially the cars, which seemed to be used exclusively. We left Johannesburg on the morning of 21St and flew to Bloemfontein where we refuelled and had some lunch and then were off again to Beaufort West 306 st. miles in a south westerly direction. Having refuelled there we set course on the last leg to Capetown. We arrived at Youngs Field at 1730 after climbing to 11,000 feet to cross the mountains north east of the cape. Though we had never seen it before, Table Mountain stood out and there was no mistaking what it was. We were very cordially received at Youngs Field and I left the aircraft in their care to do the necessary inspections and give it a wash and brush-up.

We had covered 7,695 st. miles since leaving Fairoaks at our leisure in 18 days and hadn't so much as looked at a spark plug the whole way down. The aircraft had behaved marvelously throughout and we had all enjoyed the trip immensely. The Andrews, who had only had one short flight before setting out were by this time completely sold on transport by air.

So if you ever find yourself with some time on your hands and a small aircraft standing idle, I suggest you try this change of latitude. I feel sure that it will work wonders for you as it did for me in sweeping the cobwebs away.

Regrettably, the detailed account of the return half of this journey is missing and not available for inclusion here, but a lot can be found in the main book.

Somewhere in Africa.

The Beechcraft with the Andrews family.

John Colman and the Andrews family in Cape Town.

John Colman driving us around the coast of Cape Town: Mrs. Andrews and daughter.

The rondavel we slept in at Kasama.

Frank & Elizabeth with the Beechcraft.

With the Andrews family & guide at the pyramids.

Appendix 4

AIRCRAFT OWNED BY GARTH

Piper Cub Coupe	G-AFVF
Piper Super-Cruiser	G-AJGY
Miles Mohawk	G-AEKW
Beechcraft Traveller	G-AJJJ
Percival Proctor IVC	VP-TBR

Piper Coupe G-AFVF two-seater, 65 HP, continental engine, bought from M.O.D. and overhauled by me while in the R.A.F.

110 Lycoming engine Piper Supercruiser-G-AJGY, brand new, first post-war import. I had to prepare it for its certificate of airworthiness (# 110 H.P.)

Beechcraft Traveller - G JJJ 450 H.P. Prat & Whitney engine. Shared ownership with Mr. Spanton, shown with his wife, which I flew to Cape Town and back.

Miles M12 Mowhawk (flown here by Charles Lindberg)
200 hp Monasco Buccaneer B6S Engine.
Span 35ft. Length 25ft 6in. Wing Area 183 sq.ft.
Weight Empty 1606 lbs. Max AUW 2630 lbs.
Max Speed 185 mph. Cruising Speed 170 mph.
Range 1400 miles.

In 1936 Colonel Charles Lindberg, who nine years earlier had made the first solo west-east transatlantic flight, was in Britain. Requiring a fast, long-range light aeroplane in which he and his wife could make business trips between European capitals, he asked F.G.Miles to build one for him.
The Mohawk was a tandem enclosed two-seater of wooden construction with fixed undercarriage and a 200 H.P. supercharged Menasco Buccaneer engine. It had a range if 1,400 miles.
The Mohawk No 298, registered G-AEKW, was first flown by F.G. Miles on January 28th, 1937. After many non-stop flights around Europe, Lindberg said that the aircraft was precisely what he wanted. In November 1941 it was impressed for communication duties with the RAF and became HM 503. In May 1946, it was reconditioned by Southern Aircraft Ltd. (Gatwick) and in the following year was flown in the Folkstone Trophy Race. It was then advertised for sale at 2,500, which was considerably more than the price ten years earlier. It was bought by E.G.F. Lyder and in July 1948 sold to B.P. Pini of Brosbourne who had it converted to open cockpits. In February 1950, it was sold in Spain. I bought this, hoping to fly myself home, but could not find suitable radio equipment.

Madge in the cockpit. Gerald and myself against the Beechcraft.

Percival Proctor IVC - VP 140 H.P Gypsy Major Tbr, imported into Trinidad & Tobago. Off to Tobago with two hostesses and Keith Melville, fellow pilot.

Myself with the Super Cruiser.

www.ingramcontent.com/pod-product-compliance
Ingram Content Group UK Ltd.
Pitfield, Milton Keynes, MK11 3LW, UK
UKHW041831200726
13854UKWH00002BA/981